FORGING A MAN

A Collection Of True Tales ~ And The Lessons Wrought From Them

Alf Herigstad

ISBN: 0692868925
ISBN-13: 978–0-692-86892-8

BetterMan Publications
Www.beingabettermanpodcast.com
www.beingabettermanpodcast.com/forgingaman
@Alfbeingbetter
@AlfHerigstad
Alf@beingbetter.men
https://www.facebook.com/bettermanpodcast/

Cover Photo: Alf Herigstad
Photography & Lighting: Reier Herigstad, Lulie Herigstad

Dedication

To my parents, Ron and Jan Herigstad, it is because of you that these stories exist. Thank you for the heat. Thank you for being the hammer when I needed it most. I love you, and I am eternally grateful.

Alf Herigstad

CONTENTS

A NOTE TO MY READERS

First, thank-you for reading this book, I appreciate it so much. After all what good is a great story, if you have no one to share it with?

This is a collection of true stories from my own unusual life. I say it was unusual simply because most of you reading will not have shared the exact same experiences as me. That should make it interesting, and you should also be able to relate to it as well because, regardless of the circumstances of each story, at the core of them all are just honest, authentic human feelings —and we are all human. Some of these stories are sad, some are happy, and some are...just weird. However, they are all true to the best of my perspective and memory.

As I said though; these aren't only stories, they are stories **with** the lessons learned from them attached. That is where the true value lies in my opinion. You could call it the moral of the story, but I prefer lesson. Every thing that happens in life contributes to the individuals we become. I believe there is something to be learned from every experience, in every moment that we live. We have to be tuned into the lessons though, we have to be paying attention, or we could miss the lessons, and that would be tragic.

Its true, these are my stories, but my intent is to share the lessons I learned from them, with you. It may cause you to think back to a time when you learned a particular lesson. You may be led to remember a totally unrelated story from your own life. Remembering a story, re-living it, is almost as good the second time around as it was the first.

I have a podcast called "Being A Better Man," I invite you to listen to it. You can do so for free on my website at: www.beingabettermanpodcast.com, or you can go right to iTunes and look it up. The stories in this book are compiled from the Wednesday episodes of that podcast. I started telling these stories on Wednesday as kind of an experiment, then they turned out to be popular. So, I decided to put them in a book, and now you are holding it.

I would love to know who you are, and hear your thoughts on the book, which story was your favorite and stuff like that. If you would like to take a couple minutes and send me an email I would appreciate it a lot. You can ask me questions and tell me your own story if you like. If you send me your own story include your permission for me to use it if you don't mind. I might be able to use it in another book. Writing me will also put you on my mailing list, don't worry you can opt out at any time if you like. But being on the mailing list will not only open a line of communication between you and I, but you will also receive news about new projects I have going and whats happening on the podcast and the general state of manhood around the world.

Here is my email address: alf@beingbetter.men   I look forward to hearing from you.

Now...sit back, relax,and enjoy the story.

.

CHAPTER ONE
Electric Man

The year was 1970, I was 8 years old. The year before my family had moved to a 10 acre farm and it was my boyhood dream come true. We had all sorts of animals: cows, chickens, pigs; and life was 'pretty awesome'.

Being 8 years old I had become fascinated with comic books, I read them voraciously. When I wasn't outside playing or working, I was reading comic books. I began to develop a deep bond with many of the characters, especially the superheroes.

I would fantasize about them frequently, imagining their adventures, and becoming aligned with the things they stood for. Eventually, over time, I found myself wanting to become a super hero myself. As more time went on I began thinking that perhaps I was actually intended to be a superhero! Almost as if becoming a superhero may have been the purpose for my creation. Eventually these thoughts of becoming a superhero took over my young brain and it was all I thought about. I started looking around, everywhere I would go, looking for that one 'thing' that would help turn me into a superhero. Few of the super heroes started out as one, they all had something unusual happen that helped them become who they were.

Spiderman was bitten by a radioactive spider. Batman's wealthy parents were killed by a criminal, which caused him to turn against crime and want to avenge their deaths. Superman is the exception, as he was born on another planet and it was the rays of our sun that gave him his power.

It was always something; a lab experiment gone wrong, or some other particular set of circumstances that transformed these people into superheroes. So now, I was on the look out for what MY thing would be.

I tried flying, a lot. I would get up on something high and concentrate really hard; then I would jump off, and crash to the ground. I used to do this all the time. I just kept thinking I needed more practice, or I had to concentrate harder. (I'm lucky I never got seriously injured in my flying attempts.) I would run as fast as I could, then I would launch myself into the air in a horizontal position while concentrating very hard— and then I would hit the ground. Surprisingly, I never got discouraged by my failures. I believed the right formula was out there. I knew that if I could concentrate harder, in the right way about the right things, that eventually it would work! I would dust myself off and try it again. That's how my life was in the summer of 1970.

One day I was just sitting here thinking about stuff and all of a sudden it hit me. Like a lightning bolt out of the clear blue sky—it came to me. The realization that the answer had been around me the entire time. This whole time I had been surrounded by the very thing that could transform me into a superhero, but I just hadn't seen it.

Of course the answer my brain had finally recognized, was the electric fence. The electric fence that encompassed our whole property to keep our cows from wandering off. I was thrilled and ecstatic at this new revelation. I was certain this was the answer I had been looking for!

My plan was fairly simple; I would hang onto the fence until I had absorbed enough electricity to become: ELECTRIC MAN. Then I would be able to "zap" things, criminals specifically, and THAT would be my super power.

I would go through the world righting wrongs, liberating the oppressed and downtrodden, and basically being a force for good in the universe. I didn't yet know if I would shoot lighting bolts from my finger tips, or my eyes, but I was ready to find out.

I went directly to the wire and found a spot where the electric fence was in the shade, where it ran underneath an apple tree. I took a couple minutes to prepare myself, then without hesitation I latched onto that electric fence wire with both hands. The electricity pulsing through this fence was not a constant current. It oscillated through the wire at regular intervals about once every second, kind of like a heart beat.

When the first jolt hit me, all of my joints buckled and twitched. My face muscles contorted, but I kept hanging on. Every time the electricity went through me my entire body would convulse slightly; my knees and my elbows would jerk, my cheek on the right side of my face would flare up into a half smile but I just, kept, hanging on. I kept hanging on because the whole key to this working, was to absorb enough electricity. I stayed there, twitching under that apple tree for about 30 minutes that day before I finally decided I must have absorbed enough electricity.

Did it hurt? Heck yes it hurt! It was extremely uncomfortable, but I was also extraordinarily committed to the principles of truth, justice, and 'The American Way'. When I finally let go my entire body was buzzing, humming with electricity. After taking a moment to gather myself, I decided to try out my new powers.

I pointed my finger at a fence post, because I didn't want to accidentally kill something that was alive. I concentrated very hard, this was a serious moment. I imagined electricity gathering together in my body to exit my finger in the form of electric bolts and then— nothing happened. I tried both hands at once and still, nothing happened. I was starting to get a little frustrated, and then I decided it must be the eyes. Yes, I would shoot lightning bolts out of my eyes. I started staring at the fence post intently, concentrating very hard, imagining all the electricity in my body just bursting to be released but alas, nothing happened. Then I thought that perhaps because the fence post was a dead, inanimate object, maybe that is why it wasn't working. Maybe I needed a life force to connect with? So then I proceeded to try all the same things out on a living tree sadly, with the same effect, nothing.

I began to realize that it wasn't going to happen today, but I wasn't discouraged. I just naturally assumed that I hadn't absorbed enough electricity. Nobody ever said this would be easy after all. So, the next day I went out and did it all again, and the day after, and the day after that. Every day I would go out and hang onto the electric fence for about 30 minutes (because that was about all I could take) and then I would try to zap things in a variety of different ways.

I would experiment with a different combination of variables. I would do different things while I was hanging on in the hope that I would discover the perfect set of circumstances. I tried eating an apple with one hand while hanging on with the other. I tried peeing with one hand while hanging on with the other. I just kept trying every day, with as many different sets of circumstances that I could come up with. I did this for an entire month, perhaps as long as a month and a half. Still, nothing was happening. I remained electrically impotent, unable to zap anything. So convinced was I though, that this had to be the path— the way to become a superhero, that I just kept doing it, thinking I had not yet absorbed enough electricity.

One day my dad was walking by while I was hanging onto the fence, I didn't hear him coming. As he was walking by he looked over and saw me there, twitching and convulsing as I held onto the electric fence.

After watching for a while he walked up to me and said; "Hey... what in the hell are you doing?"

Well, if you know anything about superheroes, then you know that it was impossible for me to tell my dad what I was doing, because that would totally blow my secret identity. Safeguarding the secret identity is one of the first rules of being a super hero. I had to think quickly, because he wasn't going away. I looked up at him, I managed a twitchy grin as current was going through me, and I said; " I...I like it."

My dads eyes got big for a minute, then his whole face was clouded with a mask of sadness, and disappointment. He didn't say anything. He just slowly shook his head, and walked away. He was probably thinking; Oh...my poor idiot son. As I watched him walk away I was still hanging onto the fence.

A couple weeks later in the morning, my dad and I were out changing irrigation lines in the field. It was a summer and the ground was wet from dew. I was barefoot as I often was in the summer. My dad stopped in the middle of what he was doing and pointing, said to me; "Hey, why don't you go grab that electric fence there?"

I couldn't believe my ears! In my 8 year old brain I thought my dad had figured it out. He knew what I was doing...and he supported it. He wanted to fill the role that Alfred did for Batman. He would be the civilian advocate for my super hero activities. I was very excited, because I couldn't think of anyone I would want by my side more than my dad.

What my dad knew (that I did not realize at the time) was that all through spring when I had grabbed the fence, I had been wearing shoes. Tennis shoes with a rubber sole that had somewhat reduced the amount of electricity entering my body. Today however, I was barefoot, and the ground was wet, and my dad put all these facts together, but I did not.

I ran down to the fence and enthusiastically grabbed on with both hands. I think the first jolt of electricity I felt actually made my heart stop. When the second jolt hit, I thought I could taste my fillings melting in my mouth. By the third jolt, I collapsed, which also made me release my grip on the fence.

I lay there still on the ground, just looking at the sky. My whole body was throbbing from all the voltage I had just experienced. All I could hear was my fathers maniacal laughter. He thought it was the funniest thing he had ever seen and, it probably was. Some sadness came over me then. I lay there thinking that it was the end of a dream. It was the end of my dream of becoming Electric Man. I was also sad because I realized that my dad had not figured it out, he didn't want to be my civilian advocate, he didn't want to be my Alfred. He just thought it would be funny.

That's the end of the story, but what is the lesson? I'll tell you what I think I learned. I didn't fully realize it until I grew up, but what I learned was this: Whenever you have a passion or desire that you throw your entire self into, as long as your intentions are noble and good...it will yield a good result. Even if you don't achieve your initial desire, passion or objective.

I wanted to be a super hero, and I did not become one. However, during that spring and early summer I spent all that time hanging onto the fence imagining, visualizing, fantasizing and thinking about becoming a super hero. Spending time actually believing that was my destiny...doing all that, altered me in a way. It cemented in me certain principles. It filled me with certain ideas of right and wrong, good and bad, responsibility, justice, and humility.

As a kid, when you spend two months believing you are

something, you kind of really do become that thing, on the inside. I believe this whole experience had a profound effect on who I ultimately became as a man. I'm sure there are other morals to this story, for example: "Don't hang onto an electric fence." After thinking about it, this is the lesson that really sticks out to me.

CHAPTER TWO
The Walnut Tree

Before we moved to the ten acre farm where I did most of my growing up, we lived on a little 3 acre place in the small town of Kelso, Washington. In those days I spent my summers like a feral child; seldom wearing shoes, spending every possible moment outside, imagining— just having adventures, playing with the neighbor kids and exploring the world around me. The year was 1968 and I was 6 years old.

Occasionally, I would have to become civilized once again when my parents would take us somewhere. There was a whole routine involved which included a bath, more of a scrubbing really. Also, the putting on of the so called "good" clothes including shoes, and mom combing my hair if my buzz-cut was grown out enough to comb at the time. I hated it all so much. It wasn't just the fact that my entire day of adventure and exploration was blown, it was those clothes! Once you put the good clothes on it was like you were in a prison; you couldn't go outside, you couldn't play, they wouldn't even let me eat for fear that the good clothes might get dirty. So, I hated my good clothes with a deep, abiding passion. Not to mention the fact that they felt like cardboard and the necktie made it hard to breathe.

On one such day it was announced that we had somewhere to go, probably a funeral or a wedding or something. First thing in the morning my mom got all of us kids ready to go. Then she had to get herself ready. Dad was already together. The problem with getting us dressed first was that it was impossible for my mom to get ready to go in less than three hours. I never figured out why, it just took forever. There would be this steady cloud of hair-spray rolling out from under the bathroom door, occasional grunting and other indistinguishable noises. My dad pacing in the hallway, stopping at the door every once in a while to ask, "How much longer?" To which my mother would always reply. "Almost ready!" in increasingly agitated tones.

So while the drama of my mother getting ready to go played out, we kids were on lockdown. It was dad's job to make sure we were as motionless as possible during this critical phase while mom was out of the picture. This for me, was pure hell. When I was 6 years old boredom would set in after about 5 minutes, from there it got worse and worse. Dad knew he had to watch me like a hawk. I simply wasn't designed to sit for three hours in cardboard clothes with nothing to do. I was losing my mind.

On this particular day, something distracted dad for a minute. Seeing my chance, I wandered out onto the front porch to get some air. It was a beautiful, sunny summer morning. A morning that beckoned to every molecule of my being. The next thing I knew I was down in the yard, just standing there, no harm in that, just standing there on the grass.

Suddenly, somehow without really meaning to I found myself deeper in the yard, standing at the base of our big old walnut tree. I loved this tree, I spent hours in its branches each day pretending it was a space ship, or a viking longboat, or being a monkey, or Tarzan or any number of other fun things I could transform into. I looked around. My absence had not been detected yet. I looked up into the tree, it was calling to me. In that moment I rationalized that a short climb wouldn't hurt anything, I would just climb to the first crook in the branches and then come back down. That is not what happened. I suddenly found myself resting peacefully in the tree's uppermost branches, in a state of zen meditation, just enjoying the birds, and the breeze and the sun. Then my dad's yelling ripped me from my meditative state.

"Alf...we're ready to go, c'mon."

I knew I had to get down as soon as possible, so I started scrambling. If I was caught up in this tree in my good clothes it would mean certain death. When I was halfway down, the search party, which consisted of my mother and father, came out the front door, so I stopped. I could not get caught exiting the tree. Panicked now, I climbed back up to a more concealed perch, and waited for a better opportunity.

The next three hours were very surreal. It was like watching a movie, except everyone in the movie were people that you know. I had a perfect view of the house and yard, and for three hours I watched my parents, and a couple neighbors too, frantically searching for me. I watched them go through every possible emotion, again and again. Really, it was sort of like watching your own funeral.

I had kind of detached myself from the reality that they were looking for me. I was prepared to stay in that tree until I grew up if I had to. I couldn't even imagine what fate would befall me if I came down now, that simply wasn't an option. By now my mom was just crying—wailing really, she was a mess. My dad was wandering back and forth, a combined look of fear, confusion and helplessness was on his face. He would stop every now and then, raised cupped hands to his mouth and bellow my name toward every different direction.

Eventually, his search led him to be standing directly beneath my position. I was prone in the branches, looking straight down at the top of my dads head. I became a breathless statue. He bellowed once more, and then as I watched he stiffened and jerked. His arms went down to his sides and his head slowly began to rotate upwards, upwards, like he was studying every inch of the trees trunk as it went up. His head continued to rotate up until his eyes came to rest directly on mine. I was still frozen, no doubt an old instinct from being hunted by prehistoric predators. Maybe if I didn't move, or blink, or breathe, he couldn't see me. So I stared back with unblinking eyes.

Dad started to tremble a bit. Veins began to bulge out on his forehead and neck that I had never seen before. His lip twitched and one eye began to blink independently of the other. He pointed to the ground in front of him and said, "GET....Down," in a low, guttural voice that was more of a growl than a scream.

The jig was up, so I switched gears. Now the only course of action left was for me to act as though everything was completely normal. If I acted like I had done nothing wrong and wasn't in huge trouble, then maybe he would forget that I was. Although that was a gallant effort—it didn't work. As soon as my feet touched the ground I was levitated by my neck through the air and brought into the house. At least my mom was happy to see me, until she calmed down, and then she got angry, too.

That day I was in the most trouble I had been in up to that point of my life, so it was a pretty big deal, but I survived it.

That is the end of that story, but what is the big lesson, what is the moral of this story? Some lessons have to be learned over and over again many times until they sink in, I think this was one of those lessons that contributed to me finally learning that no matter what, it is always better to own the things you do IMMEDIATELY.

We all make mistakes from time to time, but the faster we are able to own up to our mistakes, the sooner we can move forward. Nothing good ever comes from trying to cover up or hide what we have done. It's best to own the things we do both good and bad right away— doing so will help us be better men today than we were yesterday.

That's what I got out of it. Part of the reason for telling these stories is so that you can reflect on your own life, to a time when you may have learned this lesson. Remembering a lesson learned helps to cement it even firmer in our minds.

CHAPTER THREE
Sink Or Swim

I was blissfully ignorant to all the turmoil and strife the world was in. I was just a kid having a fun life. The year was 1968 and I was 5 years old. It was the first summer vacation after kindergarten. One day my mother told me that she had arranged for me to take swimming lessons. The kind of kid I was, whenever there was water around I always wound up in it, and she knew it was only a matter of time before I would get in water that was too deep. So these lessons were a life saving precaution on her part. Plus the fact that she had never learned to swim herself, and because of that, water had become a phobia for her, something she didn't want for me.

We arrived at the Kelso, Washington YMCA pool while it was still cool outside. There were probably 50 other kids of all ages there as well. It looked more like a prison than the YMCA. The pool was separated from the rest of the world by a high chain link fence, which the parents were asked to sit behind on some bleachers and observe. There were two pools; farthest away from the fence was a deep pool with a diving board, near the bleachers was a shallow kiddie pool.

The instructor in charge was addressing all the participants but my mother couldn't hear what was being said. By a show of hands, he asked, "Who doesn't know how to swim at all?" I raised my hand appropriately. Then he asked, "Who knows how to swim a little bit?" Not wanting to appear inferior, I raised my hand again. Lastly he asked, "Who are the good swimmers who want to learn how to dive?"

Even at 5 years old I hated the idea that these other kids knew how to do something that I didn't. So I raised my hand once again. It hadn't occurred to me that I would soon have to prove it. My mother, watching intently from the bleachers, had noticed that I raised my hand three times but she didn't hear what the questions were. Then she noticed me walking off with kids that were generally much older than I was. Her faith in the authorities at the YMCA, (people in charge had 'authority' back then) made her confident that I was in good hands.

The instructor asked us to form a single-file line facing the pool at it's deepest end, so I got in line. I was about 7 people back from the pool edge. One of the instructors demonstrated what they were going to have us do, which was stand on the edge of the pool, jump in performing a shallow dive, and then swim to the other side of the pool.

The first kid in line was asked to perform this simple task, and then the instructors would give pointers to the group, and then it was the second kids turn, and so on. You might think that I was getting nervous at this point. Well...not really, because I was studying everything the other kids were doing, and it didn't look that hard. I figured as long as I did exactly what they were doing, exactly how they were doing it, that I would get the same result and everything would be fine.

While this was going on my mother had gotten into a conversation with one of the other mothers in the bleachers and had not been paying close attention for a couple minutes. When she focused again her eyes found me, and to her horror she realized that I was in a line of kids that were diving into the deep end of the pool. She began screaming, trying to get the attention of the instructors but with all the other noise going on, she was just too far away. She had to run some distance to the opening in the fence so she could get to me before it was my turn. It was my turn now.

I walked confidently to the edge of the pool, looking the instructor in the eye and acting like this was something I did every day. I could hear some woman screaming in the distance, but I was focused on the task at hand. Quickly, I went over in my mind what I had seen the kids before me do, I had memorized their movements, then I launched myself into the water just like they had done.

Something was wrong. Instead of stroking gracefully under water and swimming to the other side, my scrawny little 5 year old frame sank like a rock— apparently I had zero buoyancy. I didn't get one stroke in, I just sank like an anchor.

I came to rest on my hands and knees under 12 feet of water. The pressure was giving me a sensation in my ears and head that I had never experienced before, but luckily I knew enough to hold my breath. So there I was, just looking around, wondering what I had done wrong. I also started wondering what I should do next.

It all happened so quickly that no one really knew what was going on. The instructors were standing there looking down at my wavy reflection at the bottom of the pool when a frantic woman ran up to join them, she was screaming "he can't swim, he can't swim!" My mother had seen me jump as she was approaching and the poor woman was terrified, I'm sure her fear was heightened by her own fear of the water.

As I was becoming aware that it would be really nice to start breathing again, this big hook, sort of like a shepherds crook swung in next to me. It went around my waist and started lifting me up, out of water back to dry land.

Once again I had managed to become the center of attention at an otherwise routine event. My mother was crying, scared, and embarrassed. The pool staff was angry, and embarrassed. The other kids just thought I was an idiot. After it was clear I was all right, it seemed like everyone started scolding me all at once. My mom took me home then, and that was the end of my swimming lessons. I did become an accomplished swimmer later in life, I was even a life guard for a while.

That is the end of this story. So what could the moral of this story possibly be as it relates to being better men?

Every story has lessons, even if the lesson isn't learned at the same time as the story happened, it can be learned later.

I think that is the case with this event. I can't honestly say if I learned anything that day, except that people get mad at you when you almost die in front of them. But looking back at it, there is a clear lesson that we can all glean from it.

That lesson is the importance of knowing yourself, knowing who you are and what your strengths and weaknesses are. Also the fact that pretending to be someone or something you aren't almost never ends well, because eventually, you will have to prove it.

So be authentic. Know who you are and be happy with who you are, and you will have the freedom to be an authentic person. You will be a better man than you were yesterday, and you won't wind up over your head in deep water.

CHAPTER FOUR
Devil Bike

My family lived on a very long dead-end street that branched off a major four-lane arterial highway, making a 'T'. Our house was pretty far down the street, so the busy road at the end was never really an issue because I didn't wander that far away. It was the summer of 1968 and I was 6 years old.

My birthday was in July and I had received my very first bike as a gift. I loved that I had a bike, but I hated having one and not knowing how to ride it. My friend Shawn who lived a few houses down was in the same boat as me, and we decided to help each other learn how to ride. We both thought training wheels were stupid. Training wheels were like a big neon sign that said, "This guy is a little kid who doesn't know how to ride his bike". No training wheels for us, we were desperate to learn how to ride without them.

We devised a plan that was pretty simple. We took turns pushing each other across our road, the road was about 15 feet wide, so we would get about four revolutions of the pedals before we crashed into the ditch, then it was the other guys turn. This was decades before anyone invented safety equipment for kids—no helmets, no pads.

We did this several hours a day for a few days. We were getting a little banged up with all that crashing, but I started to notice that something was different. It felt like, during that brief moment before I crashed each time, that I was in some sort of control. It started to feel like I could actually keep going if that ditch wasn't in the way.

So one day I pointed my bike down the road instead of across it. Shawn looked at me funny as if to ask what I was doing.

"I think I can do it," I said. "I think I can ride this bike. Push me real fast— as fast as you can!"

"It's really going to hurt if you crash on the street," Shawn reminded me.

"I know, but I think I can do it." I said.

So, Shawn started pushing me, and I started pedaling. I was concentrating very hard, and after a moment I thought, "Wow, Shawn is really running a long way". I managed a look behind me and to my amazement realized that Shawn had stopped pushing a ways back. I could see him standing there, his mouth open in astonishment and wonder, watching me ride this bike down the road.

Then the realization hit me that I was in fact riding this bike, totally unassisted! I had done it! There I was just riding down the road like a big kid. I swelled with pride and happiness at this knowledge. My pride and happiness soon turned into terror, as I realized I had never learned how to stop, or turn, or anything else really. All I knew how to do was sit there and pedal. I was on a run away bicycle, and if I didn't figure out a way to stop it, well—that was too terrifying to imagine.

I could see the busy road ahead of me, it was still far away, maybe half a mile, but I could see the cars going back and forth as they passed my street. I started yelling. I was screaming, "Help! I don't know how to stop!" I passed several neighbors in their yard, I cried out to them, begging them to help me, but they all just looked at me very strangely, like they didn't understand.

This really confused me. I didn't understand why no one seemed willing to help me. I just kept getting closer and closer to the busy street ahead. My house would be coming up soon, on the right. I was praying that either my mom or dad would be outside, surely they would help me.

As I approached my house, I could see that dad was in the driveway. I yelled as loud as I could. He was very hard of hearing due to an illness he had when he was younger, but he noticed me. I was screaming and crying at this point. He gestured for me to come to him. I frantically tried signaling that would be impossible, because I didn't know how.

Forging A Man

To my grave disappointment, dad gave me the same confused look that the neighbors had, like he didn't understand what I wanted. Now I was on my own. The busy road at the end of the street was growing ever closer. There were few neighbors in that stretch of road and even if someone saw me, they probably wouldn't help. I began to face the fact that I was probably going to die.

Now I could hear the cars as they sped past the end of my street in both directions. I thought about my family, my grandparents, all the people I had come to know and love in my short life. I was sad that I probably would never get to be a man now, because in a few minutes it would all be over. I looked down at the bike I was riding, and my legs pumping away. A few minutes earlier I had been elated that I had mastered it's use, and now this very same thing would be the instrument of my destruction. It was so ironic.

As I got closer and closer to the busy street, a strange sense of calm came over me. I stopped crying. I realized what was going to happen and that there was nothing I could do about it. I gripped the handlebars tightly and just made a wish that it happened quickly, that I wouldn't be dragged down the street and ground up on the pavement. I hoped that it would be a clean impact at least.

I was only about 50 feet away now, that is when my fear returned. My heart was almost beating out of my chest. As I came to the intersection I held my breath, and closed my eyes, and flew into the busy street on this bike from hell that I had become a prisoner of. Time slowed to a crawl as I waited for the impact to happen...Then my front tire started bumping as if on rough ground. I opened my eyes and realized that somehow, miraculously I had made it all the way across the road without getting hit.

My bike crashed into a deep ditch with lots of brush. I was thrown off the bike and landed on my back amidst some sticker bushes. I just lay there, still—staring at the sky and wondering how I was still alive. As I lay there I heard a noise and then my dads face came into my field of vision. Even though he had not heard what I said, he could tell I was in great distress and he had chased me down the road.

After being a father myself, I bet it was much harder on him watching me cross that busy street, than it was on me.

He picked me up and brushed me off, hugged me. Then he

looked into my eyes and asked me why I didn't stop, or turn around. I told him through tears, that I didn't know how. His expression was a mixture of wonder and amusement.

The next day we spent some time going over every possible bicycle contingency there was.

That is the end of the devil bike story. So now, what is the lesson behind it? I have actually drawn upon this experience in my life, at those times when I feel panic setting in. A little fear is healthy and normal, but panic is paralyzing. If I had remained calm, and not panicked, I may have realized I could have simply STOPPED PEDDLING. Or I may have figured out that I just had to turn the handlebars.

As it was, I couldn't think clearly at all— panic had made me useless to the point of idiocy. Of course my neighbors looked at me funny, because they knew all I had to do was stop giving my vehicle power, but I didn't know that, and it almost killed me.

So like I said, I have been able to remember and use this experience to help keep a cool head when things get crazy. Our mind is our biggest ally in all situations, we can't afford to let panic rob us of our ability to think. So remaining calm in chaos, (outside or inside) is essential to being a better man in any circumstance.

CHAPTER FIVE
Severed Parts

Elementary school principles had something in their desks in 1969 that they do not have today. They had wooden paddles, and they were used in the administration of discipline against misbehaving children. These paddles had many different shapes and dimensions. By the time I got to high school I had seen them from 12 to 30 inches long. Most were made of pine or fir, but the really special ones were made from black walnut because it was hard and would retain very sharp corners. Some of the paddles were full of holes, the holes cut down on wind resistance and made a significant increase in the amount of velocity they could hit you with.

Just about all the teachers had paddles, even the women. Some of the paddles had names, though I can't remember any now—it's probably better that way. The paddles to fear most belonged to the principles. The principle of my little school, Mr. Thompson, didn't mess around. He had two paddles, just in case one broke during use. You could tell that he had crafted them himself in his garage, and took great pride in their shiny finish and fine lines.

I was one of those kids to whom a spanking was only a mild deterrent; I had gotten used to them. I don't think I was what you would call a "bad kid," but if there was something I really wanted to do I would weigh out all the consequences. If my desire to do something outweighed my fear of the paddle, then I would mentally accept the pain before I even began.

Needless to say, I got a swat from a paddle at least once a week, from elementary, all the way through junior high school. Most of my punishment seemed to have something to do with my open dislike of girls, which was actually how my closet "like" of them manifested itself. I actually liked girls—a lot, but they were a mysterious creature to me and I didn't know how to approach or talk to them, the best I could do was find new ways to torment them, and thereby have their attention if nothing else.

I lived on a farm and occasionally we would have animals slaughtered for meat. I was always right under foot, learning all I could about the slaughter man's fascinating vocation. I would ask a million questions: "What's that thing? What's it do? Why is it that color? Do I have one of those in me?" and so on. They didn't seem to mind though, and I eventually became good friends with the slaughter guys.

One Sunday we were having a couple pigs slaughtered and I got the most brilliant idea. I would take a piece of a pig to school with me and use it to terrorize girls. I giggled out loud at the thought of it, and the slaughter guy was happy to oblige me with two pig ears. I just told him I needed them for school, I didn't say why.

My mother had never told me NOT to bring pig ears to school to terrorize girls. This fact was critical in my justification of the event. I never outwardly 'directly disobeyed' my parents, but they had to be discerning about how they worded things, and also be extremely careful about what they forgot to tell me. If I was caught in this pig ear caper I could just play dumb, because no one had ever told me not to do it.

The stage was set. I had managed to wait until first recess. The ears were in a paper bag in my coat. Once on the playground I carefully surveyed a group of girls, I waited for one to stray away from the herd. There she was…Nancy.

Holding the ears up to my head in much the same position they were in life, I made my best pig squeal imitation by sucking air in backwards over my vocal cords. She looked, I charged, the chase was on. Soon all the girls on the playground were screaming. I tossed an ear to my friend Jay so he could join me in the attack.

Suddenly everyone just froze in their tracks and became silent. I continued to run around crazy with my severed ear for a bit until I noticed everyone else standing silently, staring in the direction of the school. I turned around slowly and there was Mr. Thomson standing on the steps, both hands on his hips, trembling with fury.

He slowly stretched out his arm in my direction. When his arm was horizontal a long bony finger flipped out like a switchblade and it pointed at me. Then his hand slowly rotated, finger still out, until his palm faced upward...at which time the extended finger began flexing, as an indication to come.

I had had my fun for the day. Like a condemned man who deserved his fate I gathered myself and followed Mr. Thompson into the school to meet whatever punishment awaited me. What awaited me was his paddle of course, no surprise there. The ears were confiscated and my mother was called. All the kids were huddled beneath Mr. Thompson's window hearing what they could.

I got it again when I got home, and again when my Dad got home. Apparently I was the only one in the family with a sense of humor. I was told in no uncertain terms to never bring ears to the school again, and I never did. They hadn't said anything at all about tails though, that was an adventure for another day.

That's the end of this one, but there are a few lessons in this story. On the face of it, it would seem like I was kind of a horrible child that had no regard or respect for the girls in my class.

The truth of it, in my opinion, is that I was just a kid. A kid with a good imagination who liked girls a lot, but who didn't understand them. They were so different from me as to almost appear like a different creature all together. It was as though common language was useless to me in communicating with them, but I wanted them to notice me, to be aware of me. I think I accomplished that part, but in the process I probably made them hate me, and with good reason.

I was 7 years old and my moral compass was still in construction. All I had to guide me at this point was my limited experience and what I observed, and was told by adults. Most of what I did was instinctual and compulsive...very little reasoning went into what I did at that age. Then I grew up, and as I grew I eventually mastered the nuances of human society. By the time I hit 9th grade I was quite civilized, I still couldn't talk to girls very well, but I had learned to respect and revere them, and consider them as people with value.

There is a problem I have noticed in the world today— there are guys running around that should be men, but they are still acting like I did when I was 7. I'm not sure what happened, but these guys I'm talking about never became men for some reason. They are boys inhabiting the bodies of men. It's sad, and disturbing.

Did society drop the ball somehow? Did we create an environment of zero consequence that has allowed boys to never grow up, to never be responsible for their own actions? Our prisons are full of these 'boys' I'm talking about that should be men—it's a tragedy. If you are reading this and you have a theory about it I would be interested to hear it. (Drop me a note over at my website; www.beingabettermanpodcast.com)

The other moral of this story is about justification. I was a master at using the words of others to somehow justify the things I wanted to do. As I got older and developed a sense of responsibility and my conscience came on line, I couldn't do this anymore. At some point the concepts of honor and rightness entered the picture and I gradually became a man. I could no longer live with false justifications for my actions.

There are many different degrees of this, the worst cases are in prison, or on their way to prison, but we all know someone who is on this spectrum somewhere...floating around between boyhood and manhood— and that's why I started recording my podcast, which lead to this book. If something I say can help one guy realize there is a better way to be a man, then, it's a worthwhile thing.

If you recognize yourself somewhere on this spectrum, that's good news! Because now you know you can change your behavior, you don't have to behave like a boy any longer, you can actually behave like a man.

I also believe that as a man, it's our obligation to not only be an example of manhood, but to try and make corrections where we see a need. If you know a man who is acting like a boy, tell him about it. Sometimes a guy just needs to hear it straight from someone he knows, that someone could be you. Remember no excuses, no justifications, be happy and proud that you are a good man...and can be a better man.

CHAPTER SIX
Dr. Jekyll & Mr. Hungry

We have all done things we are not proud of, things we would rather not talk about. This is one of those stories, about one of my less than shining moments. I was around 24 years old, I was a grown man with three children, facts which completely strip me of any excuse whatsoever.

Before I get into the story I'll go back a few years. You see, I was born with an abnormal appetite, kind of like a birth defect in a way. Even as a baby my mother had to feed me every half hour. Luckily I was also born with a crazy high metabolism— the bottom line was that I could eat more than any other person I had ever met. I had a huge caloric requirement that really blossomed when I was around 14 and didn't start to slow down until my late 20's.

To give you an idea of what I am talking about, at a 4th of July picnic I am reported to have eaten 22 chickens over a 5 hour time span...not pieces, whole chickens. I was almost banned from several all-you-can-eat establishments, I embarrassed my parents on countless occasions by asking strangers if I could eat their food if it looked like they weren't going to.

Luckily we lived on a farm and my parents were able to feed me with the plants and animals we grew. I would forget we ate dinner and ask my mother what was for dinner as she was washing the plates we just ate from. For breakfast I would frequently eat a dozen eggs, a half pound of bacon and a loaf of bread. I ate constantly, and never got full. When I left home for the Army my parents suddenly had more money piling up in the bank; my mom got a new washing machine and my dad got a motor cycle, just because they didn't have to feed me any more.

When I was in the Army I was starving most of the time; I would volunteer for kitchen duty just so I could eat more food. I would bring a high powered air rifle with me when we went out on field exercises and I would shoot anything in the trees that moved, and eat it. I ate 6 robins one day and an armadillo on another day. It was a constant challenge for me to get enough calories. When we were not out in the field I had to eat in mess halls. They would only serve me one meal, so I would try to hit as many different mess halls as I could during meal times. Sometimes if I ate fast I would make it to 3 halls.

My appetite didn't slow down when I left the Army after 5 years. I ate 6 big macs on the way to work one day. I would routinely order two dinners just for myself at restaurants. It was—expensive and bothersome, and embarrassing. Now here I was, 24 years old, married with three kids, and my hunger was still causing me to behave in ways that were unfortunate.

It was my oldest daughter's birthday and my family was giving her a little party. They were waiting until I got home from work.

I was working in construction at the time. It was a hot day in June and when I came home I was ravenous, as I usually was when I got home. There were hot dogs, chips, and birthday cake. The first thing I did was silently count the number of hot dogs, then I counted the number of people. It was going to be close, I could feel a bit of hunger panic rise inside me.

Then there was a knock at the open front door of my mothers house. The little neighbor girl from down the street had seen the extra cars and stopped by just to see what was going on. She was around 7 years old. In her usual neighborly fashion my mother told her about the birthday party and welcomed her in. Then she told her to help herself, and have a hot dog. My hunger panic exploded when I heard her say that, I jumped up and looked at the little girl and yelled: "NO, THERE'S NOT ENOUGH!"

All activity stopped, all movement ceased; it instantly became absolutely quiet and everything seemed to be moving in slow motion. The tiny little girl was starring up at me as if she might start crying. I looked around and everyone else was starring at me as though I had suddenly transformed into some hideous beast, which...I suppose I had.

I instantly realized what I had done, but I didn't know how to fix it, so I just stood there. My mother finally spoke and told me in a low guttural monotone how ashamed of myself I should be, and I was. Then she told the little girl to never mind me, and took her in the house and got her some food.

I really was ashamed. I was acting like an animal in front of my own children. In that moment, it seemed like everyone hated me, everyone was embarrassed and ashamed of me. I told the little girl I was sorry and I went outside.

This was a defining moment for me, I still remember it quite well, and so does everyone else. It comes up every now and then and people will talk about their memory of it, so I wouldn't be able to forget it, even if I could. As I said at the beginning; it is a story I am not proud of—but hey, it happened. It is a part of who I am and it is my obligation to learn from it and get something out of it that is good.

So what did I get out of it? My hunger had been embarrassing up to that point, but it had never made me treat anyone badly, it had never made me mean. In the first hours that followed the incident I tried to blame the hunger itself, as though a physical sensation could be responsible for my behavior. As though the hunger had an agenda, a will of its own.

Eventually I came to understand that the hunger itself was neither good or bad, it just was. With that came the understanding that it was my lack of control, my inattention, my lack of awareness of anyone around me. It was my own self-centered need and my inability to overcome it that led to me treating that little girl badly. I had to face the fact that in that moment I was not a good man, I was a bad son, a bad father, and a horrible neighbor.

It was a tough pill to swallow all at once, but I did. I changed a little bit that day for the better, I became more aware of myself, and my responsibilities as a man. I never treated anyone else like that , not even when I was hungry.

It's no fun, but sometimes it takes something like that to break us out of old ways of being so that we can become better. It doesn't work though, unless we are willing to really see the ugly side of ourselves and accept it for what it is, because only then can we begin to correct it. Everyone has done something like this, something they aren't proud of, but a lot of times rather than see the ugliness, people glaze it over so they don't have to face it. Then they learn nothing from it, it becomes a wasted lesson that they are likely to repeat.

I challenge you to go back in your mind to those moments in your life you were not proud of. Evaluate that experience and see if you learned the lesson, or if you glazed it over. It's never too late to make amends, and it's never to late to learn those lessons.

CHAPTER SEVEN

Make A Memory, On Purpose

My dad woke me up at 2:30 in the morning. I was disoriented and confused and drunk with sleep, and I was not cooperating. Finally he was able to break through to my consciousness by telling me; "C'mon…it's your birthday today, I have something to show you."

The mere mention of my birthday seemed to open up all my capillaries and send oxygen rushing to my brain. This was the day I had been waiting for, for 364 days. Instead of having just one digit in my age, now I would have two. I was one step closer to being a grown up, a man. Today, I would become 10 years old.

I got dressed and went upstairs to the kitchen where I found my dad making me breakfast. My mom usually did the cooking, so whenever dad cooked it was a special treat. He was frying eggs and bacon. He made me a plate and I sat down. I had never been awake this early in the day, it was pitch black outside. The darkness confused me and made it hard to understand that it was morning, the actual morning of my birthday. Dad was filling his thermos with coffee and packing some things into bags. He told me to hurry up and finish eating because we had to get going. He seemed excited and a bit anxious which was a noticeable change from his usual calm, collected demeanor.

I asked where we were going? He just smiled and told me, "You'll see when we get there." I asked a few more times, trying to get him to tell me what our destination was, but he would not budge. He remained happily silent, like he had the best secret in the world. I was frustrated by his refusal, but there was something about the way he was acting that let me know wherever we were going—it was going to be good.

By now it was 3:00 in the morning. We loaded into the car and took off, me in the front seat beside him. I saw that he had packed some heavy coats which I thought was odd, because you didn't need coats in July. I was determined to stay awake, I didn't want to miss anything. I succeeded for an entire half mile before sleep came to reclaim me. I slept for the next two hours as we drove.

The next thing I was aware of was Dad shaking me awake saying, "We're here." We were still driving, but the sky was brighter with the first traces of dawn. As my eyes adjusted I looked around and saw a pleasant little town, shrouded in fog and mist, the smell of the sea had filled the car. The road we were on ended at a marina, I saw boats and docks, but the fog was so thick I couldn't see much beyond them.

Dad parked the car, we got out and he motioned me to follow him. I still didn't know for sure what we were up to, I was barely containing my excitement. We walked onto a dock that had boats parked on both sides. After a little while my dad stopped at a particular boat. A man working on the boat looked up and came over to greet us. My Dad said, "Alf, this is Bud, he's the skipper of this boat." Bud shook my hand, I had never met a skipper before but he looked exactly like what you might imagine a skipper would look like, right down to his skipper hat and yellow rain slicker. Bud welcomed us aboard.

I was left to explore the boat a little, while my dad and Bud talked. It was starting to make sense, but it was still hard to believe. I saw fishing poles, big ones, much bigger than the little trout poles we had at home. Then I realized my dreams had come true; we were going fishing...on the ocean. I wasn't sure what we were fishing for, and it didn't really matter because I was here, with my dad, and we were about to embark on an adventure together somewhere out beyond that thick fog.

A couple other men joined us on the boat and we made ready to depart. I was fitted with a life jacket. The big twin diesel started up and we took our seats. My heart was about to beat right out of my chest. My dad was beaming with his own happiness and enthusiasm. We slowly left the harbor, chugging past other boats that were getting ready to depart. By now the eastern sky was pale yellow. After a little ways we were out of the fog and it was beautiful. Pelicans were flying low in groups over the water and the sea gulls that seemed to be following our boat were calling to one another.

We finally made our way to open water and Bud the skipper throttled up the engines. The back of the vessel went down a bit as the bow raised up, I could feel the cool sting of morning air on my cheeks, and now we were really moving. We were headed due west, right out into the pacific ocean.

After nearly an hour the engines quieted down and we came to a stop. There was no land...only water as far as the eye could see in any direction. Bud had a couple deck hands and they started issuing fishing poles. My dad and I got ours and I was told not to touch anything until I was told to.

Then a deck hand got us all set up with bait, which was an anchovy held in place at the end of the line by two big hooks. Talking more to my dad than me, he showed us how to let out the proper amount of line. Then dad helped me do the same with my pole, explaining how to operate the reel with all of it's little levers and whatnot. It was much different from the little spin cast reels I was used to.

I was told we were fishing for salmon, the limit was three each. The biggest fish I had seen up to this point were trout, and not huge ones; 14 to 18 inches at most. My dad told me this was very serious business out here because I might hook a fish that was almost as big as me, and twice as strong— that got my attention.

Dad poured some coffee from his thermos and handed me a soda. We sat there watching our poles. We talked and laughed and listened to each other. We talked about salmon and sea monsters and vikings and whales and all manner of things. It was during this time that I felt for the first time in my life what it might be like, to be a grown man. I felt like I wasn't just a boy right now, I was sharing a real experience with my dad, like a man. I was being regarded by him and the skipper and the deck hands, like another man on the boat. It felt fantastic, I was so happy.

Suddenly the end of my pole arched down quickly in a violent motion and stayed there, pointing at the water, trembling slightly. My jaw dropped and my eyes opened wide as my dad shouted "Fish on!" He was telling me what to do as the deck hands ran over to supervise. I grabbed the pole and with my right hand started cranking the reel with its big fake ivory ball grip.

I had never felt anything like this before. I felt like if the end of the pole was not securely in the holder that this fish could easily pull me right into the ocean. Cranking was difficult. I was strong for my age but it was a monumental task turning the reel when the fish was fighting. Occasionally the fish would swim right toward the boat and I could quickly reel in the slack, shortening the distance between me and him.

I was getting coached by my dad and the deck hands as I fought this fish. The skipper Bud came down from the wheelhouse to express his approval and add a bit of his advice as well. Minutes were flying by as I battled this Denizen of the Deep. My right arm was on fire with fatigue. When I felt like I might have to hand over my pole because my grip was starting to fail, is when I caught the first sight of the salmon. A big silver flash not too far down— I decided I could do it.

Eventually he was close enough and someone scooped him up with a huge net. There he was, there was my fish, my right arm was almost numb, but I had won. He was about 31 inches long. I could tell my dad was proud I had caught the first fish of the day. I watched as the hands marked him and put him in the big cooler below deck.

After that, the day just kept getting better. I got horribly sea sick at one point. I was throwing up over the side but I was having so much fun I hardly noticed, the vomiting was just an inconvenience. Other men caught fish, my dad caught 1 or 2. I was the only person on the boat who caught three. I didn't get the biggest, but I caught the most.

We saw every kind of sea that day from glassy calm to super choppy. At one point we were in huge swells, a wall of water on each side of us, then we would be on top of a swell sliding down sideways. A couple times the boat tipped and we took on water over the side. It was so exciting, and a bit scary. Whenever I felt scared I just looked at my dad. If he looked calm like nothing was wrong, then I relaxed.

Forging A Man

Eventually it was time to head back in. We reeled in our lines and the engines throttled up. To my surprise the skipper Bud called down for me to join him up in the wheelhouse. My dad nodded at me with a smile and I scurried up next to Bud. Bud said he needed a break and asked if I would steer us in for a bit. He took some time explaining to me how to keep on the heading we were on, he told me which instruments to look at and how to handle the wheel. He watched me for a minute, then he put his skipper hat on my head and left me alone.

There I was, operating this boat full of men all by myself, on the ocean! I had never been so proud and satisfied in my life. It seemed like I was there a long time, but it was probably only 5 or 10 minutes before Bud came back up to re-claim command of the vessel. As I walked back down to the main deck I had a new sense of confidence and bearing. It may have just been my imagination, but I felt like the other men on the boat regarded me a little differently as well.

We got back to the Marina. We said goodbye to everyone and disembarked with our fish. Several men made a point of shaking my hand or slapping me on the shoulder. Dad and I got in the car and headed for home. The still air of the car felt good after being in wind all day. We didn't talk too much on the ride home, there wasn't much to say; I think we were both just basking in the afterglow of one of the best days of our life, and being content in the presence of one another.

A couple hours later we were home showing off our catch and telling our own versions of the days adventure. It was early evening, and it was still my birthday. My mother had made me a cake and we had a little party in my honor. After we ate I was walking around outside and I looked down in the grass. There in the grass below me, was a four leaf clover, the first one I ever found. When I went to bed that night I truly felt like I was the luckiest, happiest 10 year old that ever lived. It was 10 years since I was born, but today was the birth of a brand new memory.

I'll tell you what I got from this experience—besides a great memory. I learned how profoundly we can impact other people in our lives. I doubt if my father was ever able to truly appreciate what this day meant to me. It was a monumental day in my life, and remains one of my top 5 favorite days of all time. I'm sure he knows I had a great day, but he probably doesn't understand how deeply it affected me.

Knowing this, I have tried to give my kids days like this at different times throughout their lives—but honestly, I don't know if I ever succeeded, or even came close. I can't say for certain that I ever gave them something as precious as what my dad gave me but, I have tried, and now I have more opportunities with my grandkids and I'm looking forward to trying some more.

The important thing, and what I want you to take away from this story, is to realize that this is how you become immortal. When you impact someones life in a positive way, when you give them that kind of gift, It creates a memory. The memory becomes a story. Then they will tell the story, like I have here. As long as people are telling stories about you, you aren't really ever dead. That's what I mean about being immortal.

Whether you have kids yet or not there is probably someone in your life that you could impact, someone you could make a grand memory for. It all ties back to the most valuable things we have in life; our relationships. Making impactful memories with intent, on purpose, is a great way of nurturing those relationships, and of being a better man.

Now head out into the world and make some great memories for, and with the people you love. They'll be glad you did, and so will you.

CHAPTER EIGHT
The Nickel

One warm summer day in 1968 I was riding around in our big black cadillac with the most awesome man I knew—my father.

On this rare occasion it was just me and him, no mom, no siblings, just my dad and me; his 6 year old son. I don't remember where we were coming from, but most likely I had ridden with him to the store for something. In those days what we called town was about 30 minutes from the house. We were having a good time talking about all sorts of things, making each other laugh and I was basking in the glow of this amazing man who meant the world to me.

In those days nobody wore seatbelts, in fact I don't think some cars even came with seatbelts, so the big bench seat next to him was mine to explore as he drove us along. The windows were down and it was a good day. As I was crawling around in the car, my hand felt something tucked down between the back and seat cushions, where probably only my hand would have fit. I kept reaching a little deeper until I could grab it. I pulled it out, lo and behold I was holding a nickel!

I showed my dad and he was impressed as well.   He said; "Whoa...a nickel! That must have fell out of my pocket". As he held out his hand to receive his lost property. Keep in mind— it was 1968, a nickel would actually buy quite a bit of candy. Five cents in 1968 would be like around 34 cents in 2017 (I looked it up). That is a substantial amount of money to a six year old. They were different times for adults as well, parents actually had jars full of pennies in their homes, they were tumultuous times when every little bit really did count.

So there was dad holding out his hand for the nickel. I knew what I was supposed to do, but instead I started negotiating. I asked if I could have it, since I found it. He was intrigued, but in order to build value he acted like it was out of the question, that was far too much money for me to handle after all.

Point, counter point, counter-counter point—I was wearing him down. I think he was enjoying the debate and watching how my brain worked. Finally, with great mock exasperation he relented, and said that the nickel was mine. This was the first coin that I had ever thought of as mine. I can see it so clearly in my mind. I sat there turning it over and over, studying every word, every number on it, every picture embossed into it's surface. If I remember correctly it was a 1961 minting.

I was turning over something else in my mind as well, the whole concept of ownership. At 6 years old I don't think I had ever owned anything before, but I owned this nickel. Sure I had some toys and stuff but this was different somehow, this was value on a grownup scale. I owned it because my dad had given it to me. It was an intoxicating notion; this ownership thing. I needed to test it though, to make sure. So I asked my dad a few questions, just to make sure the nickel was completely mine. When he kept answering in the affirmative I became more comfortable with the idea that this was my nickel. mine and nobody else's.

I was thinking what I might buy with this nickel. I was imagining bringing it to school to show the other kids. When I looked down in George Washington's silver face I felt...rich. My dad asked me what I intended to do with this nickel. I thought about it before answering, Then I said, "Well, if it's my nickel I can do whatever I want with it, right?"

That wasn't the response he was expecting, he stammered a bit, then said; "Yes...I suppose so, but I'm curious what your plans are, I think you should put it in a piggy bank and save it."

The idea of saving this nickel didn't sound like any fun to me at all and I said; "Well I haven't decided yet, It's my nickel though right?"

"Yes, it's your nickel."

Forging A Man

"Then I can do whatever I want with it."

"Yes but..."

"Is it my nickel?"

"Yes."

We went on like this for a little bit...My fathers questions were making me doubt the fact that this was my nickel after all, he was trying to exercise his will on it, and I didn't like that. Finally, our little argument reached a climax. My dad had become exasperated with my defiant stance and he said, "Fine...it's your nickel, do whatever you want with it." I smiled in victory. Then, something occurred to me. The grandest most final act of ownership I could think of, I took my nickel and threw it out the open window of the car. We almost wrecked.

Dad was screaming profanities, his gaze leaving the road in front of him to burn holes in me with his eyes whenever we were in a straight stretch. All of his sentences started like: "What the...?" "What's...what kind of..." "Of all the stupid...!" My dad simply couldn't believe what I had done, especially after all the talking we did about it. Finally, he just stopped talking, like he did when he was extra mad. I was sitting there, knowing I had done something wrong and I was upset because he was upset, and I wasn't talking either. We arrived home and dad hurried into the house and started telling my mother all about it.

I had only one defense, but it was a good one: Dad said I could do whatever I wanted with it. He couldn't argue with that, but it didn't make him any less upset. Mom eventually intervened and got everybody calmed down and it was fine. For my dad, it was a lesson in the fact that when he was talking to me, words meant things.

So that was my first experience handling money. It didn't go so well. What was the lesson? You might think the lesson was learning the value of money and how to be more responsible or something like that. You would think I went on to be a master at handling money, maybe a banker or an accountant— nope. I wish it went something like that, but it didn't.

Those were the lessons my dad was hoping I learned, that's what I was supposed to learn, but I was six. It wasn't until years later as a teenager when I was getting paid to work that I started to learn some hard lessons about money. That doesn't answer the question though. There has to be some reason this nickel incident was burned into my brain all these years, I must have learned a lesson of some kind. And It wasn't until I was preparing this chapter that I figured out what it was.

My dad and I were having a great time together that day, then I did something, and then we were not having a good time together. That made me really sad, and that is when I started learning that everything you do has consequences, it was also when I started learning how to consider other peoples feelings, instead of just my own.

It taught me another lesson as well that I could use later in life when I had kids, and that was; don't teach kids lessons that are not age appropriate and expect them to stick.

Now to get the most value out of this story, you might ask yourself: "When did I start learning these same lessons?" Try and think of a time, a story in your own life, when these things showed up for you, because remembering them is kind of like learning them all over again.

CHAPTER NINE
Hobo Norm

It was the summer of 1972 and I was 10 years old. By this time I had earned a certain amount of freedom in my life. We lived on a little farm out in the country and I spent a big part of every day riding my bike down all the backroads and trying to find places I had never been before. There was a river just a couple miles from our house, and train tracks that went over the river on an old wooden trestle. This was one of my favorite places because you couldn't drive to it. The only way to get there was to walk down the tracks or ride a bike down a long dusty trail that ran parallel to the tracks.

It was kind of a magical spot, one of those spots that gets burned into your memory and will remain with you until you die. There was a tall clay bank where someone had put a rope swing. On a hot day you could swing out over the river and let yourself go into a deep pool, then the current would catch you and sweep you to a nearby sand bar.

There was another little creek only about 6 feet wide that emptied into the river at the same spot, the water from the creek was warmer than the river, and you could go back and forth from the warm water to the cold water. The fishing was good in this little spot and there were lots of crawdads too. Little mini-fresh water lobsters — I would bring some home every week and my mom let me cook them myself.

Sometimes I came here with friends, but most of the time I would find myself there all alone, just enjoying the nature and the sound of the water, it seemed like it was my place, like I owned it. I had made a little hut on the bank out of willow branches and I would lay in it and pretend like this was where I lived.

One day I went to the trestle like any other day and as I was sitting on the bank I heard a noise behind me. Startled, I spun around and saw a man. At least, he seemed like a man. He didn't act like any man I had ever known though. He was smaller than most men I had known, and he was sitting on the ground hugging his knees up to his chest, he was shivering as if he was cold. His clothes were dirty and tattered. His eyes were wide and had a look of fear in them— like a child who is lost.

I just starred at him for a moment, watching him. Then I said, "Hi". He said, "Hi" in return, and then we continued to stare at each other for a few more moments. Since he was the adult I was waiting for him to explain himself, or give me some instruction, or to take the lead in some way, but he didn't. He just kept sitting there hugging his knees. He was a pitiful sight, and the more I looked at him the more I realized he wasn't doing well. I had never seen a man in distress before so it took a few minutes to put it together. Finally I said, "Are you OK mister?" By way of a reply he looked at me and said in a shaky voice; "I'm so hungry."

It had not occurred to me up to this point that this man did not have a house full of food where he could feed himself. Not only that, but he was sitting in a wild garden full of berries that he could eat, in front of a river full of fish and craw-dads. For an adult to be hungry like that confused me a great deal.

Then I said; "My name is Alf, Where did you come from?" He let out a long sigh, and for the next few minutes he told me his story.

He said his name was Norm. He grew up in New York City. He didn't speak well of the city, he said it was dirty and full of mean people and concrete, and noise. So one day he was by the train yards and there was a box car with an open door. He climbed in with some blankets and a little food. He didn't know where he was going, all he knew was that he was leaving the city. He told me about many of the adventures he had and about other people he had met who were also riding trains. Getting chased by railroad workers, finding new empty trains to ride.

He told me about all the amazing sights he had seen out the

open boxcar door as it rolled through the country: the mountains, the vast oceans of grass, the dark forests, and the bitter cold nights. His food had run out quickly and he had been surviving on the kindness of strangers and other travelers who shared their meager meals with him.

As he told me this story I was transfixed, riveted to my seat listening as his story unfolded. I had read stories of hobos and railroad bums, but I thought it was all old history and yet, here I was talking with Norm, the Hobo. His story eventually brought him to where we were. He said the train had slowed down almost to a stop. He looked out and saw a place that looked like it should be in a fairy tale, with a sparkling river running through it. He was talking about my special place. So he got off the train and just stayed there.

He had not had food in days, he hadn't had any money in weeks, and if he was going to die he would rather die in a pretty place like this instead of inside a smelly old box car. He said, "I don't even know where I am. Where is this place?" I said, "We are in Washington State; Olympia, Washington." His gaze trailed off into the distance and he said under his breath; "I've come so far..."

As his story ended we both sat in silence for a few moments. I don't know what he was thinking, but I was trying to wrap my brain around the notion that someone would expect to die of starvation in a warm sunny place with food all around them. I had never encountered a completely helpless person before, much less an adult —for me it was like discovering an entirely new species.

That's when I took charge. I told him to stand up, I had something to show him. He stood up shakily, warily. I walked about 10 feet behind where he had been sitting to where Himalaya blackberries as big as my thumb were hanging in a cluster. I picked one and handed it to him. He looked at it like he didn't know what to do. "Eat it." I said. He put it in his mouth and his eyes got wide. Then he started picking them all and stuffing them in his mouth. He was laughing as he ate, I also noticed he was crying at the same time.

Norm didn't have any provisions, nothing. He had literally been reduced to the clothes on his back. No toilet paper, no tooth brush, no comb, even his blanket had been stolen by another hobo. I told him I would be back with some things and took off on my bike. As I rode towards home I was elated! I had my very own hobo! I was the luckiest kid on the planet.

When I got home I filled a backpack with everything I could think of that Norm might be able to use; extra clothes, soap, toilet paper, I even found an old toothbrush. My mother just thought I was on one of my pretend military missions and paid me no mind at all, she was used to me doing things like that.

Then I made him some sandwiches, my favorite; peanut butter & home made jelly. Next, I went out to the garden and loaded up on produce, there were radishes and cucumbers and some green apples from the tree. A dozen eggs from the chicken pen. Then I raided my fishing tackle box and got everything he would need to catch some fish, I found an old pan and a couple pots mom never used anymore for him to cook in. When I was all done my boy scout back pack was stuffed to the gills, it was actually over flowing, and it was pretty heavy. It was difficult riding my bike with it, but I managed.

I'll never forget what it was like when I showed Norm all the things I brought him. It was like he had won the lottery. It was like a drowning man, who's feet touched the bottom and he realizes he won't drown. It was like someone finding their child who had been lost—it was like I saved his life.

He went through everything like a kid on Christmas morning opening packages. When he got to the cucumber he held it up and asked me what it was, I told him. He asked what you do with it. I said, "You eat it." He laughed and said he had never seen one before, and that it looked like a big pickle. Over the next couple weeks I visited Norm every day. He was like my very own personal pet Hobo that I was completely responsible for. I was shocked every day by all the things Norm did not know about the natural world. He was like a baby to whom everything was new and fascinating. We made him a pole and I taught him how to fish, and how to catch craw-dads. At first he felt bad about killing and eating them, but he got used to it. I taught him how to build a fire, I taught him how to do everything.

He would run out of things like butter and toilet paper and sandwiches, and I would resupply him everyday. Every day we would talk for a long time. I would teach him things about the world around him and he would tell me stories of a dark, terrifying place where there was no joy.

After a couple weeks Norm looked a lot better. He was clean and healthy looking. He wasn't scared or cold anymore. One of the clearest memories I have, was on a day we were sitting there by the river being warmed by the sun, we had just eaten. Norm looked up at the sky into the breeze, his eyes were closed and he had the biggest grin I had ever seen, and he said; "Life is so good." I think that memory sticks with me because I have never heard anyone before or since say it like that, and mean it so much, the way Norm meant it on that day.

One day, maybe three weeks after I had found him, I went to visit Norm, and he was gone. The camp was cleaned up well like I had taught him to do, all that remained was the little fire pit. I called out to him, but he was gone. I found a note under a rock, written on paper I had brought him. His penmanship was like that of a 5 year old, but I could read it. The note just said. Thank you Alf, for everything. I have to go, There are things I need to do in the world. Have a good life, Norm.

I sat there for a long time, grieving the loss of Norm. I thought he would just stay there forever and I could take care of him. I had felt so important...and now I was just a 10 year old kid again. Being able to help Norm and teach him things had made me feel special. For a little while it was like I was the adult, taking care of a child. The future seemed very boring and meaningless by comparison.

When I told my mother about Norm a couple years later she freaked out pretty bad thinking about all the things that could have happened. I suppose she was right, it could have gone a very different way, but it didn't. I have always treasured my memories of Norm, and that summer of 1972. I still go to that spot occasionally and never without thinking about Norm and wondering what ever became of him. Wondering if he ever did the things he needed to do in the world.

When I consider the lessons that I learned from Norm and this whole experience there are truly too many to contemplate. It would be impossible to try and list them or name them all, because they are the special kinds of lessons you only learn when you are teaching or helping someone else. When you are sharing your knowledge or helping someone else learn something, you learn so much about yourself in the process. For lack of a better term, you are expanded, as a person.

Perhaps that is the lesson; never miss an opportunity to share your knowledge with another person. When you give of yourself with no expectation of reward, it is then you are rewarded in ways that you cannot imagine, or define.

I hope that makes sense to you reading, I don't know how else to say it.

When you go out into the world and share your strength and your knowledge it can make someone's life better in the process, and also yours as well.

CHAPTER TEN

A Horrible Surprise

This story took place in September of 1980, just a couple months after my 18th birthday. I enlisted into the Army on the actual day of my birthday, and there were several reasons for that.

1.   I had a disagreement with my boxing trainer, and being young and foolish, and maybe a little hot headed, I figured I would show him. Instead of turning pro, I would just join the Army.
2.   It was peace time, but the Leader of Iran had taken 52 American hostages and things were heating up in the Middle East. I was feeling very patriotic and figured if there was going to be a war that I should be part of it.
3.   I decided to join on my actual birthday because I had been saying for a couple years that I was not going to be dependent on anyone else past my 18th birthday. I also talked a couple friends into joining on the same day.

So there I was, in the Army. My basic training experience was going to last three months, because It was in a combat job, my basic and advanced training were all done together. I had been there about two months and had a month to go. We were in Georgia at Fort Benning, it was late summer and terribly hot and so humid. The weather was the hardest thing for me to get used to because it was very different from my home state of Washington. Otherwise, I enjoyed basic training. I enjoyed the physical and mental challenges, and the camaraderie. I enjoyed the game of not being last and not being the worst at anything.

One sultry Sunday we were all hanging around the barracks, there was no training going on. Suddenly a drill sergeant walked into our barracks and everyone jumped to their feet and assumed the parade rest position, because that's what you did when a drill sergeant showed up. The drill sergeant did something strange then, he just leaned against the wall and said in a very casual, almost normal tone, "Relax guys, hey I just came by to invite all of you down to the assembly area, there is something we need to tell you."

Then he left. We just looked at each other in stunned silence. These drill sergeants never opened their mouth without something loud and menacing coming out of it. He was acting like a regular person, and treating us like regular people—it was very strange, and it made us all very curious. There was no way we could turn down a friendly invitation like that, so we all went down to the assembly area to see what was going on.

The assembly area was a big open place where we all gathered. There were some bleachers there in a circle formation, right outside the first sergeant's office. We had four companies of around 30 men each, so there were about 120 of us milling around in the shade on this hot Georgia afternoon. The officers were there, and all the drill sergeants, even the captain. It was very surreal...they were all just hanging out like us, there was no saluting, no barking of orders.

Then First Sergeant Gonzales walked out and stood in front of us. He was a small man, but extremely tough. He had black belts in several disciplines and had done three tours in Vietnam; we all respected him. He said, "Men, thank you for coming. There is something very important we have to tell you." He had our full attention now, he went on. "It is my duty to inform you, that at approximately 1500 hrs yesterday, the president of the united states made a declaration of war against the country of Iran and it's allies." He let this sink in a minute— you could have heard a mouse fart 100 feet away. He continued, "We got orders this morning that this training unit will be sanctioned as a complete fighting unit. You will not go to another duty station, we are all being deployed to the war as a group, in approximately one week. The executive officer will explain our mission."

Forging A Man

As we waited for the XO to replace the First Sergeant in front, there was stunned silence, nobody was saying anything. I felt like something huge and heavy had hit me in the chest and I was still trying to wrap my brain around it. The XO rolled down a big map of the middle east that had been staged there, he was holding a pointer, and he began to speak.

He said in seven days time we would be flying in a C130 with all our gear to an undisclosed location, where we would board another aircraft that would fly us all the way to an aircraft carrier in the Persian Gulf, stopping for fuel once along the way. From there we would get issued our ammo and other ordinance and board an amphibious assault vehicle. We were going to storm a beach just like they did in World War II. He said that intelligence reports showed there were enemy troops already in position along that coastline, and we were expected to encounter heavy resistance. Our mission, along with neighboring units, was to eliminate these enemy positions so we could set up a base camp for future war operations.

The XO sat down and the Captain came to the front. He told us he realized this might all come as a shock, but we were in the Army, and this is what we joined for. He told us to take the rest of the day to write letters home.

He told us to look to the man to our right and left. After we did, he said half of these men next to you won't make it back. Or, you might be the one that doesn't make it back but, we were a good unit, and if we looked out for each other, remembered our training, and kept our nerve, we had a chance. Then he said that was all, and dismissed us. The officers all left but the First Sergeant and Drill Sergeants remained just casually hanging out.

For a while we all just sat there, each man in his own thoughts. I became aware that several men around me were crying, not sniffling, they were bawling. Like I said earlier, at first the shock of it was like something big, physically hitting me, I was stunned. My next thoughts were of my family, my parents and siblings. I thought about them as I digested the very real possibility that I would never see them again. I grieved for my mother, knowing her sensitive soul would be distraught at the news I was going to war. I thought about a lot of things; my dog back home, my friends, my girlfriend. I thought about the fact that I might never marry, I may never have kids.

Eventually, I got done thinking about all the things I might never be able to do, and I started thinking about the reality of what we were going to do. I would have to kill people. I would see my friends killed, I might be killed or worse—horribly wounded. I started to get angry then. My anger was focused on Iran, what I saw as the source of all this. This country that stole 52 Americans, for what? The more I thought about it the angrier I got. I thought who does Iran think they are? They can't do this! The Captain was right, this is exactly why I joined the Army. Before I knew it I was frothy with rage and I was actually looking forward to the trip.

I don't think this was bravery necessarily, rather I think it was the way my brain figured out to cope with the fear and dread of something awful, something I couldn't avoid. I would say most of the guys coped with it similar to myself; they were resigned to make the best of it, but everyone coped differently. Like I said, some guys were bawling. Three guys jumped off the bleachers and just started running away, as if they could just run back home. Some guys were trembling, not coping at all...they were just afraid.

After a while the First Sergeant and the drill sergeants called us all together again, the guys that ran off were retrieved. Then the First Sergeant told us quite simply, that none of it was true. They had made it all up— but, it could happen just like that and not to forget about it. Then they just left.

Wow, talk about relief. I think I might have cried a little when I found out it wasn't true. Now we had a whole new set of emotions to deal with; anger at them for tricking us like that, profound relief, and the joy that I would get to see my family again.

The whole experience established a new level of brotherhood among us, because we realized in those few moments that a time could come when we really did depend on each other for our life. We all learned a great deal about ourselves that day, and about each other. The guys who didn't handle it very well were dealing with the shame of that. Even our training and our classes took on a new level of importance and relevance, because now we knew we were learning things that might save our lives.

I have never forgotten that moment in time, the memory of it helped shape me. Looking back on it now, 36 years later as I am putting this book together, I think that might be the actual day that I became a man. When I woke up that day I was still a snot nosed kid just out of high school, but when I went to bed that night I was not thinking the thoughts of a boy any longer.

As far as lessons go though, one great thing I learned from this is that I don't like these kind of surprises. By that I mean being surprised by my own reactions, it's very unsettling for me. To this day, because of this experience I try to be prepared emotionally and mentally for any eventuality. I do that by imagining worst case scenarios, actually all scenarios, and then deciding how I will feel and react in every case, before it happens. Then, when something does come up I'm not caught off guard, I can think clearly and behave calmly because I've already imagined this and decided how I would feel.

Of course its impossible to imagine every single possibility, but I do my best, and it has helped me many, many times. Times when others are in crisis, I am able to remain rational and be a help for those that aren't. I think that's an important thing for a man to be able to do, it is an important service that you can provide others around you. It's another way of sharing our strength, and one of a man's highest callings, in my opinion.

This kind of preparation isn't easy, it takes practice— a habit of assessing all potential outcomes has to be developed. It's totally worth it though, because I look at being surprised by my own emotions and reactions the same way I look at being in a boxing ring totally out of gas and unable to defend myself. For me, they are equally horrible feelings, and I have done them both.

So think about it guys, if it sounds like a good idea, if it seems like being emotionally and mentally prepared for anything would serve you and the people in your life well, then do something about it.

I'd like to take a minute here to recognize and acknowledge all of our present day service men that have been involved with war. You guys have all gone through what I went through and much, much more. From the bottom of my heart...thank you for your service.

CHAPTER ELEVEN
The Almost Perfect Day

There is one day I will never forget, that day was May 13, 1979, when I was 16 years old. It also happened to be Mother's Day, and it was a Sunday. I was having an exceptional day. One of those days where you really feel like you are the king of the world, everything just keeps going right—everything, even the weather was beautiful in the Pacific Northwest!

On this particular glorious day I had spent the early hours in Seattle with my boxing trainer. I was working out in a professional gym, I had gone about 25 rounds that day, 4 of them sparring grown men that outweighed me by 50 pounds, and I had done very well. My trainer told me I had been turning heads, impressing the other people in the gym. The future looked bright.

On top of that, I was driving around in my mother's car. It wasn't anything special, a pumpkin orange Volkswagen square-back sedan with a lot of miles on it. She had given me full use of it for the day so I was taking advantage of the freedom it offered.

After I dropped off my trainer at his house I stopped at a fast food place and got a burger, then I drove out and surprised my girlfriend at her house. I took her for a little drive and we spent the afternoon hanging out.   It really was a perfect day, and I felt... fantastic!

I was driving home now, because it was Mother's Day and I was sure my family was going to celebrate it somehow. I was heading south on the road home that went by the little Olympia airport, driving about 35 miles an hour.

I saw a flash, an obstacle suddenly in my lane just a few feet in front of me. There wasn't even time for my brain to register what it was, it happened so fast. Instinctively my hand cranked the wheel to the left. The next thing I knew I was sort of coming out of a fog, I was alerted by the sound of glass tinkling. Nothing made sense, but in that moment, I didn't require it to. I was still sitting in the car, the steering wheel looked like a pretzel, and I couldn't see the passenger seat, because it wasn't there anymore.

Unalarmed, and very calmly, I climbed up over the steering wheel and out the hole where the wind shield used to be. I turned around sitting on the hood, my legs dangling over the dash where I was just sitting, I put my elbows on the roof of the car and rested my head in my hands, perfectly content, and feeling very happy, even peaceful.

I'm not sure how long I sat there like that, but I eventually became aware of a horrible sound, it was the sound of a woman screaming. Slowly, realization started creeping back into my brain. Oh no I thought, looking around again, I've been in a wreck! The car was destroyed, it was not recognizable. My next thought was one of panic, thinking that my dad was going to kill me.

I thought I was ok, at least I wasn't feeling any pain yet. The woman's screams were getting louder and I decided to investigate. I climbed out of the car and started following the screams. On the way I met a man, a smallish older man who was staggering along, he had a tiny cut on his chin. He stopped me, and stood there swaying forward and back the way people do when they are really drunk. Then he asked me in a thick drunken slur "Hab you sheen my little dog? I can't find my dog."

I couldn't believe it! "The hell with your dog, what about that woman?" I said, pointing toward another steaming hulk of a car. He said, "Oh she'll be ok...I need to find my dog." Then he just wandered off, looking for his dog.

I ran up to the car and looked in. There was a woman, a huge woman, 400 pounds if she was an ounce, in the passenger seat. She was screaming like she was on fire, and I could see why. At impact the floorboard on that side had been pushed in a couple feet in a millisecond, her legs were pulverized, they didn't even look like legs with all the blood, flesh, bone and fat all stirred up together into something frightfully un-natural. The shell of the car had closed in around her, and I knew immediately she would have to be cut out. I told her I would get help and took off.

The cars had come to rest in front of a veterinary clinic that had living quarters attached on the back of the building, I knew this because we had brought cows and pigs here to be treated before. I knocked frantically on the back door until someone answered. When the door opened the woman standing there let out a little scream, I thought that was odd. I told her I needed to use their phone. She told me they had already called the ambulance, That was good I thought, but I wanted more than anything to call my parents, so she brought me the phone (there were no cell phones in these days) the phone was wrapped in towels...I thought that was odd too. I called home, the phone rang and rang...nobody answered. I figured they must be out shopping for the Mother's Day party.

I thanked the woman and went back out front to where the cars were. As I was walking up the fire trucks arrived, and a few ambulances, and some cops. Four medics attacked me and made me lay down and started working on me. I didn't even realize anything was wrong with me yet. I protested, and a medic got real stern with me. She told me I was covered with blood and they had to figure out where I was hurt. That explained the woman's fear when she opened the door of the house.

So I lay there and let them work on me. The gravity of the situation started to sink in, I got a little scared. I just wanted to see my parents. The medic was concerned because apparently blood was pouring out of my mouth. It was my tongue, when my head hit whatever it hit, my tongue had flown all the way out of my mouth, then my chin hit something and my teeth had almost severed my tongue, way toward the back of my throat. I could tell too, because it was swelling really bad now, It had gotten so big I couldn't close my mouth all the way. My speech had become almost unintelligible.

So I'm laying there, my head turned to the side so my mouth would drain, getting poked and prodded when I see something that made my heart leap, my parents. They had been driving home and saw the wreck. They didn't recognize the car but my dad knew the License plate number. He wheeled around and almost got in his own wreck.

I was so happy to see them, but they hadn't seen me yet. I watched them as they walked onto the scene, they both saw me at the same time. My mother threw her hands up screaming and fell to the ground in a clump, It turns out she thought I was dead. Meanwhile my dad looked frozen, with an expression I had never seen before, all the color left him, he was white as a sheet.

I tried to call out to them as best I could, to let them know I was still alive. Now medics were tending to my mother. Mom eventually settled down and dad got his color back. The medics finished up with me and sent me to the hospital.

I was right about the woman; they had to bring in special equipment to cut her out of the car, and her legs were destroyed from her feet to her hips. Apparently she had come across a man with a dog and a bottle of whiskey hitch hiking. Not only did she stop, but she let him drive, even though he was drunk.

He was flying down the road about 75 mph, passing every body. When he passed the last car, that's when he ran into me. Luckily I had cranked the wheel to the left, it was still a head on collision, but just on the passenger sides collided, that's why I couldn't see the passenger seat, because it was sent to oblivion. They were driving a heavy Camaro muscle car and it essentially cut the Volkswagen in half. If anyone had been with me, as somebody usually was, they would not have had a chance.

Once at the small town hospital, the on-duty doctor didn't even look in my mouth. He did a few other test and sent me home. I thought it was odd because the medics said I would be in the hospital for a few days...but, he was the doctor, so I went home.

The next four days proved to be some of the worst days I had spent on earth, even to this day. The lazy doctor should not have sent me home because I couldn't swallow, because your tongue moves when you swallow. Not only that, but my tongue had swollen up to about five times its original size, and had turned black and hard, it reminded me of a parrots tongue.

I thought for sure I was going to wake up and my tongue would be lying beside me in the bed. I couldn't eat or drink, I was severely dehydrated, my mom was doing her best to squeeze a straw filled with water past my tongue to the back of my throat, where she thought it might trickle down and keep me alive.

Forging A Man

I'm sure you are all wondering, "Why didn't my parents take me back to the hospital!?" All I can say is that they were different times. People didn't question authority like they do today. The doctor had originally told my parents I would be fine, so they were going with that, almost like taking me back to the hospital was prohibited. My mother wondered about it herself years later.

At the time of impact I was in the best shape of my life. At 16, I weighed 195 pounds and only had about 5% body fat—I was a specimen. In fact they said the only thing that saved me was my musculature holding me together, my chest hit the steering wheel hard enough to mangle it but I didn't have any broken ribs or bruised organs, I was very lucky.

Four days of not eating or drinking will wreak havoc with your fitness. My body cannibalized itself, eating my lean mass. After four days I had lost over 20 crucial pounds of lean mass, I only weighed 171 and I was weak as a kitten. I had been running 8 miles a day, now I got winded walking to the bathroom, it was horrible.

Thankfully the tongue is the fastest healing organ, and on the 5th day I was able to drink a little, and form words again. It took months and months of very hard work to gain back all the body muscle I had lost, though.

I went to school an hour early every day, and walked as far as I could on the track. The next day I walked a little farther, the next day, a little farther. Eventually I was able to run a little, and I just kept going farther every day. It was the same with weights; I just kept doing a little more every day. It took me a year and a half to get back to the same weight I was on the day of the crash.

That's pretty much the end of this tale. The woman in the other car tried to sue my parents to pay for her injuries of course, but that was thrown out of court. Nowadays my parents would have sued the hospital for sending me home, but people didn't do stuff like that back then.

So what's the moral of this story? You know, just telling this story was a little emotional for me, it brought back a lot of memories. I think there is quite a list of things I learned that day, and in the days that followed.

I could say the moral of the story was in my recovery, how raw determination and persistence will always yield a result, and I would be right, that's true.

I could say the lesson learned is that tomorrow is not promised to you, your life can change or be lost in the blink of an eye, so the present should always take priority—that also, would be true.

I could say a lot of things. I learned a lot of lessons here that have stuck with me my whole life. But there is one that stands out.

Here it is; when we are at our worst, when it seems like the bottom of life itself has fallen out and we are alone, when we are just another creature in peril on the earth, there is one thing that can always pull us back from the brink and that, is family. It doesn't have to be blood family, but people who genuinely care about you. The raw love and care of other people directed at you will quicken your spirit, give you hope and be a light in your darkest moment.

That's one reason you hear me talk so much on my podcast about the value of our relationships; they are the greatest thing we have in this life. As good men, we should remember that, and treat them accordingly.

CHAPTER TWELVE
The Tough Guy

I had spent my early years in elementary school at a small wooden country school. It was painted white and had a dedicated bell tower with an actual bell like a smaller version of the liberty bell. The Principal would ring the bell with a long rope attached to it. He would ring it to signal the start and end of things like the school day, recess, and lunch.

There were only about 100 kids in this little building, from kindergarten to 5th grade. In a small country school like this the pecking order among students is very clear, because everyone knows everyone. There are clear leaders, and clear followers. You have the weird kid, the pretty girl, the quiet guy, the class clown, the smart girl, the teachers pet— it's like there are certain roles that must be played, and there are always kids to fill these roles.

One of the coveted roles was that of the 'tough guy'. Not the mean guy, that's something else entirely, just the tough guy. The boy who could physically handle everyone else in the school. The position of tough guy was determined by the almost daily ritual of fighting during recess. We called it fighting, but it was more like wrestling, no punches were thrown. Two guys would square off and begin grappling, whoever could throw the other guy down was the winner.

By the time I was in 5th grade I had claimed the rank of the tough guy, and life was good. It was kind of like being the king, or a celebrity of some kind. I had the respect of the entire school but I was constantly having to defend my title. With each successful title defense, my prestige grew.

With the advent of my 11th year on earth and the subsequent promotion to 6th grade, I had to be bussed into the nearby town to attend the city's middle school. It was a completely different world. I was now a 6th grader in 1973, at Tumwater Middle School. Sure the 30 or so kids from my grade at my former school were there, but we were all swallowed up in the great throng of humanity that was Junior High. It seemed like I didn't know anyone, everything was new and it was very unsettling. Not only that, but suddenly not only was I not a king or a celebrity, I was now at the bottom of the food chain. We were the youngest kids at this school. Above us were the 7th graders, and above them, the terrifying 8th graders who almost seemed like adults to us.

So I wandered around sort of lost for a few days, trying to figure out how I fit in. I missed my days at the little country school where I was the master of all I surveyed. I missed it a lot. Then one day I made a decision, I devised a plan that would enable me to recapture the glory of 5th grade. I started asking my classmates who was the toughest kid in 6th grade.

Almost without exception I kept hearing the same name in response. I won't use his real name here, for the sake of this story I'll call him John, lets call him John Duncan. Over and over again everyone I asked said that John Duncan was undoubtedly the toughest guy in 6th grade. He was a city kid and I didn't know who he was, but apparently he was a champion of schoolyard scraps who's reputation preceded him.

My path was a simple one; I would have to find this John Duncan and challenge him to a fight. Once I won, I would gain instant notoriety and high acclaim among my peers, it would be like 5th grade again. Eventually I tracked John Duncan down. He was pointed out to me, I walked up to him, and by way of introduction I said, "Hey, let's go fight".

He said, "I don't even know you…why do you want to fight?"

I didn't have a good reason prepared so I just said, "Because… let's go."

He said, " I don't want to." And he just walked away leaving me stunned and puzzled at this flagrant lack of professional courtesy.

Forging A Man

When I was in 5th grade I accepted all challengers, it was an obligation of the title.

I continued to pursue John over the next couple weeks. Every time I saw him I would present my challenge, and every time he denied me. I started telling other kids that he must be afraid. I even went so low as to say he was a chicken. Looking back I don't think he was being a chicken at all, he just didn't want to fight me, he had no reason to, he had nothing to prove.

Finally one day I wore him down. He said, "Fine! After school by the bus stop." The fight was on. Word of the impending battle spread like wildfire through the school. Everybody came, even the 7th and 8th graders. I had never seen a gathering like this, it was sure to launch me to instant stardom. Keep in mind, in my fighting career at the little country school I had never thrown a punch, I thought that was just for movies. So you can imagine my surprise when the fight started and John landed a beautiful punch right on my nose. I staggered back, wondering what was going on, then he hit me again, and again. The whole world was spinning around, at first I didn't understand what was going on but the realization that I was in an actual fist fight was becoming more clear with every impact.

I knew I was bleeding, because I could see blood everywhere and taste the copper. John kept on hitting me. I tried swinging back, but not having any experience throwing punches, my efforts were woefully inadequate. In fact every time I would swing wildly at him all I did was create an opening for him to blast me again. The action slowed, and stopped for a minute. We were both tired, he was tired from punching me, and I was tired from getting beat up and trying to punch him. I could feel my face was already swelling, my nose was bleeding badly, and I had not landed one punch.

As we stood there panting John was to my left. I thought he might be in range, this was my best chance to land a punch so I whipped out a fist at him, but I was short by about two inches. He looked at me, it was almost a look of pity, then he proceeded to continue pummeling me until the teachers finally broke through the crowd and broke it up. In those days kids didn't get in any real trouble for fighting, fighting was considered to be a relatively normal circumstance of childhood.

They put me on my bus, John got on his bus with much

victorious celebration. I sat down, still breathing heavy. My clothes were ripped, I was covered in my own blood, my face was swollen and I had one eye closing up, my nose hurt. Above all the physical discomfort, the worst thing was the shame. The shame of defeat, the shame of loss. The embarrassment that came with the knowledge that I had brought this on myself. I didn't know how I could ever return to this school under such a heavy cloak of failure.

Of course my mom freaked out when she saw me and was ready to burn the school down but, after I told her the whole story she realized that I and I alone was at fault. Both of my parents helped me a lot during the next few days; rather than get mad at me, they helped me understand the situation.

The lessons learned from this event were of enormous importance. What happened at school that day served to shape me in ways I couldn't imagine. For one, I never started another fight my whole life, not to this day— though I have finished several. I learned that having right on your side is critically important whether you are in a physical fight or a struggle of some other nature. Being on the wrong side of something will always put you at a disadvantage. I became an advocate for other kids that were being picked on. I realized that being friendly to everyone made a lot more sense than being a jerk. I became kinder.

Never wanting to repeat this event I decided that I should learn how to defend myself, and that led to me becoming a boxer.

I learned that one doesn't earn respect through force, but rather through strength of character. I was never really the same after that day. With that beating on the school grounds my entire world view was changed, I grew up just a little, I saw myself in a different light and ultimately I think it made me a better person, because the lesson I learned about the consequences of my own bad behavior was so painfully clear. I can still remember that fight like it happened yesterday. John Duncan and I never fought again, in fact we went on to be friendly towards one another later, if not friends.

I think the ultimate lesson here is not that you have to get beat up, or have some dramatic fight. That happened to work in my case but only because I made it work. That's the lesson, every experience we have in life both good and bad contains two potentials; the potential for positive growth through the lessons learned or, the potential for negative decline. It's up to us— what we get out of the experiences life hands us is up to each one of us individually. It's a choice you make, like what shirt to wear.

It's the difference between letting life happen to you, or you living by your own design. I've found it best to live by one's own design, and strive to make the best choices with every experience, squeezing the good out of everything.

CHAPTER THIRTEEN
Naughty Bird

When I was 6 years old I had a group of friends around the same age, there were 4 or 5 of us that used to hang around together. It was almost like a club, we traveled around the neighborhood in a little pack. It was very "Lord of the Flies".

We got into some trouble, but not too much. Mainly we were just discovering the world together, a bunch of little six year olds. We didn't have a definite leader, but a couple of us took charge more than the others. We all had our role to play in the group and those roles were constantly changing and shifting as we grew, both as individuals and as a group. We were after all, 'baby men' so we spent a great deal of time pretending to be men. We were imitating our fathers and trying on our burgeoning masculinity as though it were a new suit. It was all very natural, the way things are supposed to be, in my opinion.

It was the summer of 1968. My house had a design flaw; it had a huge picture window in front. That wasn't the problem, the problem was that it also had a huge picture window in the back, directly opposite from the one in front. You could stand there and look all the way through the house. I guess that isn't a huge problem, unless you are a bird. Birds were constantly killing themselves trying to fly through our house, breaking their necks on the glass. My mother would hang things in the window to deter them, but after cleaning she sometimes forgot until the next bird hit.

One day myself and my little band of merry men were hanging

out at my house and we heard this big 'bang.' We ran over to find a freshly dead bird, a robin. Usually when we found a dead bird it was cold and had been dead a while. Some of those birds became science projects, we would learn about anatomy, dissecting them with borrowed kitchen knives. It sounds bad, but it's a pretty normal boy thing to want to see how things work, and it was all in the name of science, and curiosity.

The bird we found today was different, or at least it seemed different to us, because it had been alive just seconds ago, it was still warm. Its eyes were still bright and shiny. We passed it around, all of us taking turns holding it and examining it, marveling at the fact that it was dead when it still looked and felt alive. Death it seems, is a complex thing for a 6 year old to wrap their head around, but we were trying to understand it.

I came up with an idea. I suggested that we bury the bird and say a prayer for it so that it could go to Heaven. It sounds nice, but this too, was another form of experiment—because the second half of my plan was that we would dig up the grave the next day, to make sure that the bird had gone to Heaven. My partners all agreed. We gave the bird a nice funeral while it was still warm. Afterwards we all felt pretty good about ourselves. It seemed to us as though the bird had a much better chance of getting into heaven being so freshly dead, and lucky for that bird we sent it straight up to Heaven—that's almost like not dying at all right?

The next day we gathered and went to the bird's grave. We started digging, and were shocked and very confused to find the body of the bird still in the grave. We all looked at each other, not understanding. Someone suggested we didn't pray long enough, someone else suggested it wasn't buried deep enough. I put forth the idea that perhaps this bird, was a bad bird. Maybe it had done something bad and couldn't get into Heaven, maybe it was a naughty bird?

The more I thought about that it didn't make sense to me—how could a bird be bad? It must be that we just didn't pray enough, or maybe someone in our group didn't close their eyes? So we decided to re-bury the bird, and pray even harder, and that's what we did. Everyone swore they closed their eyes. They next day however, it was still in the grave, and the day after that, and the day after that, and, the day after that.

For five days we kept digging up the increasingly ripe bird, re-burying it, praying harder and harder. No matter what we did it just couldn't get into Heaven. My friends decided they didn't want to keep digging up the smelly bird anymore, they were prepared to write it off as a naughty bird. I couldn't though, I became obsessed by the puzzle. I was consumed with the question of why this bird could not go to the Great Beyond. So, operating on my own now, I continued to dig the bird up every day, and everyday I would repeat the ritual. I tried lots of different things; I made a little cross, a headstone. I tried wrapping it in cloth, then a shoebox. I knew there had to be a formula.

Two weeks went by. By this time the bird was only recognizable because of its feathers. Maggots had arrived, and I wondered if the bird did make it into Heaven, if the maggots would end up there with it.

My mother had gown curious because I had been asking a lot of odd, round-a-bout questions. I never asked her these questions directly, because...well, I'm not sure why. There are just some things you want to figure out on your own I guess. One day she kept her eye on me. When I wandered off clutching a garden spade she followed. I started digging and to her horror she watched as I exhumed the rotten bird. She screamed of course, I spun around. I didn't think I had done anything wrong but she was pretty upset, so that made me get upset.

She hurried me into the house and scrubbed me...hard. Then she asked me what I was doing with that dead bird. When I explained everything to her, she immediately got it, her tone softened, and then she explained to me her version of the body/soul/spirit thing. She assured me that the birds spirit had been in Heaven since the first day, but the bodies stay here to return to the earth.

The way she explained it, it made perfect sense. I was able to go on with life knowing the bird would be OK. I told all my friends about my discovery. I had a new sense of things after that, I was a little closer to knowing how everything works.

The lesson from this extended encounter with death was, well, I learned a lot going through this obviously, but I think there was one thing I took away from the experience that has never left me. That is that perseverance will always yield a result. Every problem has a solution, as long as you are diligent and patient in seeking the answer, you will be rewarded. Perhaps not always with the answer you seek, but you will be rewarded nonetheless.

I could have quit when my friends did, the bird would have remained a mystery for several more years. Instead I just kept trying to figure it out and that ultimately led to my mother discovering me, and providing me with an answer. There is an answer to every problem, and if you are diligent, perseverance will always yield a result.

Don't quit, be diligent, and never stop seeking your answers.

CHAPTER FOURTEEN
The Long Day

The day in question was rather recent, March 9, 2016. As you may or may not realize, in addition to being a podcaster and author with a small farm to tend to, I also choose to do various jobs during the day — I enjoy the rewards of physical labor. This particular spring I was driving big trucks. Usually dump trucks hauling dirt and rocks and stuff like that but occasionally I also drive long trucks that haul wood chips. (As I'm compiling this book, I am driving a school bus to fill my time... I can't seem to get away from driving!) These 'chip trucks' are bigger than normal trailers that trucks pull, they have a big belly on them so you can put more chips in them. When loaded they weigh around 96,000 pounds. The chips are used for making paper or for burning in big furnaces.

This day started out kind of crappy. The miserable March came in like a lion and had not let up, driving cold rain and high winds, very blustery and wet. On my way to work I stopped by the barn where we keep the sheep. We had a ewe that was extremely pregnant. She was laying down and would not get up, she seemed like she was in a very bad way. She had given birth to triplets twice before and it looked like she was in great distress. I would have stayed home to make sure she was ok, but they really needed me at work so I went in, worried about her but hoping that mother nature would take care of things until I got home.

I let them know at work that as I needed to go home as early as possible so that I could tend to this sheep. Where I was working was in a seaside town about an hour and a half away from my house. The day was going OK, I was getting things done pretty quickly and I was on my last load almost ready to head home.

I was fully loaded, going about 15 miles per hour around a sharp right hand turn when I felt the whole truck shake and swerve in a weird way. I got around the corner and looked in my mirror to see wood chips hitting the ground. The only thing I could think of was that the back door had come open somehow.

So I stopped the truck right where I was and got out to investigate. What I saw was the last thing I expected; The trailer itself was ripped in half. It was still connected, but there was a huge rip from the top all the way down the side to the bottom, you could look into the rip and see the wood chips, and the belly of the trailer was sitting on the street. The trailer was old, and in use non-stop at the chip mill. Through wear and tear it had become faulty, and it gave under the weight of the load at the apex of the turn.

I just stood there for a minute, gaping—trying to understand what was happening, because you don't see that every day. I immediately called the boss to let him know what was going on and see if he had any advice for me. While I'm still on the phone the storm seemed to get worse and I was getting soaked with rain.

Meanwhile, there were log trucks and other vehicles that were trying to come down the road in both directions, but I was stopped in the middle of the road. When the trailer ripped, the back axles got turned slightly so the rear end wound up over the center line of the road. Vehicles going around me had to drive out on the muddy shoulder.

So now I am talking on the phone in driving rain while also directing traffic around my truck. Of course the boss wants me to send him pictures, but now my phone is so wet that it won't respond to my fingers on the screen. Eventually, I finally got a break in the traffic, managed to dry my phone off, and take some pictures.

I really needed to get the truck off the road, but I was afraid to move it. The rip that went down the side also went across the bottom and I was afraid that if I moved it, the whole thing might separate into two pieces leaving 25 tons of wood chips in the middle of the street.

I called the boss back and he told me to go ahead and try to move it, very carefully. Luckily there was a gravel pull-out near by. I had over shot it though, so I had to back up a few feet and then pull off the road. Another trucker had stopped so he was watching traffic as I attempted the move. Going very, very slowly I managed to pull it off of the road, but the whole way I heard terrible popping and groaning from the trailer, and I expected that any second it would rip into two separate pieces, but luckily it didn't.

Now I was off the road, sitting in the truck with the heater on because I was wet and freezing. I had not brought any rain gear with me because I didn't expect to be directing traffic that day. The boss told me that people were on the way to help, but they were an hour away, and that is when I remembered my poor sheep at home, in distress, trying to have babies.

I had really wanted to get home early this day and now it seemed as though I would never get home, because the truck obviously couldn't go anywhere, I was over an hour from home, soaked to the skin, and shivering. I began to get in a very bad mood. I had the truck running with the heater on full blast but I couldn't seem to get warm. I was just stuck there until someone came to help me...and I couldn't imagine what they would do when they got there, it seemed like a hopeless situation.

Have you ever heard of 'like attracting like'? When good energy will attract more good energy, and bad vibes attract more bad vibes? I believe that it is a real phenomenon. It happened to me on this day. As I was sitting there waiting, in a bad mood trying to get warm, I had nothing to do except monkey with my phone. Being a relatively new podcaster at the time I kept a pretty close watch on how many people were downloading the show. It really makes me feel good when I am seeing a lot of downloads, I feel like I am doing something good and providing value to the world.

On this day...while I was sitting miserable in the truck I was checking the downloads on my phone and it looked like they had come to a screeching halt. It was as if everybody suddenly just stopped listening to my podcast. This put me in an even darker mood, I felt like I had been abandoned by the whole world, forgotten about by my listeners, and physically attacked by mother nature. I also felt horrible wondering about how my poor mamma sheep was doing at home, the creature I was now powerless to help.

Eventually, people came. Then they brought these big vacuum trucks to suck all the chips out of the trailer. A guy from the shop came to pick me up and take me to the dump truck so that I could finally drive back to the shop.

During this whole ordeal I had come to the conclusion that I didn't want to come to work the next day. I needed a day off to get caught up on all the stuff I was unable to do that day. I needed to tend to the farm and get caught up on podcast work…I didn't have time for this.

The hour plus drive home was miserable as well; I had the heat on full blast, but all that did was evaporate the water in my clothes and make the windows fog up so that I couldn't see. I was forced to drive with the windows rolled down, heater on high, rain smacking me in the side of the face and I was cold all the way back to the shop.

Once I got back and parked the dump truck I was just sitting there, getting ready to get into my pickup and go home. First I had to use the bathroom really, really bad, and I was also going to call my boss and tell him of my plans to not come in the next day. My phone rang, it was the boss. He said they needed me to drive my personal truck all the way out there in the morning and get in another chip truck because they were short handed. I told him I didn't think I was coming in. He asked why, and I proceeded to tell him, in a not so nice way.

Then suddenly, through my bad mood and surly attitude it hit me; I was being presented with a great opportunity to be a better man. I stopped what I was saying to my boss, and then I told him I needed a couple minutes to calm down and I would call him back. He said OK.

I got off the phone, went in the bathroom and got cleaned up a bit, and took a minute to evaluate everything. I realized how fortunate I actually was. The truck broke in the most perfect spot it could have on a little side street, instead of out on the highway. It could have happened in the middle of town, which would have been a nightmare. Or it could have happened on the highway going 45 miles an hour, which would have caused a bad wreck for sure. I was actually very lucky. In that moment I changed my bad energy. I realized that my boss, who was also my friend was just the messenger, and that he was just trying to do his job, and I had been a little hard on him on the phone.

I called him back and apologized for my previous attitude and told him I would be happy to work the next day. My wife texted me and let me know the sheep was doing OK. When I got home my wife had a big fire going in the wood stove and the house was warm, dinner was good, and there was a cold beer with my name on it. Then I sat there relaxing after a meal and a hot shower thinking about how fortunate I was and feeling sort of embarrassed too. There were a lot of lessons in this day for me.

I had let a combination of stresses and problems get to me. Had I not caught myself, I might have said something I regret to my friend and boss. Luckily I caught myself before that happened. I also learned that sometimes things happen that seem really bad, but they are actually the best possible thing when you consider the alternatives. I was also reminded that I am in charge of the energy I put in the world. If I remain positive and optimistic, the world responds in that way, and if I am in a bad mood—it's my fault. I can't blame situations or circumstances for how I feel. I am totally responsible for my attitude, no one else.

The reason I decided to share this story with you is because it's a good example. Everyone has a bad day from time to time and it's an example of being able to turn a bad day around, a reminder that we have the power to choose how a bad day is processed in our brains.

If I wasn't so self aware and constantly thinking about being a better man because of my podcast, I might have missed that opportunity. The whole day could have spun out of control and gotten much worse. So the next time you start having a bad day I hope you remember this story, remember that you have choices, and that a bad day is really just another great opportunity to be a better man.

CHAPTER FIFTEEN
Hell Week

In 1967 we lived in the small town of Kelso, Washington. I was 5 years old and it was time for me to start kindergarten. I was all for it, I was excited, but my mom was much less so. Being her first child she was nervous to send me out into the world, away from her protection. It turns out—she was right to be nervous.

Wallace Elementary School was a prison-like structure made of red brick. It was surrounded by chain link fence and grass that no one was allowed to walk on. It was not a friendly place. Even though Kelso was not a big city, there were parts of town that were not especially...nice. The school seemed to be right in that part of town. I was bussed in from the other side of the tracks.

Up to this point I had led a pretty sheltered life. Oh sure I had gotten a few spankings but for the most part I was a well adjusted loving little kid. No one had ever been mean to me, no one had ever yelled at me, no one had ever called me a bad name. All I knew was affection, and maybe some good natured kidding. I was the epitome of innocence in 1967, and I had many things to learn.

It started off pretty well, I was a star pupil, I loved getting the right answers and I loved coloring. We were learning how to write the letters of the alphabet, and our teacher, Mrs. Dalyrimple had given us all some 3 x 5 cards to take home and practice the letters we had learned. I saw this as my moment to shine— I decided I wouldn't just write letters, but entire words! Riding the bus home that day I was looking all around for a word I could copy. Low and behold, there was a word scratched into the upholstery on the seat in front of me. I had seen this word before painted on walls and such, I recognized it, and decided it must be a very important word to be written everywhere so frequently. So I copied it onto one of the cards and when I got home I carefully transferred it to all the other 3 x 5 cards. My teacher was going to think I was a genius!

I proudly turned in my cards the next morning. That afternoon my mother got the first of many calls from the school, summoning her in for an emergency conference. She hurried to the school and sat across from the kindly Mrs. Dalyrimple. She was handed the cards I had turned in that morning. On each card, written very neatly were the capital letters: F — U — C — K.

Mrs. Dalyrimple was a nice old lady who was quite shaken up by the whole thing. My mother managed to convince her that I had merely copied the word from somewhere, and I would be afforded another chance. It was only the second day of school and I had already learned something important; words mean things, and some words are good, and others are bad.

On the third day of school I got beat up. You see, being innocent as I was, I thought it would be a good idea to taunt older kids and try to get them to chase me, because getting chased is fun, right?

I had several methods of infuriating the older kids. Its kind of embarrassing now, but one of my favorites was a chant I would do. I would stand a little ways off and yell in the most annoying 5 year old voice I could muster: "BRASS BUTTONS, BLUE COAT, CAN'T CATCH A NANNY GOAT." I would then end the chant by making a farting noise with my tongue. If I got no reaction, I would repeat the chant with more and more fervor, until they just couldn't take it any more. I never considered what would happen if they caught me. It was a tough school, full of tough kids. On the first day I saw an older kid on the bus tear off his fingernail with pliers because someone dared him. Taunting these guys probably wasn't a good idea.

Most of these older kids would just chase me for a few steps and quit. Eventually I made one of them, a third grader I think, mad enough to chase me until he caught me. He sat on my chest, using my hair as handles, and beat my head repeatedly into the concrete. He did so until a playground lady made him stop.

I was bloody, but conscious. My mother was called into the

school again, but this time a heated conversation ensued with the Principal. Apparently it was my fault, because I was "mouthing off." By the end of that first week I had become disenchanted with public education. I was not having fun. It seemed like everything I did was wrong and nothing in my life had prepared me for what I was going through. It had been hard on my mom too, we were both looking forward to the weekend.

It was Friday, and Mom was waiting by our front window for me to walk down from the bus stop with the other kids. The normal time for us to have arrived had come and gone, and she was getting a little nervous. Finally, she saw a group of children come down the street. They were all huddled together walking in a tight group. That's odd, she thought. She tried to pick me out of the crowd, but couldn't see me. Suddenly seized with panic, she ran out to the group of kids to ask where I was. As she got closer she realized they were all in a tight group because they were carrying something, then to her horror, she realized it was me they were carrying. I was pretty beat up, and couldn't walk.

From what she could learn from the other children I had been "back talking" and being "Smart Alecky" to several of the older kids that rode the bus. They had put me down on the floor in the isle and took turns jumping on me from the seats, landing mostly on my legs. Though badly beaten, and unable to walk I didn't have any internal damage. After we got home from the hospital I spent the weekend convalescing in the warmth and safety of home.

It was all about cartoons and ice cream, as my mom did her best to help me get over the trauma. By Monday I was able to go back to school, but I was bruised and sore for several days. This was the beginning of bitter relations between my mom and the school staff, who all blamed me for being so vocal. The bus driver didn't even get a warning for leaving me in that condition, in fact it was his idea the other kids carry me. The school Principal's final words to my mother after their meeting was... "If this ever happens again...you let me know". Brilliant.

I went into my second week of academia much quieter, more subdued, but wow! I sure learned a lot of great lessons that first week. I learned that there were mean people in the world, people who didn't give a crap about me. I learned that life was not fair. I learned that f — u — c— k is a bad word. I learned to be nice to other people, especially bigger people who might try to kill me. I learned that school grass was not intended for walking on. I learned that I really liked sitting next to that girl named Sheryl. I learned that nobody liked me as much as my mom did, and that she would always have my back. Unfortunately, I also learned that I did not like school very much.

You know, not all lessons we learn as children are good, or accurate. Many of the lessons I learned that week I have hung onto all the way through my life until now, accurate lessons, like life not being fair for example. Some of the other lessons I learned that week were things I had to get over later in life and re-learn— like having not liking school turn into liking it.

It's something we can all ponder. Maybe we have some negative behaviors because we had learned an inaccurate lesson at some point? Its worth thinking about, as we strive to be better men everyday, maybe there are some lessons we just learned wrong. If we realize that, then we can fix them.

Another great lesson I learned that week was how important times like these are in children's lives. It changed the way I did things with my own kids. For one thing, I tried to make sure they were prepared for anything.

As you go through your day, maybe think about some of the hard lessons you'd learned: the good ones and the bad ones. Make corrections where needed. We can't fix anything until we determine it needs fixing.

CHAPTER SIXTEEN
Confessions Of A Former Bully

Back in chapter 12, I told a story about a fight I got in during 6th grade. I talked about how I instigated a fight and then got beat up, and the lessons I learned about that. Today's story is kind of a follow-up to that. Sometimes we have to repeat the lessons of life from different angles before we've learned them entirely. This story took place the following year— now I'm in 7th Grade and I'm 12 years old.

Being 12 my brain was starting to get washed with testosterone on a regular basis. I was becoming very interested in girls but I didn't have the first clue about what to do about it. For some reason I was completely uncomfortable around girls, I couldn't talk to them, didn't understand them, and if they talked to me I became paralyzed. So part of what I did was study the other guys, to see what they were doing about it.

There was a guy in my school, for the purposes of this story I'll say him name was Tom. Tom was always surrounded by girls. He was with girls more than he was with guys. To my astonishment he seemed comfortable with them, and they seemed to genuinely enjoy his company as well. This fascinated me, and also made me quite jealous.

I would watch them during lunch; Tom and his group of girls. They would laugh and talk together, they would even hug and show other signs of physical affection. I became quite perplexed by Tom and his natural prowess with females. The reason I was so perplexed is because I was operating almost entirely with my lizard brain. In my primitive, testosterone washed 12 year old brain none of it made sense to me. Tom was not a large boy, he wasn't strong or particularly athletic, in fact he didn't display any of the masculine characteristics that I naturally assumed would make him a winner with the girls. On the contrary, he was slight of build with fine features. He played the flute in band. He never participated in the normal schoolyard one-upmanship with the other boys. He was sensitive and kind and devoid of any trace of macho bravado.

I just couldn't understand. It all seemed counter intuitive to me. In my neanderthal brain it seemed like the girls should like the boys who were most masculine— the boys who were the strongest, fastest, and bravest. After all, I was attracted to the girls who were the most feminine, the most unlike me. I natively thought the same would be true in reverse. Nobody taught me this, It's what I came to from my own prepubescent logic.

Slowly I began to form a plan. I had to do something to win the affections, or at least the attention of the girls. I had to break through that barrier. I decided that the best way to do that was to flaunt my masculine supremacy, and the best way to illuminate that, would be to contrast it against Tom.

Before I go on, I have to say I am not proud of the plan that ultimately emerged. In fact it is something I still feel bad about every time I think of it. It's a memorable moment in my life of embarrassment. The reason I'm sharing it is because what it helped me learn might be valuable to someone else.

I sat behind Tom in science class. My plan was simple; during class I would seek down under my desk where I would have access to the case that held Tom's flute. I would unbuckle the flute case. When Tom stood up to leave, the flute case would open up spilling the contents. Tom would naturally become enraged and want to beat up whoever did that. I would claim responsibility, and a battle would ensue, of which I would be victorious. All of the girls watching would naturally be impressed and swoon at my masculine display of dominance over Tom. From then on they would want to hang out with me, where their safety would be assured. In other words, I was thinking like a caveman.

Needless to say, this was the worst plan I ever came up with and it did not yield the intended result. In fact it backfired horribly.

It all went wrong when Tom stood up and the components of his shiny flute that his parents probably paid good money for, went cascading across the floor until they tinkled to a stop.

Tom was not enraged as I thought he should be. Rather he was surprised, and sad, and worried about his instrument. I didn't let that stop me. I stood up and informed Tom that it was I who had unbuckled his flute, then I braced myself for his attack—the attack that never came. Instead of being angry with me, Toms eyes were full of hurt, and confusion. His eyes filled with tears as he tried to process why I would do such a thing. It was at this point I realized I had made a huge mistake.

I looked at the girls then. There was a wall of them standing there watching the ill-conceived drama that I had fabricated. They were all looking at me with such contempt, as though I was a pile of the most disgusting stuff they had ever seen. And in that moment, I probably was.

The peculiar thing about this, is that it was never my intention to be mean, believe it or not. I wasn't trying to hurt Tom's feelings. I really had nothing against him personally. I had only been considering this plan from my own twisted perspective and was focused on what I thought the result would be. I was so intent on the result, that I failed to consider how it would be received in reality.

As I stood there watching Tom shaking to hold back his tears, as I endured the scornful gaze of the girls, I suddenly realized exactly how wrong I had been. Sadly, it was too late, the damage had been done. Instead of the girls swooning over me, now they hated me. I had become their enemy.

In a lame attempt to fix what I had done, I said I was sorry, and knelt down to start picking up the pieces of the flute when one of the girls pushed me back and told me not to touch anything. They all gathered around Tom then, like a shield against something evil—a shield against me.

They left me standing there flustered and incapacitated, the final victim of my own bad behavior. The event was eventually forgotten by most, but not by Tom or myself. I tried to be friendly to Tom on several occasions but he would never speak to me again after that. He later moved away and I never saw him again. As an adult I have tried to reach out to Tom on social media, but I have never gotten a response.

So, the lessons I learned from this: there are so many! In spite of how uncomfortable the memory is, I am thankful for what it taught me. At an early age it helped me make a distinction between my biology and my intellect. I was able to learn that just because my hormones are informing me of something doesn't make it right or good, my behavior must ultimately be governed by my intellect.

What else did it teach me? It taught me that my vision of people up to that point was totally incorrect. No one responded as I predicted they would in this situation; not Tom, not the girls...not even myself. It caused me to rethink the universe, to look beyond my own experience and understand that every other person has a unique perspective that should be acknowledged.

In particular it helped shape the way I related to females for the rest of my life. Up to this point, all women outside my immediate family were mysterious creatures that I was inexplicably attracted to yet, who I didn't really identify with. I began to realize that day that females have feelings, and opinions, and power all their own. They are not objects to be won but rather humans with whom I could communicate.

Tom probably still thinks I'm a monster, but I'm not. People learn and change and grow. I was bullied quite often by older kids, and this experience helps me as an adult to take a much softer view of my own childhood bullies. I won't hold them responsible for the bad choices they made when they were teenagers because now, hopefully, most of them are different people.

Sadly, there are still grown men being informed by their hormones rather than their intellect. They didn't have the advantage of learning this lesson as a boy for some reason. There are guys trapped in the macho, arrogant, aggressive stereotype and they continue to treat women like objects and they treat people who are physically weaker than them as inferior.

I doubt if too many men like this are reading this book, because those guys aren't overly concerned with being better men. However if you are reading this, and you think you might be one of these guys, I hope this helps you see the error of your ways.

And for everyone else who may have been mistreated at one

time or another, I hope it can help you see that people are capable of change and growth. That guy who stuck your head in the toilet in 5th grade might be a really decent guy now.

It all comes back to the most valuable things we have in our lives, which are our relationships with other people. Our relationships with people really tell the story of the KIND of man we are. The relationships we have are reflections of us. As a man, if you regard all of these relationships as something valuable; If you treat others who cross your path with kindness and respect and extend common courtesy and hospitality— then you will develop relationships that reflect this fact, that you are a better man.

It wasn't easy telling this story. It's no fun painting myself as an ignorant bully. The importance of it isn't in that part but in the fact that I no longer am one. Even at 12 years old I was able to learn a lesson and make corrections in my behavior and become a better person for it. And what one man can do...another can do. Now go out there in the world and be an ambassador of manhood every day, and in the process you could become a better man.

CHAPTER SEVENTEEN
The Power Of Life And Death

I was 7 years old in 1969, and all my dreams had come true. My family had moved to Olympia Washington, and we were finally living on a little farm. I had always wanted to live on a farm, I dreamed about it, and now here we were. We had some cows, a couple pigs, a big garden, and quite a few chickens. In addition to that we had our own woods and pastures that me and my imagination would get lost in for hours.

I had a younger brother and sister, but they weren't much fun yet because they were still so young, so I spent a lot of time on my own, imagining I was an Indian in the forest, or a cowboy, the barn became my pirate ship and I had a lot of thrilling adventures, and I found lots of buried treasures. Another thing I would pretend is that I was a big game hunter. In order to facilitate this, in my mind the chickens became exotic antelope, or Ostrich, even tigers and lions. The chickens were very versatile; I could change them into anything I wanted.

The bales of hay were held together by baling twine, we had lots of it around from the hay we used. I would collect a long piece of it by tying the ends together until I had enough. Then I would fashion a slip knot in one end, something that my dad taught me how to do— but not for this reason. I would spread the knot out so it made a loop, just like in the cartoons. I would sprinkle some chicken food in the loop for bait and lay on my stomach about 20 feet away with the other end of the twine, waiting for my prey.

When a chicken stepped in the loop I could pull the twine and the slip knot would tighten around its leg. Then I would reel in my prey while it clucked and fussed. Then I would untie it, study it for a minute, then let it go and repeat the whole process all over again. It was great fun. The king of the chickens was a huge white rooster. He was mean too. You always had to keep your eye on him because he was known to attack without provocation. One day I was out trapping chickens and letting them go, when who should step in my trap but the big white rooster?

I wasn't sure what to do at first, I was kind of afraid of him. In my mind he was kind of like a big, mean Rhinoceros. I decided if I trapped him that it would be my finest, bravest moment, and it might teach him who was boss and maybe he wouldn't be so mean.

So I pulled on the twine. The knot tightened around his leg, and then the whole world went crazy.

It startled the rooster so bad that he flew up into the air. Now I'm holding onto the twine like I have a kite in a strong wind. The rooster is screaming and flapping and trying to get away with such ferocity that I was unable to reel him in to release him. It was all I could do just to hang onto the twine. Meanwhile, all the hens had lost their minds in response to his panic.

After a couple minutes of this complete chaos, the rooster settled back down to earth. I ran up to him, he was just sitting there. I quickly picked him up and undid the twine from his foot, but he wasn't doing anything, he was just sitting in my arms. Then he let out a few weak clucks and collapsed right there in my embrace. I'll never forget the way his head swung back and forth like a pendulum attached to his limp neck.

The once great and mighty king of the chickens was dead. He died of a heart attack by my own hand. I had seen dead things before. Animals we slaughtered, the dead robin when I was 5, all manner of snakes, and road kill, but I had never killed anything before.

Slowly, the realization of what I had done crept into my 7 year old consciousness. Then came the grief of my actions, and the guilt. Guilt like I had never imagined. I expected lightning from the sky to strike me dead at any second and purge my evilness from the face of the earth. I lay the rooster down and ran to that one constant source of comfort in my life, my mom. I busted in the house crying and screaming "I killed a living thing! I killed a living thing!"

That isn't something you want to hear your seven year old screaming, so my mom spent a few minutes calming me down enough so that she could understand what I was saying. I explained everything to her. She calmly listened, and then told me that she knew I didn't MEAN to kill the rooster, it was an accident, but it was an accident that could have been prevented if I would not have been trapping chickens. She told me she thought I should find a good place to bury the rooster, and that it would be my job to do it and give him a funeral.

I spent the next hour crying, wandering around in my grief looking for the perfect place to bury the rooster. I picked a place by the barn. I dug an adequate hole and then I picked a big bouquet of dandelions, my face now muddy with tears. I conducted the funeral like my mother had said. In attendance were my brother and sister, and my dog Lady.

I don't remember how the eulogy went exactly, but it was long, and heartfelt. I talked about what a great rooster he was, how big and strong and pretty he was. I talked about how he would crow, and about how sorry I was that he was dead. I also talked about all the hens that would miss him. Mainly though, I told the rooster and the universe that was listening, that I didn't mean it, that I was sorry...and I truly was.

That's the end of the story, so what is the lesson I learned here? Well, it turned out to be a pretty profound day for me. I learned what a fragile balance exists between life and death and I became aware for the first time what my responsibility was to the creatures around me. The knowledge that I was capable of taking life instantly filled me with a sense of responsibility and care that I had not possessed before, but that I carried with me into my manhood.

The other lesson I learned was about consequences, and that there is a consequence for everything we do, both good and bad. Unfortunately I kept on learning that lesson over and over again as I grew up, but I eventually got it. Sometimes it takes a lot of lessons to learn something. Now go on with your day, but remember the responsibility you have to every one, and everything around you, and be mindful of the consequences.

CHAPTER EIGHTEEN
A Bad Idea

When I was a kid I loved laughing, and I liked making other people laugh too. In fact I was kind of obsessed with it for a while, you might even say that at times I tried too hard to make people laugh. I was that annoying kid who would make up horrible jokes that didn't make any sense and expected grownups to think I was hilarious.

It wasn't just jokes, I would play tricks on people too, tricks that I thought were funny. Sometimes they were, but most of the time they were not. Its kind of embarrassing remembering some of the stupid things I did.

One summer day when I was 7 years old I got a brilliant idea. There were two components of my idea; one was that I would always pick wild flowers for my mother and she would put them in little vases all through the house. The other component was that my mother was absolutely terrified of snakes. I combined these two facts and came up with an idea that I thought would be hilarious and fun. In fact I started laughing as soon as I thought of it.

My plan was to get a shoe box and fill it full of flowers for my mom. The funny part, was that underneath the flowers would be two harmless garter snakes. I was an expert at finding snakes so that wasn't a problem, I put them in a shoe box and covered them with an assortment of flowers I found, mostly dandelions. Then I walked into the house, and in my most precious little boy voice I offered my mom the box of flowers.

My mom was thrilled as usual. She told me how pretty they were and thanked me profusely. She said she would put them in water in just a few minutes. I ran outside and sat below the window where my mom was sitting, I was listening intently for that magic moment when my plan came to fruition and my mom discovered the snakes in the box.

As I sat there I was very proud of myself at first. I was proud of the masterful plan I had concocted, and the flawless execution of it. As time crept by I started to feel differently though. As I imagined my mom discovering the snakes that she was deathly afraid of, I began to question my judgement—it started to seem less funny. The more I thought about it, the less funny it became.

I loved my mom, I didn't want her to be upset and afraid. Suddenly I realized that my brilliant plan was nothing more than a mean trick. It was a bad, bad idea. My heart was pounding, several minutes had gone by and she still had not discovered the snakes. I wondered what I should do. Did I have time to run in and get the snakes out?

I was just getting up to run in and get the flowers when the entire world reverberated with the most blood curdling scream I had ever heard, it was coming from the window above me. It was a scream unlike any other. It was a scream of absolute terror, mixed with frenzied desperation and panic.

I ran into the house and saw my mother standing on the kitchen table, frozen like a statue. When she looked at me I didn't see anger in her eyes, I saw relief. I was someone who could help her. She said one word; "SNAKES!" Tears were running down her face and she was trembling.

I immediately started looking for the snakes. The flowers were everywhere, they had been launched from the shoe box when the snakes were spotted. The snakes could be anywhere, but I had to find them. After a couple minutes of looking I found the snakes and released them back outside. I came in the house and helped my mom down off the table. She was still trembling from the fright of it.

I expected this was the moment where I would be in huge trouble but, I wasn't. She was so glad and relieved that the snakes were gone that she never even pondered how they got there in the first place. Instead of being the guy that almost gave her a heart attack, I had become the hero. She hugged me and thanked me and the whole time I kept waiting for her to come to her senses and realize it was all my fault but strangely, she never did.

I felt horrible, and totally undeserving of my moms gratitude. I was riddled with guilt. In my seven year old brain this turn of events was difficult to understand. Looking back now, knowing my mother and what a trusting soul she was, I think it never occurred to her that her loving son would do something so despicable on purpose.

Many years later after I grew up and we talked about the incident she seemed hurt and saddened to realize that it was I who put the snakes in the box. Yes, it was a bad idea and no, it wasn't funny at all, but I learned a couple things that day that made my life better going forward. I learned the value of thinking things through and looking at situations from other peoples perspective.

I had not considered the reality of how this would affect my mom until I was sitting outside her window. Up to that point I was only thinking of myself and how funny it would be, totally disconnected from the reality of it, as though I was watching a cartoon. I had not inserted the actual human emotions of others into the equation.

This was a game changer for me. I suppose it has to happen to everyone at some point, we aren't born with the capacity to view things through the eyes of others, its something we have to learn. And I learned it in a big way with this one. Everything we do has consequences; some are good, and some are bad. The value of thinking things through thoroughly and considering other peoples feelings before you act will give you less bad consequences, and more good ones.

Now as you go through your day, try on being more mindful of the things you do. It's good to think things through before you act, and don't forget to consider the impact of your actions on those around you.

CHAPTER NINETEEN
First Date

In 7th grade I was directly between being a boy and being something that resembled a man. I was 12 years old, and it was probably the most difficult period of my life. I had acne but not too bad, not like some people did. I was athletic and strong so I had that going for me, at least, but there was one thing I did not have that a lot of other guys had—a girlfriend.

There was something about having a girlfriend in Junior High that elevated you socially. You didn't even have to be cool, as long as you have a girlfriend, and can prove it by walking around the hallways holding hands, then you were somehow above the ridicule that people without girlfriends had to endure. If you had a girlfriend it was as though at least someone in the world see's value in you, and there is the social proof of that holding onto your hand.

I was overcome with jealousy in those days. I would look at the guys flaunting their girlfriends down the hallways, I would picture myself in their shoes. Most of the time I was also confused, because many of these guys I saw as somewhat lesser than me, they had less to offer; they were less athletic, they were less funny, some of them were even less good looking than me and yet, they had a girlfriend, and I didn't. Some of those "lesser than" thoughts was probably just the jealousy talking.

What all these guys had that I didn't have at the time besides a girlfriend, was confidence. They obviously had the ability to talk to a girl long enough to persuade her to be his girlfriend. I didn't have that. For some reason I couldn't talk to girls at all. If a girl said "Hi" to me I would just stand there looking stupid and not even reply. The prettier they were the less able I was to talk to them.

I used to say I was shy as a kid, but now looking back I can see it was raw insecurity, something I abandoned long ago, but I can still remember vividly what it was like to live in that space.

I knew I had to get a girlfriend. I had to make a move of some kind. For me 7th grade was a time when I was in constant conflict with myself. I was constantly trying to force myself to do things I was afraid to do. In my brain was a continuous dialogue of what was wrong with me and what I needed to do to fix it. It's a wonder I was able to get any schoolwork done at all.

Finally, after much internal deliberation I settled on a target. Her name was Nancy, and I thought she was beautiful. There was something about her face, her expression, and the shape of her mouth that made her seem to me like a mythical creature, like a fairy that had abandoned her wings.

I came up with a plan. I would ask her to go to the movies with me. We were 12, so we didn't drive, whatever plans we made would have to be facilitated by our parents, but those were just details. For now the main objective was having the nerve to ask her. The time had arrived. We were between 2nd and 3rd periods, and Nancy would be at the end of the hallway. I knew this because I had been tracking her movements for days.

I was in position— and there she was right on cue. This was it! This was the moment, right now! I marched up to her and unleashed the speech I had practiced for days.

It went something like this.

"Hi Nancy."

"Hi."

"You want to go to the movies with me on Saturday at 2:00 at the capital theatre?"

"Ok."

"Oh…really? I mean…Ok, well I'll see you then."

"Bye."

"Bye."

I was on cloud nine! I never really expected her to say yes. I had made an actual date…the first one in my life. It was Tuesday, so I had three full days to prepare. I didn't have a job, I was 12 after all. I had no way of paying for the movie and obligatory snacks. I was depending on my parents for this aid. The problem was, I did not discuss girls in any way, shape, or form with my family. Primarily because I did't want to be teased about it. If I was going to keep up my facade of sexual dis-interest I would have to play it pretty cool.

Friday evening rolled around, the day before my inaugural date. After dinner I asked my dad if I could have five dollars because I was going to the movies with my friends. My dad thought about it a minute, he wasn't the type to just hand out money. He said ok, but first you'll have to pull some scotch broom. I agreed to his terms.

For those who don't know, scotch broom is an invasive bush from Europe that takes over entire fields if left unchecked. The best way to pull it was to use a claw hammer, dig in at the roots and then pry it out of the ground. I figured I could pull a little scotch broom before I went to the movies.

The morning of my date with Nancy I got up around 7am and met my dad out in the field. He had a big roll of bailing twine and some stakes. He told me he was going to stake off some land with the twine and I had to pull all the scotch broom inside the twine. To my utter shock, horror, and dismay my dad proceeded to rope off an entire half acre. Looking at it I estimated about ten hours worth of work, but I only had 6 hours before I would have to leave to meet Nancy. I didn't waste any time, I threw myself into the work like a crazy person. I was attacking the brush as though it had offended me personally.

After about three hours I looked at what I had done—it was impressive, but no where near what I would need to do to complete the task in time. I started to panic, what would I do? I could not stand Nancy up, that would be horrible! There was only one possibility: Mom. I ran to the house and told mom I had to talk to her. I told her the whole story from start to finish, with the understanding that I was speaking in confidence. She listened patiently until I was done.

When I got done talking my mom had a peculiar smile, even though I was close to tears. She told me not to worry. She would talk to my dad and she was positive he would gladly help me out. I was resistant to her telling anyone else of my plight at first, but she convinced me she could pull it off. As I learned in later years, my lack of showing any interest in girls so that I would not be teased had given my dad the impression that I might be more interested in boys than girls. So he was constantly on the lookout for any indication that I liked girls— that's just how it was in 1974.

Sure enough, after my mom went and talked to my dad. The next thing I know he's walking up grinning from ear to ear with a ten dollar bill in his hand, twice as much as what I asked for. He told me I better get cleaned up and he would drive me to the movies.

I asked what about the scotch broom? He just waved his hand like it was a silly thing, and said don't worry about that, it will still be there tomorrow.

I couldn't believe how luck had turned in my favor! I ran off to take a shower and get ready for my date. My dad dropped me off outside the movie theatre on time. There was Nancy, standing by the door and looking beautiful. I walked up to her and said "Hi." She said "Hi" back. I paid our way in, we got some popcorn and then went into the theatre.

I was so nervous. I could hardly maintain my composure at all. I wasn't sure what was expected of me, all I knew, was that I was here, and it was happening.

As we entered the theatre I awkwardly sat down in the first seat I saw that was empty, Nancy sat next to me. I think the movie was "The Amazing Mr. Limpet", starring Don Knots. We sat there, watching the movie and eating popcorn.

I was thinking about putting my arm on her shoulder or holding her hand or maybe even kissing her, but I didn't do any of those things. In fact we didn't exchange one word of conversation during the entire movie. When the movie was over we walked outside. Her parents were there to pick her up, she said goodbye, and I said goodbye back and that, was the end of our date.

Even though it might have been the lamest date in the history of human existence, I rode home that night with a sense of accomplishment. I had asked her, and that was a big deal! I had worked my tail off trying to earn the money. I had confessed everything to my mom and the world didn't end. My dad seemed really happy with me, ecstatic in fact. So the day was definitely not a loss.

Forging A Man

I never went on another date with Nancy. We ran in different circles but Nancy paved the way for me to enter a new phase of my life. I learned a couple valuable lessons, like the insecurity I felt was unfounded, and stupid. I learned that there is almost always a way to work out any problem. I learned that my parents really were on my side after all. Mostly this is where I started to learn that life really is what you make of it. It's not just a saying, it's really true.

I could have chickened out, not asked Nancy out and stayed at home and none of this would have happened, but it all did happen, because I made it happen. That day I learned that I have a degree of power in my life; the power to make things happen.

It's a good lesson to remember from time to time if you want to make things happen in your life!

CHAPTER TWENTY
Look Before You Leap

When I was growing up there was a river about a mile from our house. It wasn't a big river like the Mississippi, but it was bigger that a creek. Parts of it were 60 feet wide and it might get as narrow as 10 feet in some places. For me the river was like a creature unto itself, it had a personality, and a temper. It's banks were lush and thick like a jungle in the summertime, and it was on or around this river where many of my best memories were made as a boy.

My friends and I had found a beach, the most perfect spot. There was a bend in the river and the water had carved out a swimming hole about 15 feet deep. There also happened to be a huge tree leaning out over the water in the perfect place for a rope swing, right over the swimming hole. There was one cliff we could dive from, a sandy shore, and there were lots of crawdads and the fishing was good, too. I remember thinking as a boy that I hoped Heaven was like this place...

My friends and I kind of owned this spot. We were around 13 and 14. The older kids were off chasing girls and driving and this spot was only accessible on a trail by bicycle or walking. The younger kids wouldn't think of moving in on us, so we had it all to ourselves.

On one particular glorious summer day my friends and I were at the river. We were swinging from the rope and diving off the bank, just hanging out like boys do, swapping lies and stories and laughing a lot.

We had seen a couple kids we didn't recognize. They had found the trail to the river but they weren't bothering us, they stopped a few hundred yards upstream from where we were. One of my friends said they were from a different school and we couldn't figure out what they were doing in our neck of the woods.

All of a sudden out of the blue, the peaceful day was interrupted with cries for help. We all stopped and listened. Sure enough, it was one of the boys from upstream and he was yelling for help. He was around the bend so we couldn't see him, but he was really screaming, it sounded serious but we were suspicious at first. We thought it could be some kind of trick.

The screaming continued and became more desperate, almost like there were tears in his voice. One of us yelled back then, asking what was the matter.   The voice came back, something about someone being hurt.   We were all a bit confused— we knew the riverbanks well, so at their location the water was only chest deep at the deepest spot. How could they hurt themselves up there?

At the same time we all seemed to instinctively agree that there must be a real emergency.   We bolted single file down the trail toward the sound of his voice. There were about 6 of us. We arrived to find the boy who had been screaming standing chest deep in the middle of the river.   He was holding onto his friend with his arms around his chest under his arms.

We couldn't see the trouble, his friend was conscious, his eyes were open. That's when we saw that the boy holding his friend was on the verge of tears. His voice was trembling as he told us that his friend couldn't move.   He was losing his grip.   The current had gradually moved them into deeper water and the deeper the water got the less purchase his feet had on the bottom with the current of the river bearing down.

We were still standing there, not sure of what was happening. The boy screamed again for us to help him bring his friend to shore, so we all waded out to them, and brought them both in. It was a strange thing, to see a boy about our age, fully conscious, but having no control over his arms and legs. We laid him on the bank and asked the other boy what had happened.

"He dove in from there." The boy said, pointing to a high bank just 20 feet upstream. I knew immediately what had happened. I walked into the water where the landing point of such a dive would be and right there, the water only came up to my ankles. Beneath me were big flat granite slabs, just below the waters surface. From where he had stood on the bank, the sun on the surface of the water had hidden the rocks. It must have looked like a deep pool, and they hadn't checked first.

We were all quiet now, no one was making eye contact, and no one was looking at the boy on the ground whose pleading eyes were searching everyone's face, looking for some clue as to what was going on with him. Only the boy's friend was tending to him now. The injured boy could talk, but not very loud, it was a whisper really. He kept telling his friend over and over again that he couldn't feel anything. He was clearly afraid, and panicking, but even his panic seemed impotent in the stillness of his body.

Without a word, one of my friends ran back to our spot and jumped on his bike to go get help. There were no cell phones in those days so he would have to go from house to house until someone let him use their phone. So, we waited. After about 30 minutes we could hear the sirens. Then the crush of brush as the medics hauled their equipment down the narrow trail toward the river.

We all stood back as the medics worked. They kept touching him in different places asking if he could feel it. I caught the grim expression the medics shared with each other as their eyes met. All they had was a stretcher, so they strapped him on it and then they asked us all to help carry it back up the trail to the ambulance, since there were only two of them. Then, they were gone. We all stood around in stunned silence. We were old enough to realize the possible magnitude of what just happened. Then, quite shaken, we all went back to the safety of our homes.

I told my parents about it and they were very concerned, my mother had warned me all my life about the dangers of the river. The next day they found his name in the paper. Within a week we learned that he was likely going to be paralyzed from the neck down for the rest of his life. The dive had broken his neck.

We never heard anything about the boy again. Not surprising since he had gone to another school in a different part of the county. As fate would have it years later, after I was an adult I attended an inspirational gathering in our community where they had people speaking.

A speaker came out, he was a man in a wheelchair, he was controlling his chair with only his chin, and he proceeded to tell the same story I just told you, only from a different perspective. It was him, it was that boy we saved from the river. I went and talked to him afterwards. I told him I was one of the other boys that day. He thanked me and he cried—I may have cried too.

I have re-lived this story many times in my mind throughout the years. It was my first glimpse at how fragile the line is between things like walking and not walking, between health and happiness and sorrow and misery, even between life and death. One minute you are a healthy kid with your whole life in front of you, the next second you are reduced to a head sitting atop a lump of flesh you have no connection with, and in that head reside all the same thoughts, memories, desires and aspirations you had just a moment before.

That's one lesson I learned very well that day; that tomorrow, even the next second, is not promised to us. The only thing we have that we can truly lay claim to as ours, is the moment we are living in, so we better make it count.

The other lesson I learned, and one that I have employed countless times since that day, is to look before you leap. It just takes a moment to check the water, or the situation, to see how deep it is. What might look like a deep inviting pool, could be a granite slab. The same is true of every situation that is new. It just takes a moment to check the water.

This was an unfortunate tale, a sad story, but a necessary one. We need to have stories like this one too—some of the most valuable lessons come from the hardest things.

CHAPTER TWENTY-ONE
Bottoms Up

I was 14 years old when I was a freshman in high school. It was a horribly awkward school year for me. It was really, really tough trying to fit in, and manage where and how I belonged in the matrix of other adolescents going through the same thing.

Part of fitting in for me was joining the football team. I saw some success on the gridiron, we had a pretty good football season, but then the season ended. Some of the other guys got involved with other sports to stay in shape until next year, so I decided to join track.

I wasn't really sure what to do in track, mainly I was there to keep my cardio up. I was never a competitive class runner but I did get a lot of cardio during the practices.

I had a routine; every day I would arrive early for practice and put on my jock strap, followed by a pair of shorts, and that would be topped off with my sweat suit. In the middle of the gym waited a 5 gallon bucket of analgesic balm, something like 'Icy-Hot' before they invented Icy-Hot. I would go to the bucket and take down my sweat pants then I would bend over straight legged and rub down my legs with balm in preparation for practice.

The West wall of the gym is where the girls locker room was.

One fine day I arrived at the magic bucket of balm before anyone else. I took down my sweat pants and started applying the ointment to my legs as I did every day. Suddenly I heard a shriek, followed by laughter from behind me, in the direction of the girls locker room. I stood up and turned to look. I saw a couple girls who had come out and they were locked in some sort of convulsion of hilarity of one sort or another, nothing unusual there. By now a few other girls had come out. I went back to the work of prepping for practice.

I hadn't been bent over two-seconds when all the girls seemed to be laughing simultaneously at the same joke. There were screams and shrieks and laughter the likes of which you don't see that often. I stood up again and looked around, hoping to catch a glimpse of whatever it was that had them in such a state. By now all the girls were out, there were maybe 25 or 30 of them. I couldn't see anything, so I went back to rubbing my legs. Again, on cue...as soon as I bent over the entire gymnasium erupted in a cacophony of feminine hysteria. With the acoustics it was really quite deafening.

I just couldn't understand what could be going on, I figured something must have happened in the locker room that had them all in stitches. I stood up looking at the mob, trying to get some clue as to what was so funny.

One of the girls, almost blue from laughing so hard raised an arm to point at something. She was pointing in my direction, so I turned to look on the other side of me but there was only the empty gym.

Then, I looked down. To my shock and terror, I saw that in my haste I had forgotten a step of my routine. I had put on my jock strap and sweat pants, but I had forgotten my shorts. Which meant that when I was bent over my bare bottom was positioned in such a way that the girls could probably look right up my spine, from the inside... if you know what I mean.

I was frozen for a moment. Then I felt my body temperature rise about 20 degrees in two-seconds, it started at my feet and shot to my head like the mercury in a thermometer. At the same time I started sweating profusely. My brain was stuck for a minute, I couldn't even think and I'm sure I stopped breathing.

It was obvious that the girls realized that I had figured it out because their laughter increased proportionately with my realization of what had happened. Then, faster than I have ever moved before or since, I reached down and snatched my sweat pants from around my ankles, pulled them up, and started running. I just ran in the direction I was facing, which was away from the girls. Across to the other side of the gym.

Forging A Man

There was a door there, one of the doors with an alarm that is not supposed to be opened unless there is an emergency. Well, if this wasn't an emergency I didn't know what would be. I crashed through the door and just kept running. I could hear the alarm going off behind me but I barely noticed it, I was just running, fueled by the awful adrenaline of embarrassment that was coursing through my veins.

I didn't stop running for about five miles…and then I walked very fast for a while and then continued running. Eight miles, all the way home I ran. When I got to my house I ran inside and went straight down into the basement, into my room, my sanctuary. I landed on the bed and just laid there in the darkness for a long time contemplating what had become of my future.

It was over— my life— I was sure of it. Nothing would ever be normal again. One thing I knew was that I could never return to my school, that was out of the question. Perhaps I could talk my parents into moving? I didn't know what was going to happen, all I knew for sure was that I could never see any of those girls again for the rest of my life.

My parents called me to dinner, I refused to come up saying I wasn't hungry. They kept attempting to get me to come up the rest of the evening and I kept refusing. I didn't want to see them, because I knew they would make me tell them what happened. I would have to break it to them that I wasn't going back to school either way, but I put off re-living the nightmare for as long as I could.

Finally my dad, in his stern voice commanded me to come up stairs so, I complied. They sat me down and had me tell them the whole horrible story. It seems like they were trying not to laugh, which was infuriating. There wasn't one thing funny about this.

When the issue of school came up, that's when the war started. I was prepared to be beaten if I had to, but I wasn't going back. Before I went to bed that night we agreed that I wouldn't go to school the next day, which was a Friday, and then we would talk about it over the weekend. That satisfied me for the moment, it was the best offer on the table.

It's amazing, the effect time can have on a situation. When I woke up the next day I almost didn't remember the incident at first, but then it came falling back into my brain like an anvil in a cartoon.

Then Saturday came and went, and Sunday. My parents were wise people, they somehow knew that I would be much more pliable after a couple days went by.

They assured me that those girls had probably forgotten all about it, that I probably wouldn't hear a thing. They followed that up with the fact that I was going to school and there was no way out of it. I went to school that Monday, expecting the worst, keeping my eyes down. Surprisingly I didn't hear any comments. I had imagined the whole school would be buzzing about the intimate details of my nether regions, but no one said anything. At track I didn't go to the gym, instead I went straight out to the field and practiced. I managed to make it all the way home without hearing anything about it. Huh... my parents were right!

That is the end of the story, but as you might imagine I can remember it like it was yesterday, because it was such a big deal to me in the moment. And that's one of the lessons I learned: when something is a huge life-ending deal to me, it doesn't mean that it is to anyone else.

I learned something about perspectives in this situation. To me it really seemed like the end of the world, but to those girls it was probably just a funny thing, and when they saw how I reacted they might have even felt bad for my embarrassment.

Knowing about perspectives is important, because every body has a different one and being able to see things from other people's perspective is a very useful skill.

The other valuable lesson I learned was about time. The ability of time to dull the memory or put round corners on things where sharp ones used to be. It's pretty interesting, something about the mere passing of one moment to another, and another, can actually alter your perspective. I've used this many times. In the heat of the moment when I might want to explode and say what's on my mind I just wait a few moments. I will gain a different perspective, one that I control instead of the situation controlling me. It's a very valuable thing to know, and one that has served me well as a man.

Now head out into the world and keep your pants up, and look before you bend over but mostly, take advantage of the magic of time, use it to gain control over emotional situations— it will serve you well on your path.

CHAPTER TWENTY-TWO
Too Close For Comfort

I was 12 years old, it was summertime , and the year was 1974. We didn't have any cell phones, DVDs had not been invented yet and things like mp3 players, memory sticks, and flash drives were still in the realm of science fiction. What we did have was tape recorders. Tape recorders were pretty cool in 1974. My friend and I would turn it on in secret, and record the adult conversations without them knowing. We had one you could play backwards and it was fun trying to make it say things in english by speaking nonsense into it.

We lived near some railroad tracks, which was also pretty fun because you could tape things onto the tracks like coins or beer cans and then go back and see what they look like after the train ran over it. This provided hours of fun because there are a lot of things that will fit on a train track. One day my friend and I got the bright idea to combine these two fun things; Trains and the tape recorder, into a brand new fun activity.

My mother never condoned me playing around the train tracks, she thought they were dangerous. I knew that was just silly because you can hear the trains coming, they have horns and everything. So, because of my mother's irrational fear of trains I just never brought it up when we were planning to spend time on the tracks.

For some reason my friend and I decided to execute our new idea in the middle of the night, I don't remember why. I suspect that it had something to do with elevating the excitement, but I'm not sure. Our plan was to record a freight train going really fast, up close

—really, really close. When the time was right we slipped away on our bikes under the cover of darkness. The train tracks crossed the river a couple miles down, at the same spot where I found my pet hobo named Norm a couple years earlier...but that's another story. There was a bike trail that ran along the tracks all the way to the river.

It was dark as pitch out there. We couldn't see any electric lights of civilization from where we were, and there was no moon because the sky was overcast. We stood there on the tracks for a few minutes, my friend and I, with the tape recorder of course. This is when we started having a difference of opinion. My friend carried the tape recorder to the tracks and set it down. I asked him how he was going to turn it on. We didn't know exactly when the train was coming. I thought someone would need to stay with the tape recorder to operate it.

My friend said he wouldn't turn it on until we heard a train, then he would run up and lay it down by the tracks and then run back to safety. I didn't like that idea. I asked, "What happens if you trip? You could fall and hit your head on the tracks and not have enough time to get up."

"Or", I reasoned, "Your foot could get stuck or something. It's too dangerous to be moving around while the train is coming."

We went back and forth for a bit, but we finally agreed that my way was better, and ultimately safer. So it was settled, and since it was my idea I was the one who would operate the recorder.

We were sitting on one of the tracks discussing this— and we could feel it before we heard it, a vibration. It was a train, but it was still pretty far away, we didn't even know what direction it was coming from yet, or how fast. Not wanting to take any chances I decided to get in position. Clutching the recorder to my chest I lay down as close as I could to the rail itself without touching it. I was only about three inches away from it, on the creosote soaked wooden ties. My finger was on the record button ready to go.

My friend and I were yelling back and forth about the location and direction of the train. Finally he said in was coming from the South, which was the side my feet were on. Time went very slowly while I was laying there, partly I think because I was so uncomfortable. Now I could hear it too, in the distance, it sounded like a fast one. This is the part where I started having second thoughts. I started wondering about what could go wrong, or if we could get into trouble for it. I had excited anxiety because I knew I was about to experience something I had never experienced before. My friend was excitedly shouting but I had stopped paying attention to what he was saying, I was too wrapped up in the drama of what was about to happen. When I considered the tons of steel that would be speeding by just inches from my head I was nervous, and scared, and excited all at the same time.

Now I could feel the vibration of the approaching train easily beneath me, and I could hear its engine getting closer. I double checked my finger position on the red record button. I had been laying on my back, staring up at the dark overcast sky, but suddenly I could see something else, a faint light from the trains powerful headlight was illuminating the mist above me.

My heart rate started increasing, I was sweating in spite of the coolness of the night. I lifted my head and looked over my feet...I could see it, maybe only a half mile away now. For just a second I considered rolling away and scrambling to the safety of the wood line, but just for a second. Where I came from chickening out wasn't really an option and besides—I would have been too disappointed in myself. I lay my head back down and waited.

The vibration was becoming violent beneath me, increasing with the roar of the engine as it approached. Now the night sky above me was lit up like it was daylight— this was it! I lifted my head once more to look at the train. It seemed as though the headlight was trained directly on me now. I could see the window of the engine. I could see the engineer! What I had not counted on though, was that the engineer could see me, too. I saw his expression of fear and panic as he realized a person was laying right next to the track. I saw him reach up to grab the chain and I saw him pull it, releasing the longest, loudest horn blow I have ever heard. The noise of it seemed to penetrate every part of me.

Then all at once, as though I had been swallowed by a black hurricane, that train was upon me. The light gave way again to darkness, and the sound of the horn was replaced by thousands of tons of steel grinding against steel as the train raced past me. All of this at the same time overloaded my senses. It was more than I expected and more than I could process. My fight or flight instinct turned on and I sat up quickly to run away, but the rushing train displacing all that air seemed to create a vacuum. When I sat up it felt as though I was getting sucked in toward the trains wheels. I quickly laid back down.

It was a long train or, at least it seemed like a long train, but eventually the last car went by. I was left drenched with sweat, trembling, and my heart about to beat right out of my chest. My friend ran up hooping and hollering, and helped me up. I was trying to act like it was no big deal, but I was visibly shaken. That's when I remembered the recorder still clutched tight to my chest. We both looked at it and lo and behold, the red button had been pushed. I was so relieved because I had no recollection of pushing it, I was afraid I had forgotten in all the excitement.

We went back down to the bike trail and sat with the recorder between us. We looked at each other and smiled—this was our prize. This was our reward, and we were about to share it together. He pushed the rewind button, paused, and then pushed play. Let me tell you...to a 12 year old boy what we heard come out of that tape recorder was pure gold. We had captured the essence of a giant freight train moving fast, It was exactly what we were going for. We were both surprised about half way through the recording, when you could hear a terrified scream above the noise of the train. For a minute I was very confused wondering who it could have been, because I didn't remember screaming but, it must have been me.

That is the end of this story — except for the part where we played it for my mom a couple years later. Her reaction was priceless. So what did I get out of this? Was there a lesson? After all, I was doing something that was...OK it was kind of stupid. It was probably illegal, and if my parents had known about it at the time I probably would have gotten into big trouble. A sobering fact about this incident that I learned much later, is that sometimes there are things sticking out, hanging off the train. One of those things could have hit me and drug me all the way to Seattle, and I would have been quite dead when I got there.

So am I advocating misbehaving? Have I become a champion of stupid decisions? No, here's what I think; I must have learned a great deal of things about dangerous situations, because I never did anything like this ever again, but the real lesson, the one I used through the rest of my life, the one that partially shaped the man I became is that sometimes, you have to take risks. Sometimes you are faced with a risky situation and if you don't take that risk, you will forever be plagued with not knowing what would have happened if you did.

I took the risk that night and I was rewarded with an awesome recording that was around for years, and I was rewarded with the experience itself, and the story. It also cemented in my brain the fact that almost every good thing in life comes with a risk. I can't think of anything great that comes easy. I'm not saying you should go put your life in jeopardy, but there are lots of risks that won't kill you. Take every risk that comes your way. Sure there are consequences along with the rewards, but the fact remains that there is a risk somewhere between you, and every great thing you will ever do.

Now go out there and take some risks. Weigh the consequences against the benefits then do what it takes to make something great happen in your life.

CHAPTER TWENTY-THREE
Show And Tell

In 1969 we put a man on the moon. I was in second grade and I was 7 years old at the time. It was in second grade that I was introduced to a new activity and I fell in love with it immediately, it was called, "Show and Tell". I don't know if they still do show and tell in school, but what an amazing concept it was. For those of you who may not know, during show and tell, one at a time whoever wanted to would get up in front of the class and share some part of their life. Sometimes kids would bring something cool from home and talk about it. They would pass it around and let other kids hold it. It could be anything from a picture of your uncle when he was in the war, A cool rock you found, or your grandmother's gall stone.

If you didn't have anything cool to show then you could tell a story about your life, what your family did on vacation, or whatever.

I think show and tell is awesome for a couple reasons; for one it was a great way to really get to know your fellow classmates in a way that you wouldn't get to otherwise. It also got kids used to public speaking and being in front of an audience. Not only that, but when a kid brings something to school from his home, or tells a story about his life and the other kids show appreciation for it, it does a lot for a child's self esteem.

My show and tell career started out like everyone else's; I brought a few things I found at home, and that was cool. My parents had some interesting stuff—but somehow I felt like I was only scratching the surface of my potential. So one day instead of sharing something I brought, I told the class about a dream I had. I may have embellished it a little bit for the audience's sake, but the other kids loved it. In the next couple weeks I went through all my favorite dreams but, I was running out of material. I started to panic a bit, I had become addicted to the emotional feedback of my audience.

So, over a weekend I racked my brain and I came up with the solution. I was an imaginative kid, and I was always making up stories so, I would tell a story. Not just any story, but a grand story, the kind you can't finish in one installment. Every day would be a continuation of the story until it was completed. When I was a kid one of my favorite TV shows was Gilligan's Island and I got a lot of inspiration from that show.

Before I go on I suppose I should mention that my teacher hated me. In fact she hated all boys and was reported to have even told a parent that. It was something everyone knew. Her dislike of me was palpable, because I was as 'boy' as you could get. She had grown tired of my show and tell style and she was reluctant to call on me. She would call every other kid with their hand up and then only called on me when everyone else was done, so I always went last.

Then, the entire time I was delivering my show and tell she would either be rolling her eyes, shaking her head, or grinding the palms of her hands into her eye sockets, that's how I knew when I was really onto something good.

So Monday came, and I was ready. I was called last as usual, I got up in front of the class, looking extremely serious...paused for effect, and then I began. I started out my story by saying that as I was walking home from school one day, I found a book in the ditch, it was bound in human skin. I took the book home and started reading it. It turned out that the book was all about my family, and it said that we came from a long line of witch doctors. The book was full of spells and incantations and other magical enchantments. I said I tried some of the spells, and they worked!

By this time I had exhausted the days allotted show and tell time and we had to return to our regular lessons. All of my classmates were on the edge of their seats. They couldn't wait to hear what the spells were and what I could do, I told them I would continue telling the story the next day. You would think at least a couple kids would have said I was lying, it was kind of an amazing coincidence after all, finding that book, but no one protested. They must have thought, "Who would lie about such a fantastic thing? It must be true!" So for the next two days I continued the story, each day I would talk about a couple more magic spells I could do, thanks to my witch doctor ancestors.

One spell I cast could temporarily turn the mean dogs on the end of my street into zebras and giraffes until I got past them. Another spell allowed me to be able to jump all the way onto the top of our roof, and then I could float back down. My classmates favorite story, the one that really got their attention, was the spell that let me turn dry leaves into money. I told that one on Thursday.

That day during recess and then again at lunch time, all the kids in my class were bringing me arms loads of dry leaves begging me to turn them into money for them. I had to think fast. I instructed everyone to pile their leaves out in the baseball backstop. Then I told them to meet me there during our last recess of the day.

We had a lot of maple trees and alder trees around the school, and all their leaves from the year before still littered the stand of trees they were in. So finding leaves was no problem and there was a mountain of them by the time last recess came. I looked out and all the kids were waiting for me around the huge pile of leaves. I walked out confidently to join them, but on the inside I was in full panic mode.

I walked around the pile, inspecting it. Then I let all my inhibitions lose, because I had to. I started dancing on one leg and spouting some kind of gibberish—then the other leg. Then I fell to the ground and clutched two handfuls of dirt, jumped back up and danced around the pile sprinkling it on the leaves. Then I went around the pile stomping my feet as hard as I could, first clockwise, then counter-clockwise. Then for the finale I looked up at the sky and screamed—then spit on the pile.

Then I said, "Well...that should do it, there oughta be a pile of money here tomorrow!"

I looked around at the other children, afraid I would see them scoffing or laughing, but instead they were all in stunned silence, some of their mouths were open. Apparently, I pulled it off. From the looks of it they all believed they had just witnessed something supernatural, and there I was acting as cool as I had just tied my shoe or something.

The bell rang and everyone ran back to class. I could hear excited conversations between kids about what they were going to do with their money. I was terrified. I didn't know what I was going to do tomorrow when they all ran out to get their fortune and those same old leaves were lying there. I was terrified but I managed to mask it, by appearing disinterested instead.

When I got home that night I considered talking to my mom about it and telling her the plight I was in, but I thought better of it. Yeah, that wouldn't go over so well. Besides being scared, I just felt bad. They were all so happy and excited and tomorrow they would be so disappointed. I enjoyed witnessing that joy on my classmates faces and I did not want to let them down. How could I not let them down, AND also not seem like the biggest seven-year-old con man there ever was?

After dinner a notion occurred to me. I spun it around in my head a few times until it started to take shape. Yes, that was it! I had come up with a brilliant solution! I went to my piggy bank and scraped a dollar out of it with my mom's nail file. Then I jumped on my bike and rode to the school just as it was turning twilight. I went out to the backstop where the pile of leaves waited. In several trips I returned them all to the stand of trees they came from, scattering them around so they looked natural. Then, I took that dollar and wedged it into the chain link fence of the back stop...down low, about 6 inches off the ground. I made sure the dollar was secure, then I got back on my bike and sped back home.

I lived pretty close to the school but the next day I rode the bus because I wanted to hear everything that was being said and most of the other kids also rode the bus. Every one in my class was busting with excitement, and I was excited for them. They couldn't wait for the bus to stop, and when it finally did they all jumped off and ran straight out to the back stop. I didn't run though. I just walked calmly as though I didn't have a care in the world.

When I got to the backstop I arrived at a very solemn scene. All the kids were standing there, silent, staring at the bare patch of dirt where the pile of leaves had been. I became alarmed then, "I don't understand!" I said. "I know I did everything right, what could have happened?" Then the questions started coming; Where are the leaves? Why isn't there any money? What happened Alf? Maybe somebody stole it.

That's when I "saw" it. I was staring down towards the ground, slowly approaching a spot in the corner of the back stop. "Look here every body" I yelled. When I had everyone's attention I continued. "The leaves did turn into money, but then the wind came along and blew them away. There's one of the dollars that got stuck in the fence. It looks like they were blown that way." I said, pointing to the woods. Being able to see that one dollar stuck in the fence was all the proof they needed. They were excited again, not because the money was in their hands but because they believed at least, that it existed. Without another word there were 25 kids out tromping through the woods looking for money before the bell rang. There were kids out in the woods looking for money for several more days actually, before the last one gave up.

Surprisingly, I never got into any trouble for this, I guess no one told their parents. None of the kids were mad at me either, after all, you can't blame a guy for the wind. And the real surprise to me was that none of them ever asked me to do it again, like they all instinctively knew it was a one time shot.

That's the end of the story; So what do you suppose I learned by this? Let's face it, I totally lucked out. If I had not thought of that solution my name would have been MUD. My mouth almost wrote a check that my butt could not cash. As it was though, there were no injured parties. Everyone had fun dreaming about their fortune and it was fun for them to hope and believe for a minute.

I didn't learn any lessons about not being deceitful because, I didn't start out intending to be deceitful. I started out with only the intention to entertain and have fun with a story but, then it got out of hand. That's the real lesson I learned here; that words have power, it can be a power for good, or a power for bad, but words have power. That power can also destroy the person who wields it, if he allows it to get out of hand. With great power comes great responsibility, and even though I was only 7, I could feel the weight of that responsibility. I cared for my classmates and I was on the verge of hurting them and disappointing them, making them feel lied to, because I didn't yet understand the power of words.

Under the right conditions people will believe almost anything they are told, no matter how fantastic and unbelievable. Therefore, it is the responsibility of the person speaking to be aware not only of his words, but of how they are being received. I went on to tell a lot of wild stories but I never led people to believe me again, if it wasn't true. To this day I'm kind of a fanatic about words, because words mean things. All the words we speak have power, and I think everyone has an obligation to use words as accurately and responsibly as possible.

If you look back on your life, how many times have your own words betrayed you, and got you in some kind of trouble? This is a reminder to use the power of words for good. You'll be happier, you'll sleep better, and you'll be a better man.

CHAPTER TWENTY-FOUR
Results Are Everything

In 1969 I was 7 years old. My sister was 5 and my brother was 4. Life was good and carefree as it should be for children of that age. We lived on a little farm and my mom took care of us and the house while my dad worked long hours as a sheet metal man.

My dad worked a lot. He worked all day at his trade, and then when he came home there were always chores to do on the farm. Often times he would come home from work and then be out tinkering on things until mom called us in to dinner. Then after dinner he would go back outside and work until it got too dark to see. My dad was a working man from the inside out, and he felt strong about his responsibilities. Whenever I could, I followed him around, like a little shadow, and helped when he let me, if it wasn't too dangerous. I learned an awful lot just by being around him.

In the summer it was tough sometimes though. If the weather was warm we wanted to go swimming or on a picnic, or camping or fishing, something fun—but my poor dad was always working, even on most weekends he was working around our place tending the garden or mending fences, or fixing things around the house or working on a car.

I made pretty good use of my time while I was out of school, I spent most days pretending to be all sorts of different things all over our property. Viking, indian, pirate, cowboy, you name it, that was me, that's how I spent my time. But on weekends I would beg my dad to please take us somewhere fun. I couldn't pretend all the time, sometimes I just wanted to jump in a lake and get away from the heat, or have some other kind of adventure with my family.

His refusals were kind, but firm. I could tell he wished he could do all those things too, he just felt overwhelmed by the responsibilities around our place, but every once in a while he would just say, "To heck with it." He would stop his work and tell mom to start packing because we were going somewhere. Those were the best of times. I can still remember the elation and excitement I felt whenever my dad decided to take us on one of these excursions.

I remember in particular one very hot day when we did just that. We were going to the lake! I religiously guarded all of my lake gear, which included swimming fins, a mask and snorkel, a beach ball and a shovel for digging in the sand, I had a bucket too, because you never knew when you would need one. As I was gathering up all my stuff my mom was getting food and other supplies together and my dad was loading up the grill and charcoal. It was going to be a great day. I don't know what my sister and brother were doing. They were too young to fully appreciate the magnitude of what was going on. Sure they were happy, but not like I was.

We got to the lake, which was at a beautiful state park not too far from our house. Everything was going just as I'd hoped. The water was perfect, the swimming was good. I made a few new friends with the other kids that were there. Since I lived out in the country I didn't get much playing time with other kids my age, so that was a big deal. My mom was afraid of the water, I never knew why, but my dad was out in the water with us. His farmer tan was so dark that it looked like he was still wearing a shirt, even though he wasn't. My dad had to be careful though because he was almost deaf. He had an operation on his ears when he was a young man and all I knew, was that he couldn't get any water in his ears because he could get an infection that would be dangerous. In spite of that, sometimes he would plug his ears with his fingers and dive under the water with us.

In the afternoon we were all getting hungry from swimming and playing all day, so my mom and dad fired up the grill and started cooking some food for us. While they were busy cooking I was still out in the water. It was a roped off swimming area and there was a lifeguard so they weren't too concerned about our safety.

I was over by one of the side ropes, wading waist deep. I

stepped over the rope and started looking around in the area just beyond the rope. As I was roaming around I came across something curious, just about five feet past the rope. It looked like a giant dandelion flower floating in the water. I had never seen anything quite like that before so I looked a little closer. I touched the golden fronds that were radiating out from the center...I picked them up out of the water. "Wow" I thought, that looks just like hair. Then I looked closer still at the center of the giant flower, down between where the hair started I could see something light colored, it was skin. That's when I knew this was a person floating in the water. I was only seven, but I knew what drowning was and I knew people needed to breathe if they wanted to live, and I knew this person wasn't breathing.

I reached down and grabbed the person's body and lifted up, a face came out of the water, the face of my own 5 year old sister.

Her eyes were closed. I yelled for my mom and dad, I screamed, but my screams were mixed in and drowned out by the shouts and yells of 50 other kids playing on the beach. No one took any notice. I was scared now, terrible scared. The shore was only about ten feet away and I put my arms around her and started dragging. I stepped in a deep hole and she went under again, I figured that must have been the hole she stepped into in the first place.

I got her to the shore and drug her body up on the bank. She wasn't moving. I was still screaming for help but I was just far enough away that it didn't register with anyone, nobody was coming. I wasn't sure what to do. Part of me wanted to leave her and run to get my folks, but another part of me understood that I didn't have that much time.

I had seen a lot of cartoons and other silly shows where someone saved a drowning person by pushing on their belly and then water would shoot out of their mouth and everything would be OK. Sometimes they would crank their arms like it was a pump handle and water would shoot out of their mouth, the drowned person would wake up and everything would be fine. So I did all those things. I pushed on her belly, I pushed on her chest, and I cranked her arms like pump handles. I turned her over on her belly and did it all again. I just kept moving her around any way I could think of. Somewhere in the middle of all that, somehow, by some

117

miracle, she woke up. She spit and coughed, and then she started crying.

Man...I was so happy I didn't care if she was crying, I was just happy her eyes were open. I got her on her feet and led her back to where my parents were, and I immediately got in trouble. They wanted to know what I did to her to make my sister cry.

I told them the whole story, but they didn't believe me. They thought I was just telling one of my stories, even though I insisted it was true. My sister couldn't really tell them one way or the other because she didn't even remember what had happened.

We all ate dinner then, like it was any other normal day at the lake. I was moping around, frustrated that I was the only one who knew what happened, but I had told so many crazy stories already in my life, that no one would take me seriously. I continued to tell the story for years, I stuck to it for the sake of accuracy, because I remembered what happened.   I remember it like it was yesterday. When I got older though, every body thought it was just some goofy idea I had that was left over from my childhood. I don't think anyone really believes the story to this day, not even my sister. I eventually gave up, I haven't told this story for many years, until now.

You know what though?   Its OK that no one believed me. Eventually it stopped being important to me If I was believed or not, because I knew it happened. Every time I looked at my sister I was glad I found her that day.   Glad I was able to get her out in time. When she grew up, got her drivers license, graduated from college—I was glad. My sister had a son, my nephew. He is 17 as I am putting this book together. He is shaping up into a fine young man and I'm glad that I found his mom in the water that day.

So, aside from the obvious down side of the   'boy who cried wolf' scenario—the lesson I learned from this is something I've applied many times in life, and it's very relevant to being a better man. The lesson is, as long as I know what I know—that's all that really matters.

As long as I know what is true, as long as I know myself well, as long as I am confident in the rightness of my intent and actions, nothing anyone else can say will get to me. It kind of made me immune to insults and unjust criticism. It taught me that, while personal glory and accolades are nice, they are also over rated. They don't affect the outcome of any situation. The only things that really matter, are the results.

It's powerful to be sure of what you know about the world, but mostly, be sure of what you know about yourself. Focus on the results of your deeds and not the attention. It will make it a little easier to be a better man.

CHAPTER TWENTY-FIVE
French Toast Wars

I was 13 years old, and somewhere between being a boy and a young man. My body, mind, and internal chemistry was changing and everything I did and said turned out to be an awkward attempt to balance those changes with the life I had known up until then. When a person is in a space like this, anything can happen.

It was 1975 and I was on a camp out with my Boy Scout troop. We had an active troop and we went on a pretty serious camp out every month. This time we were camping at Ft. Warden, an old retired World War II naval base on the northern coast of Washington State. There were a lot of old structures and underground bunkers to explore, it was a lot of fun.

We were having a great time, as we always did. There were about 25 boys on this camp out from the ages of 11 to 18— that's a whole lot of young testosterone. All of us were constantly trying to affect our standing within the group, trying to elevate our position in the pecking order. Some of us were succeeding, and some of us not, just like in life. That's the way is was though, and that's the way it will always be in our species whenever a group of the male gender are thrust together as we were. Whether we are men or boys, it's part of our nature. I for one, loved that element of it. I loved the challenge of standing out, I relished the opportunity to try, even in the presence of older boys who were currently superior to me, but who I also knew were once exactly where I was.

Unfortunately, sometimes my willingness to stand out and be

noticed caused me to do stupid, crazy things that would get me in trouble, and put my dad in the awkward position of trying to explain my behavior. (Not all the time, but sometimes...)

One evening we were all gathered together chatting in the firelight, and inevitably, someone made a boast. It was another guy around my same age. He was boasting about how well he could cook and he wanted to prove it by making breakfast for everyone the next day. Being who I was, I just couldn't let a boast like that go unchallenged. I told him I was a pretty good cook myself, and it just so happened that breakfast was my specialty.

We went back and forth like that for a bit. The scout master informed us that what was on the menu for the next morning was french toast, bacon and fruit. Naturally upon hearing that, both the other boy and I immediately crowned ourselves the best french toast makers in the world, and the verbal sparring continued. Finally someone came up with an idea, probably the scout master. We should have a contest, a french toast contest! We could each cook in a different kitchen area, our food would be served on different colored plates, and everyone who ate our food would vote who was the best once and for all, without knowing who they were voting for. That sounded like great fun to me and I accepted the challenge immediately, as did my new rival.

The next morning the adults got us all set up with everything we needed. We each had the same number of eggs and bread and bacon and oranges. We had identical cooking utensils and our outdoor kitchen areas were separated by a cinder block wall.

The rules of the contest were explained to us. We had to make our own batter and cook the french toast. We had to cook the bacon at the same time, and we also had to slice our oranges into quarters to be served. All of our hungry friends were waiting eagerly just a little ways off, they could not see us cooking though.

The contest began and I flew into action. In truth, I had never made french toast before, but I had watched my mom make it hundreds of times. I knew exactly what I was doing. I was working feverishly, because there was also a time limit, we had to finish preparing everything within a certain period of time. My hands were flying from the batter I was making, to the oranges, then to the bacon and back to the batter. I was very focused on each individual task as

I was doing it. I was almost ready to start dunking bread into the batter when I looked down and noticed something was wrong. In the middle of my large bowl of egg batter there was a crimson puddle of blood. Not a tiny puddle—a puddle about 4 inches in diameter and who knows how deep.

I quickly looked around, good...no one was looking. I looked back to the bloody batter, the puddle was getting bigger. I turned over my hands that were holding the rim of the bowl to discover a cut on my hand that I didn't know was there. Apparently, in the process of slicing oranges I had cut myself. It was a fairly nasty cut and it was still bleeding pretty good. I grabbed some paper towels and wrapped them around the cut finger. I applied pressure but it kept bleeding through the paper towel. I applied a new, thicker paper bandage and lashed it into place with some duct tape that was there. (We used duct tape for everything when we were camping.) The cut was under control now, back to the bloody batter.

It looked pretty gross. There was a significant amount of my blood floating there on top of the egg batter. What would I do? I had wasted so much time tending to my cut, I didn't have time to try and spoon out all the blood...I had used all the eggs I had to make my batter, so starting over was out of the question. My reputation and dignity were on the line, there was only one possible solution. After looking around once more to make sure no one was watching, I picked up the wire whisk and furiously started just blending it all together. My spinning whisk created a vortex in the bowl, a vortex made of eggs, salt, milk, a little pepper and a bunch of my blood. When I was done I stood back and looked. Yep...the batter had turned a strange shade of pink. Before anyone had a chance to inspect it I quickly started dunking the bread into the pink batter and started cooking. After I had cooked all the bread I had, there was still some pink batter left in the bowl, so I disposed of it, and the evidence of what I had done into a nearby garbage can.

The timer rang and we were done cooking. A few adults served our anonymous french toast to all the other people while we waited to hear the verdict of who had won. I was plenty nervous as you might imagine. I had no idea what effect my secret ingredient would have on the taste. Part of me felt very strange and uneasy about the fact that everyone there was eating a portion of me. Thinking like that was not helping my situation, in fact it made me nauseous, so I forced that thought out of my head.

To my surprise, when the verdict came in it was I that won the french toast contest. I won it by a landslide actually. Almost everyone preferred my french toast over that of my competitor. The victory was sweet, but I would just have to take their word for it, because I didn't eat any french toast that morning. I made due with an orange.

I never told any one of this event for years, and absolutely never told anyone in my Boy Scout troop. There is only one reason not to ever speak of a thing, and that reason is, because you know it was wrong. It was wrong of me to do that, to not tell anyone what had happened. When I saw the blood I should have told someone. The contest would have been abandoned and my wound treated. Instead I was so caught up in the frenzy of competition that doing anything other than I did, didn't even occur to me.

I was 13, so I knew better. In a rational non-competitive state I would have certainly made another choice, but that time I didn't. I made a hasty, wrong choice and then justified that choice in my mind for the sake of winning.

That day I learned a lesson about hollow victories. Sure, I won, but the victory was hollow and unrewarding. Not because I had cheated exactly, but rather to win it I had to perpetrate a deception on my friends. The guilt of that wrong act had rendered my victory impotent and unsatisfying. It was a good lesson to learn at a young age. Winning really isn't everything if what you win is less than honest and empty. Its better to lose with your honor intact.

Now head out into the world and while you are being a better man avoid any hollow victories, they aren't worth it. And if any of my old Boy Scout buddies are reading this, hey I'm sorry. However, if you've developed any super powers from eating that french toast... you're welcome!

CHAPTER TWENTY-SIX
My Greatest Enemy

The following tale is not amusing, at least not to me. Rather it is an account of my personal demons, their genesis, the suffering that followed, and the road to victory over them. As you read keep in mind that 'One man's pudding is another man's poison'. What is frightening or even debilitating to one, may not be so for another.

When I was five years old I used to sneak over to my friend's house to watch "Dark Shadows", the daytime horror soap opera. My mother wouldn't allow me to watch it because she said I would have bad dreams, it turns out that she was right. It was watching Dark Shadows that I first became introduced to the figure of the wolfman; also known as the werewolf.

What I noticed about the wolfman that set him apart from other monsters was the way he went about so single-mindedly bent on killing his victims. Oh sure, other monsters killed their victims too, but it wasn't the same. The vampire killed for food, the mummy killed for vengeance, Frankenstein killed out of self defense, the lake creatures killed because they wanted to be left alone, the wolfman however, killed for the sake of killing alone, and that terrified me.

Another difference about the wolfman was that he was virtually unstoppable. Nowhere was safe; he was just too strong, too vicious. If you were in a car he would just rip the doors off. You couldn't hide because he could smell you; crosses, holy water, garlic, none of that would work. You had to be fortunate enough to be in possession of a silver bullet and a gun to shoot it out of. That's it—that is the only thing that could stop him, and I didn't have that.

Another terrifying thing about the wolfman was that he could be anyone. They walk and live among you like normal people except for a couple nights a month when the moon was full. Knowing this makes it almost impossible for a small boy to ever truly trust anyone.

You could never turn your back on anyone at night because they could change, just like that! They could be your father, maybe the neighbor, your best friend, anybody. Anybody except a dog that is. Dogs served as the early warning devices for wolfmen. This drew me ever closer to my dear dog, Lady. At first I acted out my fears alone, because to divulge the source of my fear would be to admit disobeying my mother by watching that show. In the beginning I was still more scared of being in trouble than I was of the wolfman himself. My parents thought I was afraid of the dark, but I wasn't. I was afraid of what was hiding in the dark, waiting for the right opportunity to rip out my throat, which was one of the wolfman's favorite killing techniques.

I kept a particularly close eye on the lunar cycle for a boy so young. My parents thought I was interested in astronomy. When the moon was full I insisted on sleeping with them but I couldn't tell them why, except that I was scared. They would beg to know what I was afraid of but I couldn't tell them. I would blame it on the dark, or a bad dream, whatever was handy. It was only a couple nights a month so it didn't seem too excessive at first. As time went on and I got older my father became increasingly annoyed with my fearful ways. At the same time my fear was becoming increasingly cemented in my brain.

When I learned to read I researched everything I could find on the subject. While other kids were barely reading "See Jane run," I was digesting every account of the wolfman legend that my school library had. I learned that they had been around for some time, there were even ancient drawings depicting them.

Eventually I told my parents the name of my fear and that made it worse, because there was 'no such thing as wolfmen'. I was just a silly boy. After we moved to the farm in Olympia where I grew up, the problem got worse. I was by all accounts a fearless lad, performing death-defying stunts on a daily basis. At night however, and especially on a full moon, I was reduced to a sniveling, paralyzed coward.

My father sent me out to get firewood on one such night. It was a full moon and there just wasn't any earthly way for me to obey him. I was a dutiful son and always obeyed my father, but I had to refuse no matter the consequence. He became infuriated, even more so when I pointed out the fact that it was a full moon. He finally stomped out and got the wood himself, shaking his head and grumbling. He wasn't just angry, he was disappointed. This fact made my heart ache terribly, and the whole time he was outside I feared for his life.

By the time I was 13, I was a mess: a relatively normal boy most of the time, yet still saddled with my debilitating fear of wolfmen. It's very hard to be afraid of something that doesn't exist. It is hard because there is no comfort, no one to talk to. If you try to talk to someone they just shake their head and repeat the fact that wolfmen are not real as if that is supposed to fix everything.

I had already figured out long ago that wolfmen were not real; yet knowing that did nothing to assuage my fear. With my intellect I thought I was being ridiculous, but when the moon was full, no amount of reasoning could slow my heart beat.

I was in Boy Scouts. We went on monthly campouts that I loved, but if the moon was going to be full I wouldn't go. My life was still governed by the lunar cycle.

We lived on a farm and I was the product of a long line of rugged men who did what needed to be done without question. I was a good son who enjoyed making my father proud, but sometimes when the monstrous fear would grip me, he couldn't hide his disappointment. The only thing worse than my fear of wolfmen, was seeing disappointment in my dad's eyes. I decided finally, to do something about it. In other walks of life I considered fear to be a weakness of mind. I was a believer in the concept of facing ones fear head on, and conquering them. I had never applied this philosophy to my 'wolfman condition' though. The faintest thought of doing this paralyzed me. The time had come however; I refused to continue being a victim of my irrational fear and a source of pain to my father.

On the night in question the moon was full and bright. It was in early winter, between Thanksgiving and Christmas and the night air was cold and sharp. My plan was to wait until midnight, at which time I would walk out into the woods, alone.

I thought if I came back then I would be free. If I didn't come back, then at least I wouldn't be afraid anymore. Before I left I made sure I said good-bye to everyone. My choice of mid-night had no real significance; it was just my version of "high noon" like in the Western movies.

I told no one of my plan. I sat waiting for midnight to come. I was shaking and my entire body was covered in beads of sweat. Finally, it was time. The night was well illuminated by the moon. Everything was cast in it's eerie light. The woods began about a five-minute walk away from the house. As I walked through the pasture towards them it seemed as though my footfalls were loud crashing stomps even though I was doing my best to be walk quietly. There was a wide path around the perimeter of our woods, the plan was simple; I would enter the woods on the North end and hope to emerge unscathed on the South end, about a 20 minute walk in the daylight. If there were any wolfmen about they would certainly not be able to resist this opportunity. I just wanted it to be over.

Even though the night was well lit by the moon, looking into the woods was like looking into a black curtain— but I entered, trembling. The forest floor was littered with dead branches and knee-high underbrush. Stealth was impossible. Each step I took was a loud crash that resonated through the otherwise silent forest. Each step I took was the gong of a dinner bell, and I was the main course. I wasn't 20 feet in when I heard it, off to my left, a single footstep. My heart was beating so fast the beats were indistinguishable, it was more like a hum in my chest. When I heard that first noise I knew I was never leaving these woods alive. I kept walking though; there was nothing else to do.

Then another branch broke on my right, the brush rustled behind me, more footfalls to my left, then on the right again. It became clear to me that I was surrounded. Surrounded by the very beasts I had feared all my life; they were real after all! However, I was confused by their delay. I realized I would be dead in the next few moments, my carcass strewn about the forest floor. I wished they would just get on with it because the anxiety of being stalked was pure torture.

In my minds eye I saw them, perhaps as many as seven judging by the noises I was hearing. Maybe they were an entire family out for a kill? I kept looking down as I trampled through the brush. In the back of my brain I thought just maybe if they didn't know that I knew they were there, they wouldn't have to kill me. Maybe they had already fed and were just having a bit of fun? I also kept looking down because I was afraid that if I peered in the direction of the noises I might see them, and if I saw one, I was literally afraid my heart would explode.

It went on like that for several minutes. Finally, half way through the woods I just couldn't take it any more. I stopped. The noises that had been following me seemed to stop as well. I decided that this was where I would die; right here in the middle of my father's woods. Having accepted the fact that I would be torn apart any minute, I began to get angry. I was angry with these wolfmen for torturing me all the way through the woods. I was angry at them for torturing me in my dreams, for making me afraid my entire life, for causing my dad to be disappointed. I was angry, so I screamed at them.

I screamed at the top of my lungs for them to come and get me. I called them names and stomped my feet. When I finished screaming and the last echoes of my voice were fading I closed my eyes and waited for the inevitable—but it never came. After a couple minutes I opened my eyes. I was still alive for some reason. I thought this was either a very good sign, or a very cruel joke the wolfmen were pulling on me.

I began screaming again. It was more personal this time; I was challenging them, taunting them, calling them names, throwing things and making fun of them. I was getting all those years of fear off my chest. My confidence and courage was swelling with each passing second in which I was still alive. I was so encouraged by their absence, that if one would have finally came at me I felt like I could take him.

Finally, the screaming was over. I was done. I collapsed onto the forest floor and sobbed, I was overwhelmed with relief. Eventually I got up and continued my walk through the woods to the South end. Along the way I still heard noises, but now I recognized them as the scurrying of small animals frightened by my presence. I was laughing; laughing at myself, and for myself. It was the type of laughter that spills out of you when you are filled with joy.

I was liberated, I was free at last. The enormous burden that had plagued me was vanquished and it made the whole world look different. For the first time I was able to appreciate the beauty of moonlight on a landscape, and it was so beautiful. There was a layer of frost on everything and the moonlight made everything seem alive. I could see the lights of my home and walked toward them. I couldn't wait until the next time my father needed wood brought in.

It might have seemed silly to you to read about a kid being afraid of werewolves, but that was my perception and perception is reality. This story was the first and also the final chapter of a work called "The Wolfman Chronicles". In the extended version I also detail a few of the dreams I had.

As far as the lessons I learned from this go, there are too many to count. This time I'm going to leave what the lessons were up to you, the reader. What do you think I learned? What would you have learned if it was you, instead of me? I will tell you this; this experience changed my life, probably more than any other singular experience in my childhood. It was like a rite of passage on steroids. The kid that came back that night was entirely different, from the one who went out to face his enemy.

CHAPTER TWENTY-SEVEN
Exploding Friendship

I was 16 years old. I had a drivers license and I was finally at a point in my life where I had a little bit of freedom because I could drive myself where I needed to go. That's one drawback of living out in the country; most of your friends live in the city and unless you have a way into the city, you don't really get to hang out with them.

One of my friends who lived in the city was Ryan. Ryan was a good guy. We would hang out and get poker games together, we both liked to eat a lot and we both laughed at each others jokes, so we got along pretty well.

One day over at Ryan's house he was showing me his dads black powder rifles and pistols. You know, the old fashioned muskets, guns that you have to pour gunpowder in and then load them with a ball right down the barrel like they did in the Civil War. It is still a hobby that is practiced today by historical re-enactors. Anyway, as he is explaining his father's supplies to me, I learn that there are different grades of black powder, from F to FFFF. 4-F was the finest and most explosive, while 1-F was course and a little slower burning. Before the night was over Ryan and I decided it would be a good idea to design our own bomb, using his dad's gun powder.

We were not interested in blowing ourselves up, so we planned to start out small. We knew the size of the explosion was directly related to the amount of resistance or compression. So we got some notebook paper out of our school supplies, about a 1/4 inch thick stack of paper. We dumped a pile of 4-F black powder on it, then we folded and rolled the paper as tightly as we could while wrapping it with duct tape.

When we were done we had something about the size of an orange. It even looked like a bomb. For a fuse we decided to use fine steel wool. It's made out of magnesium and it will actually burn without creating a flame, I don't remember why we knew that. The other cool thing about steel wool was that you could stretch it out to make yourself a timed fuse. Before we ever tried it out we tested several fuses of different lengths to see how long they burned, we kept copious notes— it was all quite scientific.

To attach the fuse we carefully cut a hole in the bomb and taped it in place. Now we were ready to blow it up, which is where my living in the country came in handy because I knew a ton of places that were remote out in the woods.   That is where our bomb laboratory test site would be. That first bomb we made was probably my favorite. We put it at the base of a tree, there was a lot of thick brush around it, too. We lit it and took off running to a safe position that we had previously decided on.

We waited. We waited some more. We started to wonder if the fuse had gone out when all of a sudden, it blew. We were expecting the sound of a large M80 like at the 4th of July, but what we got was louder than we had expected, much louder.   The sound of the explosion echoed four times off the sides of different hills.   It was pretty amazing.

The problem with successfully making a bomb, was that now we were hooked. All we wanted to do now was make bigger, louder bombs; we wanted to improve our methods and keep getting better and, we did. We were only limited by Ryan's dad's supply of gun powder, but he was well stocked when we were starting out.

There wasn't any ill intent behind our bomb making, we really just loved the science of it, and the explosion of course. Our bombs got bigger and bigger and more and more devastating in their destructive power.   Our biggest bomb cleared a 6 foot circle of thick brush down to bare dirt.

There was a problem though; there wasn't really a practical use for our bombs, and they were dangerous even though we were being careful. We decided the answer to this problem was an underwater bomb. That would have a practical use because we could make depth charges, drop them in a lake from a boat and then pick up the fish that were floating around, killed by the shock wave. Brilliant!

The first thing we had to do was invent an underwater fuse, the bomb itself was already water tight. We came up with an idea that we thought would work. We took some clear plastic tubing and stuffed it with the coarse, slower burning 1-F powder. Once it was lit it would keep burning by continuously lighting the dry powder in the tube before the water was able to put it out.

We had to test our theory immediately. We manufactured a small bomb, a little bigger than an apricot. We made the fuse and attached it. Now we had to test it, but where? In Ryan's back yard there was one of those galvanized metal tubs that hold 25 or 30 gallons of water. It was circular, about 16 inches tall. We decided that since it was a smallish bomb we could just do it in his back yard.

We had become cocky, and arrogant, and desensitized to the nature of bombs and what effect they might have in a neighborhood. We were too eager to try out our new invention. For the first time since we had started making bombs, we threw caution to the wind, and filled the tub with water. It was in the afternoon. Everyone was home from work, families were sitting down to dinner all around us and Ryan's parents were both home as well.

We gave each other a hopeful look, lit the fuse and dropped it in the water. We didn't even go away to a safe distance... no, we actually stood close enough to watch our underwater fuse burning beneath the water. We were shouting "It's working, it's working!" and then the explosion came.

It wasn't as small of an explosion as we thought it would be. All of our practice and improved methods meant we could pack more power into a tinier bundle, we forgot about that part. Immediately after the explosion it was like everything in the world stopped, probably because we were temporarily deaf. Where was the water? We looked around, then we looked up and there was the water, hanging in a column up in the sky!

Apparently, the size of the bomb, the slant of the tubs sides, the amount of water, everything was just right so that when the water tried to escape the explosion it met resistance at the side of the tub, and shot straight up into the air. It was pretty amazing! The last thing the expanding water did before it left the tub was to blow out all the seams and leave it flattened like a soda pop can run over by a car. Then the water fell all around us, all at once. Ryan and I were standing there, drenched by the water, laughing hysterically at this crazy thing we had caused to happen, delighted that we had invented something that worked.

What we didn't yet realize is that the percussion had rattled the windows of all the houses for a couple blocks in all directions. All the dogs in the whole neighborhood were barking. Less than a minute had passed since the explosion and we hadn't had time to finish our celebration when Ryan's parents came bounding into the back yard from the back door. They both wore expressions of fear and panic, obviously they had expected the worst. Then they saw us, laughing hysterically, drenched in water, standing next to a flattened galvanized tub. Their expressions changed quickly to anger.

After a few moments of glaring at us his mom said, "Alf, it's time for you to leave." She didn't have to tell me twice, I got out of there as fast as I could. Luckily, they didn't call my parents. We were no longer allowed access to the black powder after that. In fact, Ryan's parents discouraged him hanging out with me too much after that, and I don't think I was ever invited to dinner again. We were still friends, but it was different somehow. That was the last bomb I ever made, and that is the end of this story.

I want to be really clear—I am in no way advocating kids making bombs. It was one of the stupidest things I ever got involved with. We were just a couple kids pretending to be rocket scientists, it was crazy and we are really lucky we both survived. Do not, I repeat **do not** try this at home.

I told you about this so I could share the lesson I learned from it. It was an important lesson about being in control of your intellect, or more specifically, not losing control of it. When it was all over I could remember some of the close calls we had, and there were several. Once I was no longer doing it I could see the progression that took place in our minds, I could see how with each successful bomb we became more and more relaxed, and careless, to the point of lighting a bomb in a residential neighborhood.

I could remember the excitement and exhilaration that came over me when we were making bombs and blowing them up and it was suddenly clear that that level of exhilaration is unhealthy. It's unhealthy because it completely takes over the part of your brain where common sense lives. It renders your intellectual decision making part of your brain useless— you get kind of addicted to the excitement of it and then that becomes all that matters.

It doesn't have to be bombs that do this, pretend bombs in video games can create the same unhealthy effect. Drugs can do it, too, or risky criminal behavior, or any number of things. Attraction to some women can even have this effect on a guy, separating him from reality.

Here is the bottom line; there is a certain type of intense excitement that crosses the line, and it is dangerous. It almost always involves potentially dangerous activities, and if it gets ahold of you many bad things can happen. I was lucky, but there are thousands of guys in prison, or dead, who were not so lucky. So be on the lookout for it, learn to identify it, so that you can avoid it. In order to be a better man, you have to stay alive.

CHAPTER TWENTY-EIGHT
Self Inflicted

11 years old is the youngest you can be in Boy Scouts. Before that, as you are getting ready to be a Boy Scout you are a Cub Scout, and then a Webelo. Finally, when you are eleven years of age you can join an actual Boy Scout troop, which I did.

That first summer after I turned eleven and joined a Scout troop, was also my first opportunity to go to Boy Scout camp. That was a pretty big deal because your troop is there for a whole week with a bunch of other troops. You are away from home. You ate in a mess hall and there were all kinds of things to do because the camp was right on a lake. At night time there was a theatre sort of place made with logs and lit only by two huge fires where different groups of guys would tell stories or act out funny skits, and of course many songs were sung. The camp was nestled in a beautiful Pacific Northwest forest with all kinds of hiking trails, and that is where I got to learn most of what I know about local native plants.

This was the first time I would be gone for an entire week, and my mother was not too pleased about it— she was nervous about me being out of her sight for that long. My father on the other hand was happy for me, he knew I would have the time of my life. On the day I left, my father gave me a gift. I wasn't expecting a gift, my birthday had already come and gone. I opened it up— it was a brand new folding pocket knife.

What you should understand is that I had other knives before, but up to this point my parents had made sure they were not sharp.

In fact they were intentionally dulled on a rock before I was allowed to have them. This knife was special, it was a real knife and it was sharp as a razor, and it was beautiful! It had real wood sides and brass rivets. It wasn't a pre owned thing, he had bought it especially for me. It wasn't a big knife, the blade was only about 4 inches long, but I loved it and I couldn't wait to start carving wood into some amazing shape.

My dad took a little time explaining how sharp the knife was and making sure I remembered all the things he had taught me about how to hold it and to never cut towards my body. He always said; "Cut from...and you won't cut your thumb." After I got checked out with him, then my mother repeated everything he had said, just to be sure.

So there I was at Camp Thunderbird. Every thing was going perfectly, and I was having an amazing time. At night I would sit with other woodcarving enthusiast around the fire and use my new knife to carve things. My scout master was an accomplished woodcarver and he was showing me some tricks.

About the third day in I was walking back from the lake with a friend. The brush was thick and lush on each side of the path and I decided to take a short cut. I told my friend I would blaze a trail through the brush with my new knife. I whipped it out and started hacking. Suddenly I was no longer a Boy Scout—I was now an explorer in the middle of a deep jungle, and my knife had become a huge sharp machete. Everything was going pretty well. My knife could easily handle most branches up to the size of a pencil. I was swinging in a wild roundhouse fashion from right to left, and then left to right, leaving a passable trail behind me with my little knife. Sometimes there were ferns or something pointing straight at me and I would have to slice downward in front of me. It was during one of these moments that everything went wrong.

From as high as I could reach, I swung down with all my force to sever a limb that was in front of me. I felt something uncomfortable —I looked at my right leg, and there was my knife, buried up to the hilt in my thigh. Four inches of steel were inside my leg.

I got one of those adrenaline surges, the kind that you can feel going through your head, then I froze for a minute, just looking at the handle sticking out of my leg. Before I went down I grabbed the knife handle and pulled it out. Luckily, I pulled it out straight. Then the blood came, and I was down.

My friend tried to help me up, but the severed muscle in my leg had contracted into a big knot, and I couldn't move it. So instead, he ran to get help and left me laying on the forest floor. I was upset that I had damaged myself, but I was more upset about the thought of my dad finding out what I had done. He had always stressed that knives were not toys, they were tools, and I had used it like a toy.

I was holding pressure on the wound so the bleeding wasn't too bad, but it was starting to hurt like crazy. I began to feel very alone and stupid laying there on the ground, waiting for help. There was a nurses station at the camp. It was attended by a nurse and it was full of medical supplies. After about ten minutes I heard people coming. My friend led them down the trail I had blazed to where I was laying. By now the pain had become pretty intense but I was trying very hard to be a tough guy and act like it didn't hurt too bad.

Now, I had never met this nurse before, I had only heard about her. She was beautiful. She had light brown hair that was bleached by the sun. The sun had also kissed her skin with tiny freckles and she had big blue eyes and a disarming smile. It's hard to guess the age of adults when you are 11, but looking back I would say she was probably 25.

It was summertime, and it was hot, so she was wearing shorts and a loose fitting halter top, and she was kneeling down right in front of me tending to my leg. Well, let me tell you—it was a miracle! Suddenly I was no longer aware of any pain. My entire universe had narrowed down to the sight of this angel in front of me and that was all I was aware of. I was seeing some things I had never seen before, and the awareness of that put me in sort of a stupid trance. So much so that I wasn't answering her questions, because I wasn't able to. The power of speech had left me and I was falling in love, or something like it, for the first time.

Unfortunately, the nurse and the men who came with her interpreted my love sickness as a serious case of shock. So, after my leg had a bandage they hoisted me onto a stretcher and carried me back to the nurses station. I didn't want to go. I just wanted to sit there the rest of the day while she worked on my leg, but it wasn't up to me. After a while on the stretcher my senses returned and I started thinking about my dad again. Suddenly I could talk. I began asking the adults if they could please not call my parents, but they informed me they had to, because it was the policy. So, I quietly awaited my doom. I was sure they would rip me out of camp and take me home and I would never be able to come back.

My parents showed up about a half hour later. They both wore somber expressions, and my mother looked more worried than usual. My dad wasn't really mad, more like confused, and disappointed. They did want to take me home but I begged them to let me stay.

The wound was dressed up nicely, I still couldn't move my leg very well and there was a splint to make sure of it. There were crutches in the nurses station and I talked them into letting me stay the last two days, though I would not be able to swim or anything. As punishment for using my knife like a toy my dad took it home with him, but he said I could have it back when I got home.

So what lessons did I learn here?

Well for one, it taught me a healthy respect for sharp things. The muscle in my leg never did go back together quite right. Even now when I flex my legs my right thigh is a different shape.

More than that, it taught me that I'm not invincible, which is an important lesson for a kid to learn. A little to the left and I would have cut my femoral artery and bled out right there in the woods, which would have been a really stupid way to die.

I had been given a responsibility in the shape of a knife, and I had failed. Being on the cusp between boyhood and manhood, and wanting very badly to be a man, I knew I had failed. It was a knowledge that weighed heavy on me, and I resolved myself to not fail like that again. I think my dad knew I felt it, and that's why he wasn't too hard on me.

Overall I think this was a turning point for me where I started to really learn that my dad knew what he was talking about. That there were things I could learn from him if I paid attention, and that there was real value to be had in doing so. I have never stopped learning from him, he still has things to teach me all these years later.

Finally, I learned that there is some mysterious power, some kind of undefinable magic that women have. It can eliminate pain and rob you of speech, it makes you sweaty and stupid. This was my first encounter with that power. I didn't understand it at the time but I have never forgotten this first brush with it. It left an indelible mark.

140

CHAPTER TWENTY-NINE
The Runaway

I was the oldest of three children. As the oldest I got some of the perks that came along with that; I was the cherished first child, I got the most baby pictures taken of me, I was the first to get to do new things like ride my bike to the store by myself. There is a certain measure of privilege that comes with being the oldest child.

The downsides of privilege are that you start to expect certain things, you can develop a mentality of entitlement. That's what happened to me. When I was 9 years old I was going through kind of a rough time. I didn't feel like I was being cherished in the way I had become accustomed to. In reality, my parents were just busy doing life and keeping our household operating, tending to the farm and my two younger siblings. They were just living, doing the best they could.

My perception was much different though. It seemed like people didn't have time to listen to my stories or entertain all the random thoughts that constantly poured out of my mouth. When my dad came home from work it seemed like he didn't have time for me. He didn't seem interested in all the discoveries I had made during the day. It seemed like no one would listen to me or pay enough attention to me. This went on for a couple weeks and I became increasingly agitated. I started applying meanings to other people's actions that were based on a false reality—the false reality I had created for myself. Once I started down that road it was a slippery slope. My imagination got carried away and I began to actually feel like a victim, and then I started to wallow in my victimhood.

I convinced myself over the course of two weeks that nobody loved me. No one cared at all about me in fact, if I just disappeared they probably wouldn't even notice. After all, no one seemed to notice the foul mood I was in, or the fact that I wasn't talking to anybody. They were all just going on with their lives as though everything was normal, which validated my beliefs.

I decided I should just run away. I had read a book about a boy who ran off and lived in the woods for a year, and I figured I could do that. I set a date and started making preparations, gathering supplies and whatnot, but the closer I got to actually running away the more I thought that maybe it wasn't the best idea. After all, even if my family didn't miss me, I knew my dog would, and I would miss her too, I couldn't do that to her. I thought about taking my dog with me, but I wasn't sure I would be able to feed her.

So, I came up with a new plan. It was the next best thing to running away. I wrote a very detailed, very emotional letter to my whole family. In the letter I explained that I was running away, and they would never see me again. I also explained why I was leaving, and pointed out specific offenses I had endured, and the lack of love and caring I had suffered. I told them all I loved them, in spite of their lack of concern for me. If I remember right, I think I signed the letter, "Your former son".

It was in early winter, and a few hundred feet from our house was the pump house, it was a structure built around the well, and the pump was in there that supplied us with water. We also used the pump house to store the winter apples. There were several gunny sacks full of apples, they would keep in there for most of the winter, but more importantly, they would provide me with sustenance while I executed my plan. So one day, on a Saturday, I taped the letter I had spent hours writing and re-writing to the window on the back door. The door everyone used to come and go in and out of the house. I figured that was a perfect spot, it would be seen quickly.

My plan was to disappear into the pump house, where I could crack the door open a bit and have full view of the house. I would wait for my letter to be discovered and then I would watch as my family frantically looked for me. I would sit there eating apples while they all grieved, racked with guilt. I would listen to their wails of sorrow and regret and then, when I was satisfied that they had suffered enough, when they had proven to me that they actually did love me, I would return. In my mind I saw them all crying with relief that I was back, all of them embracing me and telling me how sorry they were. Yep, in my 9 year old brain this was a perfect plan.

I had taped the letter onto the window around 9:00 in the morning and I was firmly ensconced in the pump house, waiting for the show to begin. About an hour had gone by and nothing had happened yet. No one had spotted my letter. I was watching the house and occasionally I could see the door open, and close, then I would wait for a scream, but none came.

Two hours went by, and then three. I had already eaten about ten apples and I was stuffed. I was starting to get bored, and a little irritated. Time just kept going by, no one called my name, nothing. At the five hour mark I was starting to realize that my brilliant plan was backfiring. In spite of what I had made myself believe over the past two weeks, I didn't really believe it. Down deep I always knew my family loved me but now—I was actually thinking that maybe it was true after all. I had been gone all day and no one noticed, nobody wondered, it was like I hadn't existed at all.

The time kept going by. Now when I saw the door open on the house I was praying that someone would notice, I was going through an emotional roller coaster, it was very serious now. I didn't just want someone to notice I was gone...I **needed** someone to notice. Finally, after 8 hours of silence I couldn't take it anymore. It was five o'clock in the evening and it was starting to get dark and cold. My sorrow and self pity had turned to anger. I left the pump house and marched toward home. I stomped up the steps and barged into the house. I looked at the window on the door and my letter was still there where I had left it. Was everybody really that blind? I thought.

I grabbed the letter off the door and went into the kitchen where my parents were sitting, and I really let them have it. I was crying with hurt and trembling with fury as I stood there and unloaded everything I had been feeling and thinking over the past two weeks. Seeing that I was obviously upset and in kind of bad shape, my parents wisely just sat and listened, glancing at one another with concerned looks. Then I held up the letter and shook it, explaining that it had been on the door all day and no one had even noticed.

My parents took the letter and read it together.

I was spent, and exhausted after my tirade. I stood there breathing hard just looking at the floor. There was a period of silence, and then my mom reached out and pulled me into her. She just hugged me for a few moments. Then she held me at arms length and looked into my eyes and told me how much she and dad loved me, how important I was to them. She said they were sorry I had felt this way, but that I should know better. She said if I ever feel like that again to just come and talk to them first.

Just like that it was over. Two weeks of emotional torment were gone in the blink of an eye. Apparently that was all I needed. I just needed to hear it. I hugged them both, and told them I was sorry, and I was. I felt kind of silly afterwards. Once I was filled back up with the love and security I had been used to all my life it was hard to imagine how I had gone down that road.

I never travelled that road again though, once was enough. The things this event taught had me never need to repeated it. One of the things it taught me was to always question my own perception. Question it, test it, weigh it against the facts and look at it from other angles because your perception will become your reality, and I never wanted to be the victim of a false reality like that again.

I also learned something about how fragile relationships can be. How thin and tender the threads of our emotions can be and how just a word, or the lack of a word, can affect them. That's an important thing for men to remember. Even though I learned this lesson it was still something I have struggled with from time to time. Sometimes we just take it for granted that other people know how we feel— to always be sharing it can feel redundant or excessive. The fact is, the other people in your life need to know how you feel; they need to hear you say it even if they already know it. They still need to hear it, just like I needed to hear my mom tell me that day.

It's another way we can take care of the most important things we have— our relationships. Remember to tell the people who are important to you, family, chosen family, loved ones— how you feel about them. It's an important part of being a better man.

CHAPTER THIRTY
Men Behaving Badly

It was around the spring of 1982, right before my 20th birthday. I had been serving in the Army at Ft. Hood Texas for 18 months, then I got orders that said I would be going to Germany. I was excited to be traveling abroad, but at the same time I was torn about having to leave my new family. I had gotten married while I was in Texas, and the marriage came with a two year old daughter, so suddenly I was a dad, and my wife at the time was also pregnant with my first biological child who would later turn out to be my son.

It felt very wrong to leave them at this point in life, if felt very unnatural, I knew I had to figure out how to bring them to Germany with me. In order to accomplish that I had to sign a new contract with the Army that would extend my tour in Germany to three years, which meant I would be in the Army about a year longer than my original enlistment period of four years. But, it was worth it to me, I couldn't stand the thought of being separated from my new daughter and soon to be born baby for that length of time.

Still, it would take several months for me to secure housing and save up enough money to bring my family over, but it was better than going years without seeing them. In those days there were no cell phones, no Skype, no Facebook, no internet. So I would truly be isolated from all my loved ones except for the now old fashioned method of writing letters, and the occasional super expensive long distance phone call.

My first night in Germany I made a complete fool of myself, as I tried to prove that German beer was no more potent than American beer. I was very wrong about that, and spent the next day suffering the consequences. A day later I arrived at my duty station, my permanent unit. As luck would have it, it was the beginning of the weekend. There I was, 19 years old, alone in a foreign country for the first time and I didn't have a clue about what to do.

A fellow soldier quickly befriended me and offered to show me the town. I was grateful for this opportunity, he seemed like a good guy, his name was Jeff. He was a tiny little wiry sort of guy, probably 120 pounds and full of energy, the kind of guy that never really stops moving.

We got cleaned up and ready for a night on the town; he was going to show me all the best spots. The town was only about a mile away, so we took out walking. We arrived at our first destination, a night club that was full of big, round tables around which were American GI's and a few German citizens drinking room temperature beer from large glass boots. We found a seat and started drinking with them. I met my first Germans then, and I was having a good time getting to know people.

After Jeff had polished off a couple glass boots, he seemed to change. He became sullen and edgy, his eyes were darting around and he seemed like a different person. He told me to get ready to leave. I stood up and put on my jacket. Then, to my horror, Jeff jumped up on the middle of one of the round tables. Then he went around the whole table kicking everyone in the face who was seated there.

It all happened so fast, I didn't know what was going on. He jumped down off the table and grabbed my arm as he was running out the door. Not knowing what else to do I followed him. We ran out of the bar and down the street. There were some people chasing us so we kept running until we couldn't hear them behind us anymore.

As we were catching our breath I yelled at him asking what the hell that was all about? He just laughed and said he had always wanted to do that, and that those people had it coming. Then he started off down the street to a new location. I began having serious doubts about my choice of companion for the evening but I followed him anyway, because I was in a strange city in a foreign country and I didn't know how to get around without him.

We wound up in another bar. We had a booth next to the dance floor. Most of the patrons of this bar were German, with just a few Americans. We had had a couple beers here and it all seemed pleasant enough, I was taking in all the new sights and sounds. Then a woman who was dancing got real close to our table. Jeff decided it would be a good idea to reach out and grab her bottom in a particularly rude manner.

She was furious, she turned around and cussed us both out in German. I could't tell what she was saying, but I knew it wasn't good. She was sitting with a very large American guy and a few other Germans. The big guy walked over to our table and told Jeff that what he did wasn't very nice, and told him not to do anything else like that if he knew what was good for him. After he left, Jeff finished his beer and again told me to put my coat on. What happened next was very unexpected.

Little Jeff walked over to where the big guy was seated, he grabbed him and threw him down in the middle of the dance floor and proceeded to beat the hell out of him. Everybody in this bar knew each other and soon there was a pile of people all trying to get a piece of Jeff—who was now on the bottom of the pile.

I was sitting there not sure what to do. Even though I didn't condone his actions, I felt some responsibility because I had come with him. I felt like I should at least try to get him out of there. So I went to the pile of people and very politely reached down to where Jeff was and picked him up with one arm and then started casually walking toward the door carrying him like he was big sack of potatoes draped over one arm.

When the people saw what was happening they weren't about to just let us leave, now they were coming for me, too. Jeff was back on his feet fighting like a wild man, and I had no choice but to do the same. There was a wall of people coming at us, so many that they got in each others way. As soon as we would knock one down another would take his place.

We were fighting our way to the door like this, it was kind of like being in a bad movie. When we got to the door we turned to run and then froze, because we were each staring down the barrel of a 9 millimeter hand gun, which were being held by the German police...

the Politzei. Suddenly we were both pinned up against the wall being interrogated in broken English by the police. I had heard stories of the Politzei. At that time they had a reputation for shooting first and then asking questions, and you did not want to wind up in German jail.

In a very calm voice I began explaining to the police that my friend was drunk, and a little crazy, and that if they let us go I would take him straight back to our barracks and they wouldn't have any more trouble from us. I must have been convincing, because gradually the cops started to become less militant, and eventually let us go on my promise that I would take him directly home.

Now we were free again, walking up the street toward the barracks. All the way I was admonishing my new companion about how much trouble he almost got us into, about how crazy he was acting, and really just about how rude he was being to other people. I was very angry that I had wound up being associated with this guy and I had made up my mind that he and I were not going to be friends.

About halfway back to the barracks we met another soldier walking toward town. When he was about 15 feet away Jeff yelled at him: "What did you say about my mom?" The guy look surprised, and before he could even respond Jeff was on top of him, beating the stuffing out of him, right there on the sidewalk.

I looked toward the street and guess who I saw driving by? The same police that had let us go only moments earlier. Their lights came on as they made a u-turns and we heard a big chirp of their siren. Jeff saw it too and yelled at me to follow him. Suddenly I was seeing a part of Germany I hadn't expected, as we were crawling through peoples gardens and climbing fences trying to elude the police who were chasing us. The chase went on for what seemed a very long time, and I didn't know where I was. I was cut and scraped up all over but we kept going because we could hear the sirens and the shouts of the police who were still trying to find us. After a while a helicopter showed up with a search light.

Eventually, somehow, we made it back to the front gate of our Kaserne and scampered quickly to our barracks. I went straight to my room without even acknowledging Jeff. I was so angry at this point I wanted to tear him to pieces. I hid there in the darkness of my room until I went to sleep.

The next day I got up and was wandering around my unit, introducing myself to the other guys I hadn't met yet. There was no sign of Jeff. Finally I asked the Sergeant on duty if he had seen him because I had a few choice words for him. He laughed and said Jeff was long gone. He had left earlier that morning to catch a plane back to the states, his time in Germany was over.

I was kind of dumbfounded. I had managed to get hooked up with a psychopath on his last day in Germany. He was going crazy because he knew he would be gone the next day, he had probably been planning this night for months, and I was just the unlucky guy that he chose to accompany him. This experience taught me a great deal about befriending people too quickly, about trusting people I didn't know. I felt foolish because looking back on it there were plenty of signs that he wasn't right in the head, but I ignored those signs because I was so eager to have a friend.

I replayed the events of that night over and over in my head, feeling ashamed that I had not behaved better. I should have made him stop, I should not have let him hurt innocent people. I should have turned him in or better yet, I should have knocked him out myself and called the military police. But I didn't do any of those things, I just went along, and in doing so almost put myself, and my family in jeopardy.

I did a lot of growing up from of this experience. I knew I never wanted to repeat anything like this, and in order to do that I had to become vigilant. I had to always be on guard and aware of my surroundings and other people, and I had to maintain a clear sense of who I was and what I stood for at all times. I had to wear this sense of myself like a cloak that I put on whenever I was in public. If I could keep this sense of who I was then nothing could surprise me. I would always be ready to react to whatever happened in a way that would not make me ashamed. I think gaining this constant awareness of myself was the final step in me entering my manhood. It was the moment I truly became personally accountable.

I don't know whatever happened to Jeff, he is probably rotting in a prison somewhere. Although what he did was horrible, and what he put me through was almost catastrophic, I can't deny that his lunacy did help me in a way. It expedited my evolution as a man by illuminating what I lacked. Only then was I able to fix it— to make sure it never happened again. We can't fix things we don't know are wrong.

So remember to look into the mirror, remember to take a nice long objective view of yourself, because we can only improve the things we we know about, the things we can see, and that's important if you want to be a better man.

CHAPTER THIRTY-ONE
Don't Be The Wildebeest

When I was nine years old I had a special relationship with my bike—a purple stingray with a metallic flecked banana seat. This bike was like my horse, and I kind of thought of it in the same way. We lived out in the country so this bike was my means of transportation everywhere I went. I spent hours on it each day, I knew it intimately. My bike was a faithful companion.

I could do tricks on it too; Of course I could ride with no hands that was easy, but I could also ride a wheelie all the way down our street. I could get going real fast and stand up on the seat with my arms stretched out for balance like a person on a tight rope, luckily I never fell while doing this one.

One autumn morning I was riding my bike around our circular drive way. I was venturing off the driveway itself and was riding out in the edges, on the grass. Suddenly I felt a sharp pain on my head, then another, then one under my shirt. The pain of each of these was very intense, like a pin-prick of fire. I didn't know what was happening, I stopped and was grabbing at the pain spots with my hands. That's when I noticed that there were yellow jacket wasps all over me, they were swarming on me now and I started getting stung all over the place, even right through my jeans. I was parked right on top of a huge ground nest and there were little holes in the dirt where more angry wasps were emerging from.

I knew I had to get away, the pain in multiple spots all over my body and the sights and sounds of more wasps coming sent me into

151

a panic. I grabbed the handlebars of my bike and just started riding as fast as I could. I didn't know where I was going. I was blinded by pain, panic and fear. I was just peddling as fast as I could to escape more pain.

Unfortunately, in my haste and confusion I drove my bike straight into a fence. Not just any fence, a three strand electric fence that was there to keep the cows in. I crashed into it, the wires of the electric fence wrapped around me and my bike, and I went down in a heap. Now I noticed a new sensation, electric shocks everywhere the wire was touching me in addition to the yellow jackets, many of whom had followed me and were still repeatedly stinging.

I was stuck. I was wrapped up in electric wire, one leg under my bike. I was thrashing like an animal caught in a trap and that's exactly what I was in that moment. Of course I was screaming, not just in pain and anguish but also in the hopes that someone would hear me and come to help.

No one heard my screams. Everyone was in the house, out of ear shot. I later found out that I had been observed from a window, rolling around on the ground, but since I was always doing odd things as a child no one paid it any attention. They thought I was just involved in another of my weird games I used to play by myself. So there I was. Alone and helpless, being stung all over by angry wasps and getting shocked by the fence at the same time.

In moments like this, moments of extreme distress and pain, it's a natural human thing to seek help from others first— to find someone who is not in your predicament to help you get out of yours. However, when no one else is available the responsibility for your salvation falls back squarely onto your own shoulders. This is a critical moment.

It is in this moment when many people give up, they quit. They succumb to whatever peril they are in because they are either too scared, too exhausted, or in too much pain to care anymore, they just want it to be over. It is in moments like this when some people die. That moment when the wildebeest stops fighting the lion.

Other people in this critical moment of peril take another course. There is a window of opportunity in which they are galvanized by self preservation. They fight harder, they summon all of their last remaining strength to free themselves and find safety. That's what I did. In that moment when I realized no help was coming, I became very focused. I stopped screaming and thrashing and I started thinking. I tuned out the pain and focused on how to get up. Suddenly the path to freedom became clear. There were a couple wires dropped over me which I quickly took off. In my panic it felt like I was wrapped up, like these wires were pinning me down somehow when in reality they were just laying across me.

After removing the wires I stood up, I was free. I started running as fast as I could, stripping all my clothes off as I ran because there were wasps underneath my clothes now. I wound up in the middle of our front yard, naked except for my underwear, trying hard to catch my breath with angry red welts rising up everywhere I had been stung. About this time my mom came running out, aware that something was terribly wrong. In the next few moments she was putting a paste of baking soda on all the stings to draw out the poison. Everything was going to be OK now. By the end of the day I was back on my bike almost as though nothing had happened.

The lesson I took away from this experience was to never be the wildebeest. Never stop fighting, never give up. When it seems hopeless, and there is no one to help you, and it would be a lot easier to just lay down and die—but escape is always possible. There is always a way out of every situation, but in order to take advantage of it you have to focus your mind, you have to think.

I have used this lesson several times in life when I got into situations that seemed hopeless, and every time I proved that it was true; calm rational thinking in times of great stress will save you, while fear and panic will profit a man nothing. Each experience like this makes it easier the next time. Our human default is to panic when hit with the fight or flight instinct but with practice you can develop a third default reaction, which is thinking clearly.

Now when you head out into the big world perhaps give some thought to this. Start visualizing yourself remaining calm and thinking under conditions of extreme stress and trauma. It might help the next time you find yourself in a tight spot, and it will make you better able to keep on living instead of becoming a victim!

CHAPTER THIRTY-TWO
Walk In A Blizzard

I was freshly out of basic training, after a two month stint as a home-town recruiter for the Army, and I was now stationed at Ft. Hood Texas. I had arrived in Ft Hood around the first part of January. Prior to leaving home for my duty station I had gone to visit my grandmother in the hospital on my way to the airport— my father's mother.

There I was, all dressed in my dress green uniform looking and feeling pretty sharp. And there my grandmother was laying in bed, stricken by cancer and unable to speak. I had been pretty close to my grandmother, she lived on our property and I would visit her fairly regularly. Ironically, she was my healthy grandmother; she was always jogging down the street and going on fishing trips, and really living life to the fullest. She had quit smoking a couple decades before, so it was a shock for everyone when healthy grandma was diagnosed with lung cancer.

I had come her hospital room to say goodbye. Even though she had lost the power of speech, her mind was still strong, she did all the speaking she needed to do with her eyes. I sat by her bed and took her hand, and stared into those eyes. I was trying my best to communicate in the same way she was communicating with me.

It was a hard thing, because we both knew we would never see each other alive again. It was just a matter of time for her, and I had my orders to go to Texas. So, I sat there for quite awhile, just holding her hand and telling her how much I loved her, with my eyes. There were tears staining both of our cheeks, the finality of it was overwhelming. Eventually, my dad reminded me that I had a plane to catch. One last long look and a squeeze of the hand, and I was out the door and on my way to Texas.

Just two months later in February I got the call I had been expecting; my grandmother had died. She was going to be buried next to her husband in Glendive, Montana, and my family wanted me there. I wanted to be there too, so I asked for and received a short leave of absence.

Being only 18, I wasn't too smart yet, but I was young and strong and invincible. My flight was an early one, around 5 in the morning, but I had decided it would be a good idea to stay up partying with my friends until the wee hours of the morning the night before my flight. Around 3 AM I realized I only had a couple hours until my flight. I was afraid that if I went to sleep now I would't wake up, and I would miss my flight for sure. So, I decided to just stay up until it was time to leave for the airport.

It was critical that I caught my flight because there were not any planes into Glendive, where the funeral was. I had to fly into Billings, Montana which was about 220 miles away from the funeral. My family was going to meet me there and we would all drive up together. Something happened, the chair I was sitting was too comfortable or who knows what, but the next thing I knew I was waking up with a start. Looking at my watch I saw that my flight left in 15 minutes. There was no way I could make it in time, it was impossible. I went on to the airport anyway.

I explained my story to the people at the airport, and they went to work finding me another flight. They found one, but it would land at 11:00 at night, several hours after my original flight was supposed to land. I took the flight without hesitation, it was the only option. It was 1981, and cell phones had not been invented yet. There was no way to contact my family to inform them of the flight change because they were on the road somewhere between Washington State and Montana. My best and only hope was that they would figure out what happened and wait for me.

When I landed in Billings a blizzard had just started up. There were big drifts of snow all over the runways and they were fighting hard to keep them clear. I had just come from Texas and wasn't exactly dressed for a blizzard. These were my cowboy days, and I looked the part. I had a pair of pointy-toed slick bottomed cowboy boots, Levi's jeans, a Western shirt, and a denim jacket with fake sheep wool on the inside...oh, and a cowboy hat of course.

I got off the plane and looked around hopefully, but I didn't see one familiar face. I wasn't sure what to do, there was a blizzard after all, and it was 10 below zero outside. Glendive was 220 miles away. Somehow, for some reason in my 18 year old brain there only seemed to be one option. I had to make it to my grandmother's funeral, regardless of the apparent obstacles. I asked the guy at the desk which direction you would go if you were heading to Glendive. He pointed in a direction, and I was out the door and on my way, hitch hiking to Glendive in a blizzard.

It took me about 15 minutes to make it to the freeway. It was very, very cold and very dark as well. There weren't a bunch of streetlights lighting the freeway like there was back home. The cold and dark hadn't phased me yet though, I was determined to make it to that funeral. The snow was piling up fast, when I started out there was only about 6 inches but now 30 minutes later there was almost a foot. I had to stop every few minutes to knock the snow off my hat.

I was starting to get real cold, so I would slide my suitcase ahead on the icy road, sort of like a bowling move, and then I would run to catch up to it. Then I would do it again, and again. I figured all that running would keep my body warm, at least until someone stopped to give me a ride. There was a fact I had not counted on though— people don't generally drive around much in a blizzard.

In the first hour I had only seen two cars, and when they came by me I realized they probably didn't even see me on the side of the road. The freeway was a sheet of ice so any driver would be focused only on the road ahead. Not only that, but the snow was coming down so hard they might not see me even if they looked straight at me.

It wasn't until a couple hours had passed that I started to get worried. I was frozen to the bone, running to my suitcase had stopped working some time ago. In fact I think it made it worse because I was sweating a little, and the sub-zero temperature was freezing my sweat, and making me even colder.

I hadn't seen a car or any signs of life in 45 minutes. It was dark, and cold, and I was more alone than I had ever been. I started to resolve myself to the notion that I was an idiot, and it was a pretty sure bet that I was going to die out here. I told myself there were worse ways of dying than trying to get to a loved ones funeral, and I just kept going.

Finally, another car came by, a pickup actually. I got as close to the driving surface as I could in the hopes they would see me. I was waving my arms frantically trying to get their attention. His headlights made two almost solid beams of snow in the air ahead of them. As they drove by I knew they hadn't seen me. The road was super slick and the pickup fishtailed for a little bit, before gaining control and moving on out of sight.

I stood there watching it go, my lower jaw clacking against the upper, as I shivered uncontrollably in the intense cold. I thought that maybe I just saw the last humans I would ever see in this life. Since there wasn't anything else to do except keep walking, that's what I did. 15 minutes later I had all but given up hope. I was in the process of saying goodbye to everyone I loved in my mind. I felt terribly bad because I knew how much my parents would suffer at the news, especially my mom.

Suddenly the air around me was illuminated. I looked around and saw two headlights cutting through the snow, I couldn't believe it, another chance! This vehicle was going much, much slower, almost as slow as a man would walk. As it got up to me it stopped, and a door opened. A man yelled at me to get in, and he didn't have to yell twice. The heated interior of the cab almost made my skin hurt as it adapted to the contrast in temperatures. I was in a state of shock mentally as well, because I had become so convinced that I was going to die. It was hard to believe what was happening. There were two people in the truck, the man driving and one of his teenage daughters. My jaw hadn't even stopped clacking when he started yelling at me.

"What in the hell are you doing out here, son?" He yelled. "Don't you know theres a blizzard going on? You could die out here."

Through a shivering chin I managed to tell him that I was going to my grandmother's funeral in Glendive, that I missed my plane, so there wasn't anyone to pick me up. His tone softened, he shook his head and muttered to himself, then he told me I would be OK. He said they would take care of me and see me off the following day.

By the time we got to his ranch I was almost done shivering. We went into the house where we met his very kind wife. We all sat down and he told his version of the story, how he thought he had seen something on the outskirts of his headlights, he tried to stop but the road was too slick. So he took the next exit and doubled back around going real slow to see if he could see it again, and that's how he found me.

His wife was fussing over me like I was a long lost relative. She made me some hot coco, and then we feasted on a banquet of fried chicken and mashed potatoes. Afterward they saw to it that I had a long hot shower. They gave me bed clothes to wear and she washed the clothes I was wearing. They took me to a room where the most comfortable bed in the universe waited for me. As soon as my head hit the pillow I was out cold.

The next morning I was wakened by the smell of bacon, and coffee. My clothes were folded and clean on a chair so I put them on and wandered downstairs to where everyone was eating breakfast. We discussed my situation. I was reminded a couple more times how foolish I had been and how lucky I was to be alive, and I didn't argue. Finally it was decided that the man's son would drive me to the nearest bus station. Again, because I was a young idiot, I wasn't traveling with any money. They said they would buy me a bus ticket to Glendive, to my grandmother's funeral.

I was awe-struck by their kindness and hospitality. I was aware of how close I had come to cashing in my chips and I was thanking them over and over again, profusely. Before the son and I left for the bus station the wife gave me a little care package she had made and a letter, addressed to my mom. "Now you make sure she gets this." She said as she handed it to me.

The roads were still in horrible shape, so the ride to the bus station was an exciting story in itself, but we made it. I settled into a seat and I was on my way to Glendive. Glendive wasn't a very big town. When I arrived I asked someone where the cemetery was and started walking in that direction. I came up on it pretty quickly.

There was a big hill that the road curved up, I could see lots of people and cars up there so I figured that's where everybody was.

As I was halfway up the hill cars started driving down, apparently the service was over, I had just missed it, just barely.

When my parents saw me they slammed on their brakes almost causing a wreck with the car behind them. My mother came bounding out of the car and practically tackled me. She was holding my face in both hands looking at me as though my expression would give her all the answers she needed. Then my dad walked up. I gave them the short story because I wanted to get up to where my grandmother was buried. I needed to say goodbye one final time and pay my respects. I got in their car and we drove up the hill to the grave site. They left me alone for a while and I conducted my own private little funeral for this amazing lady who had meant so much to me and my family. While I was there, I said a few words to my grandfather as well, as I had never been to his grave before.

After that we all gathered at a relative's house for an informal reception. That's when I told my parents the whole story. While I talked, my mother just sat there crying, knowing how close she had come to losing me. When they asked me more questions about the people who saved my life I remembered the letter. I handed it to my mother. She trembled and cried as she read it. Apparently, the letter was full of praise for me, the idiot that almost killed himself. It also contained good wishes for our family, condolences for our loss and, well— love. Just pure love was in that letter. It's the kind of letter you might imagine one mother would write to another mother. It was just what my mom needed.

My mother corresponded with this family for many years after this happened. They exchanged Christmas cards and occasional phone calls, but they never met in person. My mother held them in the highest regard and spoke of them with reverence. Because my mom knew that they were the only reason I was still alive.

I learned a lot of lessons from this, many of them obvious, like don't be an idiot, but far and away, the biggest thing I learned was how important human kindness and hospitality can be. These people were the personification of hospitality. They saved me, brought me into their home, fed me, comforted me and gave me safe passage. What they did saved my life for sure, but the ramifications of that are astounding. If they hadn't done that none of my children would have been born. None of my grandchildren, the latest one who is just a baby as I am putting this book together, would not exist. You would not be reading this book right now.

All the people who my life and my children's lives have touched, would never know us. The consequences of their actions went on and on, generation after generation—to infinity. That's what these kind people in the middle of Montana did. This is why I am hospitable to strangers. This is why I try to be kind to other people. I will spend the rest of my life trying to pay forward this gift. Who knows, in doing so I might save someone else's life, or significantly alter their future. That is the lesson of this story, human kindness, and hospitality. They don't cost a great deal to the people who provide them, but the effects they cause can change lives, if not the world.

Now, head out into the world and be kind to someone. Be gracious and hospitable because it's the right thing to do. You never know who you might be saving, and in the process you will also become a better man.

CHAPTER THIRTY-THREE
King Of The Chickens

In the summer of 1970 I was around 8 years old. Living on our little farm there was always plenty to do because we had woods to play in, we had the barn, I had my bike and my dog, we had pastures and — I had my imagination. There really wasn't any reason to be in the house unless there was a torrential rainstorm. I didn't want to be in the house anyway, and my mother didn't want us kids in the house either. She had enough other responsibilities without having kids underfoot.

Our house was not very big, looking back I don't know how we all survived in those tiny rooms with only one bathroom but, that's how it was.

Among our other animals, we had chickens. My dad had gotten in the habit of letting them out in the morning so they could forage for plants and insects all day. He swore it made the eggs taste better. At night the chickens would all go back into their coup and we would lock them up safe against predators, then the next day they were out again.

The king of the chickens was a giant white rooster. There were some younger roosters that stayed out of his way, but he was in charge and all the other chickens knew it. Unfortunately, this rooster had started being kind of mean, not to the other chickens, but to us. If one of us got too close he would take out after us, he would chase us until we were an acceptable distance away from his hens.

If you didn't grow up on a farm you might wonder why anyone

would be afraid of a chicken. Well, a big rooster can do some pretty good damage, especially on a kid. They have these big sharp spurs on the insides of their ankles, they jump up in the air with their feet forward and then swipe back and forth with their spurs in an attempt to stab you.

The rooster kept getting meaner and meaner as the summer went on. Everybody just figured he was a mean rooster. What they didn't know was that I was partially to blame. When no one was around I would taunt the rooster, I would bother him until he would chase me. That was the fun part, getting chased. Unfortunately it only served to make the rooster very, very angry all the time.

One day my brother, sister and I were all outside doing our own thing, they were only 6 and 5 years of age, so I was in the habit of keeping an eye on them, sort of. I heard some screams and ran over to find my brother and sister up on the picnic table being guarded by the rooster, he wouldn't let them down. I immediately switched into big brother protector mode and I was going to take care of that rooster. I got a rake to use for defense but when I tried to shoo him off, he attacked me anyway, hopping right over my outstretched rake. Now all three of us were on the picnic table. I decided to lure him away so my brother and sister could get to the house. My plan worked. I was eventually able to taunt him into chasing me and when he did my brother and sister scrambled into the house. I joined them in the house then because it was time for lunch.

During lunch we had forgotten all about the rooster. After lunch we went outside to play and were minding our own business when all of a sudden we were blind sided by this crazy bird. He ran right into the midst of us and almost nailed us good. My brother fell down and probably would have gotten his eyes gouged out if I hadn't been able to distract it. We all ran back into the house with the rooster right on our tail. This was a problem— apparently this rooster had laid claim to the entire yard. I looked out the window in the door and I could see him pacing back and forth in our driveway. We three were holed up on what we called the porch, which was a little room where you took off your coats and boots and stuff before you walked into the kitchen.

We waited for a while. It was kind of fun for me...like a soldier being pinned down behind enemy lines. My brother and sister were pretty scared though. I assured them he would calm down and go back to his hens soon, because that is what he always did before. After 10 minutes or so we opened the door and looked around. We couldn't see the rooster so we all stepped out onto the patio. All of a sudden he came running around toward us from behind my mom's car. Luckily we were just a few feet away so we all made it inside. We tried a few more times, but each time the rooster was out there, waiting. We were literally trapped inside our own house by something with a brain the size of a grape— or even a raisin. Finally, we all gave up and just decided to stay in the house even though it was a nice day. Mom didn't notice at first. But when she couldn't hear her soap opera's because we were making too much noise, it hit her. She told us all to go play outside. We explained that we couldn't do that. We explained that the rooster would not let us outside.

My mother scoffed, she thought that was ridiculous. "It's just a chicken," she said. We pleaded, we insisted, and eventually she came to believe that we were genuinely too scared to go outside. Then she told us that she would take care of that rooster. We followed her to the door, a little anxious about what was going to happen. We had never seen her take on a crazy rooster before. My mom marched confidently out across the patio and into the yard toward the rooster. She was yelling "shoo" and "get out of here" and things like that. The rooster stopped pecking the ground, stood up straight, and bolted straight for my mom without any hesitation. She wasn't prepared for that. Fight or flight took over and she sprinted right back to where we were waiting inside the house.

She was breathing heavily from the run, but she was angry, very angry, and she wasn't done with that rooster yet. She said something about having him for dinner as she grabbed one of our baseball bats. Now that she was armed with a weapon there would be no stopping her. Again, she marched confidently out of the house and across the yard toward the rooster. The rooster saw her coming and stood up straight. He began sort of a deliberate trot in her direction, he quickly picked up speed and was now in a full run.

The complete lack of fear the rooster displayed seemed to shake my mom's confidence a little, but she kept closing distance between them. At 30 feet apart my mom stopped and held up the bat, but the rooster just kept on coming. My mom lost her nerve. Rather than let it get close enough to swing at, she threw the bat at the rooster hoping to hit it, but the rooster just jumped over the bat unfazed, and kept coming. We were all screaming now, afraid for our mom as she was once again sprinting back to where we were on the porch. Once safely inside and she got her breath back, she calmly informed us that it was nothing to worry about, that dad would take care of it when he got home.

After watching my mom get soundly defeated, I was a little worried for my dad. Of course I would have bet on him, but this rooster was proving to be one tough customer. I started worrying about stupid things like our whole family being pinned down for weeks, running out of food, cut off from civilization. Like I said, that was dumb so I snapped myself out of it—but still, I was nervous not knowing what was going to happen.

After about 4 hours we heard my dad's car roll into the driveway. We all waited breathlessly, listening for him to scream when he was attacked. But no attack came, he just walked up to the house and came in. He found us all huddled together, he asked my mom what was going on. When she told him he started laughing. He couldn't believe we had let a rooster take us prisoner. He saw the concern on all of our faces and assured us he would go take care of the evil chicken. He told me I should come along, he would teach me how to deal with roosters. There was something about the calm way my dad handled things. When he was around it was almost impossible to be afraid. Feeling suddenly empowered I jumped up and followed him outside.

The rooster had moved off a ways, but when he saw us coming he didn't disappoint. Apparently the earlier events of the day had left the rooster feeling quite invincible. My dad didn't have any weapon, I wasn't sure what he was going to do. The rooster was charging him at full speed. Right before they came together my dad stopped and drew back his right foot. The rooster kept coming and my dad let him have it, right in the chest. Yep…kicked him just like a football.

The rooster was launched backwards into the air. He landed about 15 feet away then he stood up, got his bearings, and charged my dad again. I couldn't believe it. My dad kicked him again, even harder. Again the rooster rolled around, got up and charged again.

Forging A Man

My dad was laughing a little now, obviously impressed with this roosters tenacity. Then he looked over his shoulder at me and said you have to keep going until he learns who the boss is. Now I was concerned for the rooster, I didn't know how he could survive all those brutal kicks. I expressed my concern and dad reassured me that the rooster would know when to quit.

Sure enough, the roosters fourth attack had much less gusto in it. The fifth attack had even less...and the 6th never happened. The beaten rooster summoned the shreds of dignity he had left and clucked and strutted away in a different direction as though nothing had ever happened. "Well," my dad said, "you shouldn't have any more trouble from him for a while, let me know if you do though, and he'll wind up in the stew." We never did though, not from that rooster. Of course I never taunted him again either. After that we let the chickens do their thing, and we did our thing, and there wasn't any trouble.

I learned a few lessons here, though it would be several years before I recognized them. This is when I was introduced to the idea that 'hesitation is not your friend'. Hesitation is caused by fear and uncertainty, and it will make you appear weak against whatever you are up against. Decisive quick action is rewarded, while hesitation will almost always punish you. My mother could have easily taken the rooster, if she hadn't become afraid. The fear made her hesitate, and even to the rooster with his grape sized brain, it made her look weak. Along with that I was introduced to what an important role attitude plays in everything. The rooster was just a chicken, yes he was a big chicken, he might have weighed 12 pounds, but he acted like he was as big as a grizzly bear so that was how we treated him. He beat us with sheer confidence and attitude. Unfortunately for him, my dad had more.

What also stuck with me is what my dad said about showing the rooster who was the boss. It turns out that the rooster wasn't really mean or evil, he just wanted to be the boss because that's how roosters survive. He wanted to be the boss and he was going to be, as long as everything else let him. I've met quite a few people who are just like that rooster and just like the bird, they move on once they learn who they are NOT the boss of.

To sum it all up, I guess I have met many 'roosters' in my life, and it's likely everyone reading this has too, it's part of life. It's how you deal with these roosters that matters, though. First, don't antagonize people, because you might turn them into a mean creature, like I did. Aside from that, if one winds up in front of you, you may not have to kick them in the chest, but you can always let them know who they are **not** the boss of. They are not the boss of you.

Now head out into the barnyard of life and stand up to the roosters, don't run. Be decisive, confident and strong...those roosters will find someone else to bother and you can get on with your life.

CHAPTER THIRTY-FOUR
Ticket To Freedom

When I was a kid there was one particular event that always loomed in the distance. An event that would change my life and bring me a little closer to actually becoming a man. It was something I yearned for, and a day hardly went by that I didn't think about it, from the time I was 10 years old. That event, was getting a drivers license. It seemed like when I got a drivers license I would almost be completely grown up. It represented freedom, and maturity. I would be able to go places with my friends and maybe even go on dates with girls.

This was especially true for me because I lived out in the country and my closest friend was two miles away. For kids in towns or cities it might not be as big of a deal because everything is within walking distance and there are city busses you can take. But for us country kids, a car represented a lifeline to the rest of the world.

The time to get my license was now close at hand. I was almost 16 years old. I had gone through drivers education in school and I had my learning permit for around 6 months. Both my mother and Father had taken me out practice driving many times and I was ready, I could taste it. I had a spot in my wallet all ready to receive the new license, and I would open it up and imagine it being there.

Finally, the day came. I woke up on my 16th birthday with only one thought; today was the day I would get my license.

My dad drove me to the DMV (Department of Motor Vehicles), on July 29th, 1978. It was a Saturday, so my dad wasn't at work. After waiting for what seemed a ridiculously long time, I was finally called up to take the written test, which I crushed, I didn't miss any questions. Then I took the driving test. That was a little more tense. I was driving our 1963 Ford Galaxy. I was a little nervous about doing something stupid like forgetting a turn signal or not stopping completely but when we got back, the instructor told me I had passed!

I was so excited, and my dad seemed to be proud of me as well. Now we had to wait. In those days it took a long time with their slow equipment to produce my temporary license. The permanent one would be sent in the mail. One reason it took so long is because there were a lot of people in front of us. My dad got tired of sitting around and he told me he was going to walk a couple blocks down the road to an auto part store and look around, and for me to wait there. So, my dad took off walking and I stayed there waiting intently for my name to be called.

After a while I zoned out and was drifting off into other thoughts when I heard my name. I jumped out of my chair and ran up to the desk. I think I startled the person who was working there. He handed me my temporary license and said congratulations! Gripping my new ticket to freedom tightly in my hand, I wandered out into the sunshine of the parking lot. It was an odd moment because there I was, holding my hearts desire, and there was no one around to celebrate with.

It occurred to me that I could legally drive a car anywhere I wanted to go. The entire world suddenly seemed accessible to me. I walked over to our car. In those days we never locked our car doors, in fact we never took the keys out of the ignition. I looked in and there they were, dangling next to the steering wheel.

Something came over me then. I forgot all about my dad, I forgot about everything really. All I could think of was that here was a car, with the keys in it, and in my hand was a piece of paper that made it legal for me to operate this car. The next thing I knew I was sitting behind the steering wheel. The Galaxy's engine was purring, suddenly I was driving out of the parking lot and down the street, almost as though it wasn't a conscious choice to do so. It was more like I was being compelled to drive this car.

I had never driven completely alone before, and it was a thrill. I went up and down streets, through the city. At red lights I would nod knowingly at my fellow drivers, as though we were all part of the same club now. I got into the next town, and then I got on the freeway, which was very exciting. I was in pure euphoria, I didn't have a care in the world—I was in bliss.

At some point, the euphoria and bliss started to fade, and then a thought came crashing into my brain that completely eliminated all my good feelings. My dad! How long had I been gone? I had no idea. I left him—stranded. I immediately turned the car back towards the DMV. As I approached the parking lot where I had left I could see a rigid figure standing in the middle of the lot. It looked like a statue of a man. As I got closer I could tell it was my father. As I drove by him to park I could see that he was not smiling. In fact he looked very angry. I parked and remained seated.

He marched stiffly up to my open window and asked me what the hell I was thinking, driving off without him? Leaving him stranded and not knowing where I was, etc., etc. I heard what he was saying, but it didn't really register. I was looking at the license in my hand. When my dad stopped scolding me to catch his breath I held it up and said with a huge smile; "Look, I got my license!"

My excitement and happiness was palpable and contagious, and it was apparently stronger than my dad's need to continue scolding me. He got that look where he is trying really hard to be angry, but he was failing, trying to keep the smile from forcing its way onto his face. My happiness and enthusiasm had won. He went around and sat in the passenger seat and directed me to go home. After that, It was a good birthday.

I really wanted to tell this tale because I like this story, and it brings back some great memories, but I didn't know what kind of lessons I could apply to it. I wasn't sure what I had learned from it that would be worth noting but, I decided to tell it anyway.

Then, during the writing and the re-living of it in my mind, I started to realize a few things. I did learn some lessons from this. It was a great example of what I always say: "That the things we focus on expand." I had been focused for a long time on getting my license, and when the time finally came it was simple, it had been made easy because I was so prepared for it. I got what I had wanted because I was focused intently on it.

It also reminded me what a great dad I had. He was on my side, even though I went off and left him. He knew how much this meant to me and he was proud and happy for me, even though I had made him angry. At the time I thought his anger had crumbled in the face of my sheer happiness but looking back, having been a father myself now, I see that it wasn't just because of my beguiling ways and natural charm. Being a father myself I know that it's impossible not to smile when you are faced with the pure delight of your children. When the people we love are happy, truly happy, that is one of the best moments in life for a man. It makes all the sacrifice and difficulty worth it. As a man, when the people we love are overflowing with joy, that is a "mission accomplished" moment. This story reminds me of that, and what is one of the best things about being a man—experiencing the joy of our loved ones.

Now head out into the world, and stay focused on the things that matter. Look for joy in the people you love and experience it with them. If you don't see it, then look for ways to make it happen. And remember, you might bring them joy simply by being a better man every day.

CHAPTER THIRTY-FIVE
Broken Trust

In the last chapter I told about when I got my driver's license, in "Ticket To Freedom". Today's story happened 5 months later, and it's the tale of how I subsequently lost my driving privileges.

My friend's family had a beach house, right on the Pacific Ocean, about 2 hours away from where we lived. They were letting him have a little get together there one weekend in December— completely unsupervised.

So far, since getting my license I hadn't been in any trouble. I had not gotten any tickets or wrecked anything. The vehicle I drove was the farm truck; a 1964 Chevy. I loved that truck, for all intents and purposes it was MY truck, and in later years after I left home it became my brother's ride. As much as I loved that truck, I didn't trust it to go all the way to the ocean and back.

My parents had just purchased one of the only brand new cars they ever got. It wasn't anything fancy, it was a powder blue Mercury Zephyr station wagon but, it was brand new! The idea that my parents would let me drive their brand new car to the ocean seemed ridiculous but, I had to try. So I waited.

I bided my time until there was one of those moments...one of those points in which my parents were engaged intently in something else. A rare space when the perfect combination of conditions existed; something had their attention and they were experiencing happiness, comfort, and joy all at the same time. I spent over two weeks waiting for this perfect moment, and it finally came. When it did, I gently inserted myself into their happiness bubble and suggested how nice it would be if they could show me how much they trusted me, by allowing me to drive the car to my friends family beach house for the weekend. I also threw in how grateful I would be and how fortunate I was to have such understanding, trusting parents, and how much that meant to me—how wise they were for preparing me for adulthood like that.

I couldn't believe it...but it worked! It must have been something about my delivery, because they both kind of just nodded, not wanting to leave the happy state they were in. The way I presented it made perfect sense. I was totally taking advantage of the fact that in my house, words meant things. I knew that having agreed to my request they would not go back on it. The permission had been granted.

The next day, when they were back in the normal grind of everyday life, the reality of it hit them. They called me in and asked me again what my plans were. I told them again, as innocently as 18 years old. I told them how my friends and I, a group of 6 - 16 year old boys were going to spend the weekend at my friend's families beach house. We were all responsible young men, what could go wrong? Not having any solid evidence to the contrary, they grudgingly agreed...again.

On the morning I was leaving to join my friends my grandmother was at the house. Grams almost blew the whole gig. When she learned what my plans were as I was packing the car she became incredulous. She was telling my mother what a horrible mistake she was making letting me go off by myself in their brand new car. Then she started on my dad, pleading with him to come to his senses but, they had already given me their permission. What message would they be sending me if they went back on their word now?

We all made it to the ocean— my friends and I. My friend showed us in and we all explored the house, getting our bearings. We went into the kitchen and on the table, in a box, was an entire case of pink champagne, and there was beer in the fridge. We were only 16. None of us had much experience drinking. The champagne tasted like bubbly cool-aid, in short—it was a recipe for disaster. We all had a couple drinks and then we decided we should go bowling. The town of Ocean Shores, WA was throbbing with tourists in the summer time, but in December it was quiet and still, like any other very small town. The only people besides us were the locals.

We had fun bowling, all of us slightly lubricated by the first round of champagne. Then we got something to eat at one of the local restaurants. We went back to the house to watch movies, play games, and drink more champagne. It's funny, but I don't remember any of the movies we watched, or the games we played. I do remember drinking more champagne though. We all felt, perhaps for the first time, something like men. There we were having an entire weekend to ourselves without any supervision. Drinking alcohol, telling stories, talking about women and making off-color jokes. I think in the beginning we were inebriated by the sheer feeling of independence as much as the champagne but, then the champagne started to win.

The next memory I can recall was all of us running around in the sand dunes, naked and screaming, like wild men. The fact that it was about 35 degrees, very near freezing, didn't seem to matter at all. We had been made invincible by the bubbly pink beverage.

We were making naked snow angles in the sand and truly behaving like we had lost our minds. Then, I decided to put my clothes back on and get in the car. The beach was desolate and expansive, and the full moon illuminated everything almost as well as the sun on a cloudy day. There I was, in my parents brand new car screaming down the beach at 80 miles per hour. Then I would crank the wheel all the way to one side or the other and the car would slide sideways, the wheels plowing through the sand. I think that's how I popped off all the hub caps.

When we got tired of that the next thing that seemed to make sense was seeing how far out in the surf I could drive without getting stuck. I was driving down the beach in 12 to 18 inches of ocean water. I couldn't see to the left or right because of the rooster tail of spray the car was creating. Meanwhile, the waves kept crashing in on me. Sometimes the water got pretty deep because of the waves and the motor almost stalled but somehow, I kept it going. Unbelievably, through some divine intervention or simply stupid luck, I didn't sacrifice the car to the tide, I didn't get stuck, I didn't crash into a giant log on the beach, or roll the car. I'm still amazed that none of those things happened.

Alf Herigstad

The net day when my eyes opened, I thought I was dead, or at the very least, dying. The pounding in my head was unlike anything I had ever experienced before. Even the light coming through the window hurt. I had one shoe on, my clothes were filthy, and as far as I could tell there was sand in every orifice of my body. I looked around at my friends and it seemed we were all in the same state. There were splashes of vomit here and there, the house was in shambles. Nobody said anything, we were all too busy mourning our stupidity. That's when I thought of the car.

In pain and agony I stumbled outside. There was the car, almost unrecognizable. Covered with sand and dried salt, all the hubcaps were gone, there were a couple small dents and one of the windshield wipers was bent. The inside was worse though.

What had been a pristine new car, complete with the new car smell, now smelled like the intestinal tract of a whale. There was sand everywhere, and some seaweed too, and more vomit. The carpets were wet with sea water and there wasn't a square inch of it anywhere that looked new any longer. I had that sick feeling, like when you lose a great deal of money or accidentally hit 'reply-all' on a controversial email. I knew my life would not be the same when I got home. I didn't know what was going to happen, but I knew it wouldn't be good, and worst of all, I knew I deserved whatever I got.

After we were somewhat recovered, we all helped try and restore the beach house to how it was when we got there. We did the best we could. Then we went to a place with a big vacuum and tried to do the same for the car, but there was only so much we could do. It was going to require professional help. Then, we all made the trek back to our respective homes. My parents had been racked with worry and dread ever since I left, so they were waiting. I pulled into the driveway and parked. Then I got out and just stood there, not sure what to do.

My dad came exploding out of the house and marched up to the car—he didn't look at me. I stood motionless as he walked slowly around the car, looking at everything. His face was getting red, veins were starting to appear on his forehead. Then he opened a door and looked inside. He recoiled when the blast of ocean smell hit his nose, but the inspection continued. I was coming to grips with the fact that my life was probably over. When he was done he came to me and looked at me directly for the first time since I had arrived. He was trembling with fury, but there was something else as well, in his eyes, the look of profound disappointment. It was this look that affected me the most and tore at my heart. In that moment I felt like the worst son who had ever lived. My dad was a reasonable, rational man. He was aware of his own limits. He rarely spoke in times of extreme anger because he knew he wouldn't be able to control the things he said. This time was like that. He didn't say anything as he stood there trembling with rage and disappointment, he just held out his hand. I knew what that meant. Without hesitation I retrieved my wallet and dug out my 5 month old drivers license, and placed it in his hand. He spun around and went back into the house, and left me standing there in my shame.

It was about six months before I got that license back. Six months of being on my best behavior, and repairing the trust of my parents I had lost. I learned some amazing things from this experience. I learned what it was to completely betray the trust of someone I love. I learned how horrible that felt, and I decided I would never do that again. I learned what a valuable commodity trust is, how precious. Whenever trust is received it should be held in the highest of regard, and handled as a fragile treasure, because that's what it is; a gift. It is also one of the cornerstones on which relationships are based. Trying to cultivate a relationship in the absence of trust, is like trying to grow a garden in a parking lot, where there is no soil.

I also learned some things about the dangers of drinking, how abrasive sand can be, and that I wasn't a man at all yet.

It's so important to make trust a priority. Give trust your focus, and it will expand.

CHAPTER THIRTY-SIX
Best Friends

Right around the time I was born my parents decided to get a puppy. Her name was Lady, a little black and white mixed breed dog. She was part spaniel which gave her some long wavy hair, and part a few other things. She was our first dog and we all loved her.

Since they got her when I was am infant, and I grew up with her, she became more than a dog to me; she was more like my older sister. We were both babies at the same time but she grew up and matured much quicker than I did. We spent all of our time together, Lady and I. She was truly as much a part of my family as my parents were, she was ever present. In fact she probably knew me better than my parents did, because dogs can understand some things that people can't.

As I grew older and learned how to walk and talk and to do the sorts of things that other humans do, it didn't affect my relationship with Lady. Some people who have never owned a dog would have a hard time understanding the type of bond we had. They might think that our relationship would be limited by the fact that Lady couldn't speak, but I would disagree. Since we grew up together from tiny babies, our communication transcended speech. She always knew what I was thinking, she knew what I was saying to her, our body language and small gestures and sounds between us were all the language we needed.

When I started school it was rough on both of us. It was the first time since we were infants that we had been separated, but very quickly Lady learned the routine and knew that I would come home again each day. My human siblings were 2 and 3 years younger than me so it was Lady who was my most constant companion. During all of my adventures and explorations of the world around me, she was with me. I was never alone. Lady had some hunting instincts and would frequently go into the woods by herself to chase rabbits and other small animals, but I had developed a certain whistle. It was different from a normal whistle. When I did this particular whistle noise, it meant that Lady should drop whatever she is doing and find me right away. It always worked every time, no matter how far away she had roamed or what she was doing. When I made this certain whistle she would always show up very quickly.

When Lady and I were 8 years old I had started little league baseball. One day it was time to go to a game. We were running late and we were in a hurry. I never left home without saying goodbye to Lady, so I gave my special whistle, and I waited, but she didn't come. She had never taken this long to respond—I whistled again. When she didn't show up again I became very afraid. She had never not shown up before, ever! Something was wrong, and I knew it. My parents were urging me to get into the car, by now I was crying, saying we couldn't go to the game, we had to find Lady. My parents didn't understand the code we had, they didn't understand the importance of our whistle. How could they? No one understood it except Lady and me.

They tried to assure me that it would be OK, that she would probably be waiting for us when we came back. As we were driving out of the driveway my mother told my dad to stop the car, she thought she heard something. A distant, faint yelp or something. We all listened quietly but we didn't hear anything, so dad continued driving on to my baseball game.

During the whole game all I could think about was Lady. When we got home I ran out of the car calling and whistling but, she didn't come. I told my parents we had to go look for her, we could get flashlights and call friends to help and we could all go out into the woods and find her but, they made me go to bed instead, though I don't believe I slept.

The next day we did look for her, but found nothing. I made posters and hung them everywhere within 2 or 3 miles of our house.

Forging A Man

I called for her, I whistled for her for hours. For the first time in my life I experienced panic, and fear, and a sense of loss that was difficult to process. That first day without her turned into two, then three. Then a week had gone by and then two weeks. My memories of that time are very dark. It seems all I did was call, and whistle, and roam the woods and pastures until my mother made me come home—and I cried. Remembering that time, it seems as though I never stopped crying. I woke up crying for Lady, and went to sleep crying for her.

My parents were worried about me. To say that I wasn't handling Lady's absence very well is a severe understatement. What no one seemed to realize is how much she had become an integral, permanent part of my life. She wasn't just a pet, she was a very important thread in the fabric of my existence. I had come to rely on her, almost as though she were a part of me. I considered her in everything I did. Now, I didn't know how to live, I didn't know how to be by myself. I became listless with melancholy and had no interest in doing anything, except trying to find Lady. The only thing that kept me going at all, was a belief I had down deep that she would return, that she was still alive, somewhere.

About a month after Lady's disappearance my dad sat me down; he said he had something to tell me. As I listened, he told me through his own choking voice that he had found Lady's body. That she was dead. He told me that it looked like she had been chasing something way out in the woods and when she jumped through a fence, a wire went through her leg behind her achilles tendon, she had been trapped there until she starved to death.

It was too terrible for me to imagine, and I didn't believe a word of what he was saying. I demanded to know where he had buried her so I could see for myself and prove that it wasn't her. He told me not to go and find her grave. He demanded that I leave her alone. At my first opportunity I snuck out and wandered out to the back boundary of our land. He had mentioned he marked the grave with a stick. I pulled and dug at many sticks and finally, there was one with fresh dirt.

I could not have explained what was driving me. I was acting without thinking, the only motivating factor in my mind was grief, and the need to prove it was not Lady in the ground. I **needed** to believe she was still alive. I was digging with both hands and then suddenly, a black and white paw sprung out of the dirt beneath my fingers. The world stopped. Everything stopped. I just starred at this paw for several moments. I knew it was her, I recognized her paw, and my mind was locked at a place in which it didn't know how to move forward, I couldn't do anything, I was frozen. Ultimately my mind did move forward, just a bit, and when it did I collapsed onto her grave, screaming and crying into the earth. I don't know how long I was like that. If no one would have come and got me, I might still be there— but my dad found me, and brought me home. I don't remember the days that followed, they were lifeless, and meaningless. It was like I had died with her, but my consciousness was cruelly forced to live on, in the shell of my body.

I eventually stumbled out of this fog of grief I had been trapped in. It happened when my Dad came home from work one day. He was walking funny, his arms weren't swinging, and he was smiling. My mother called us kids into the kitchen where my dad was, but I remained on the couch, disinterested. My mother made me come into the kitchen. I sat on the floor with my brother and sister, my dad squatted down in front of us, he could barely contain his excitement. I was still not interested in whatever was going on. Then a face, a little black furry face emerged from my dads coat. It was a puppy. My mother and siblings squealed with delight as my dad set the puppy down on the floor. Initially, I recoiled in horror. I didn't want another dog, I was offended at the idea that any other dog on earth could replace my Lady. I felt it was an attack on her memory. I scooted back on my butt several feet while everyone else was welcoming the puppy into her new home.

Then, the puppy seemed to notice me from across the room. She came straight at me. When she got to me she jumped on my lap and started licking me and shaking her butt, like she hadn't learned to wags her tail yet, without the whole butt moving. I resisted, but after a minute or two the life of the puppy invaded my soul. That's when I started living again. I had not smiled or laughed in weeks, and now I was doing both. This puppy, together with the love of my parents, had restored my life somehow. She was a fat little puppy, another blend of various breeds. She kind of looked like a bear cub, she wiggled when she walked so we named her Wiggles. She remained with our family until she became old and died, some time after I had left home.

I could never talk about Lady without crying well into my adulthood. In fact I was around 34 when I wrote a song about her while I was long haul trucking around the country. I kept singing that song until I could get through it without crying. It took some time, but it was the song that finally healed me, and made me able to talk about Lady without falling apart.

This was a sad time, but like all stories, everything worked out. That's kind of the lesson I got from it. During those days between Lady and Wiggles I didn't know how to live, I didn't want to live, but the world kept spinning around regardless. The sun kept rising in the Eastern sky, as though it had no idea what was going on in my life. Plants continued to grow and birds flew, the whole world just kept moving forward in spite of me. Life marched on, as it always will, and eventually it snagged me up again and brought me along with it. It did this because I was focused again on the moment I was living in. I was focused on the puppy in my arms. Lady had become part of the past, and I had to let the past have her.

It's an important lesson to remember in times of great tragedy, and I have used it many times. There is something about realizing that no matter what has happened, life is going to continue. Time will continue to pass and with that passage of time, even the most stark and horrible of events begin to heal, some heal more slowly than others, but time is an amazing ointment. What we are left with is like a scar; a memory of the incident, but the flesh under it is healed. In that understanding there is always some hope for the future.

Now be confident knowing that whatever happens, time is on your side, pain doesn't last forever, and heartache can be healed. Focus on the moment you are living in—focus on the puppy in your arms.

CHAPTER THIRTY-SEVEN
Cars Need Oil

Some stories are not comfortable to tell, because in order to tell the story, if we're honest, we have to cast a light on a time when we were not acting smart or at our best. In fact some stories, if we are honest —make us seem pretty stupid. This is one of those stories.

I was 18 years old and I had just returned home from Georgia, I was at basic training in the Army. I was hanging out at home because I had managed to get the distinction of becoming a home-town recruiter for a month, before I would have to go to my permanent duty station in Ft. Hood Texas. As it turned out, my special recruiter duty would later be extended to two months because I was doing such a great job recruiting people for the Army, but that's part of another story.

So there I was, living at home and being an Army guy. As luck would have it, one of my buddies from basic training was stationed just up the road about a half hour away at Ft. Lewis. His name was Dave and he was from Lubbock, Texas. I was at basic training for a grand total of 3 months including my advanced training. During that time Dave and I had become really good friends. You tend to form special bonds with people when you go through things together. So I was thrilled when I got the call from Dave one day telling me that he had arrived at Ft. Lewis. He told me I should come up and see him and we could have some beers and pizza in the post cafeteria.

Even though we were not 21 yet, in those days soldiers could drink on post regardless of how old they were— I'm not sure if it's still like that now. That was October of 1980. I was super excited to see Dave, so I ran outside to jump in a car and go up to see him. I wanted to welcome him to the Great State of Washington.   My parents had a couple of cars at the time.   The one I saw in the driveway was the 1963 Ford Galaxy. It was teal in color, with some chrome highlights. It was an awesome car to drive— it was powerful, and fast. I looked around for my dad to ask him if I could borrow it. I didn't see him anywhere so I figured the car must be available because it was just sitting there all by itself. In my excitement to go see my friend I jumped in it and took off, headed for Ft. Lewis.

What I didn't realize at the time unfortunately, was that my dad was just out of sight in the garage. He was getting oil to put in the car.   Right before I had gotten outside my dad had decided to change the car's oil. He had gone underneath and removed the drain plug. When I pulled out, if I had looked back I would have seen a tub full of dirty oil laying in the driveway where the car had been, but in my youthful exuberance, I never looked back.

When my dad emerged from the garage with an armload of oil cans, his heart sank. The car was gone. Somebody (and he figured it must be me) had drove the car off without a drop of oil in the engine.   Cell phones would not be invented for a couple more decades so my dad just went in the house, and waited by the phone. He was hoping with all his might that I would notice the oil light on the dash— maybe I would notice something wasn't quite right. He hoped I would return before I caused any irreparable damage.

The freeway on-ramp was about 10 miles from our house.   I noticed the car sounded a little funny as I pulled onto the freeway, but I was thinking about the pizza I was going to eat, and the beers I was going to drink, and the laughs and memories I was going to share with my friend Dave. The sound of the engine barely registered in my brain.

When I got onto the freeway I was inconvenienced by the fact that this car, which was normally very fast would not go over 45 miles and hour. I thought that was very strange and decided I should tell my dad about it but still, I did not notice the bright red oil light on the dash board because the focus of my thoughts were elsewhere.

10 minutes later I was approaching the off-ramp for the Army base. The car was really acting up, now it would only go 35 miles an

hour but I kept the pedal to the floor regardless, I was almost there. As I got off the freeway and began slowing down, that's when I realized for the first time that I may have done something horrible. The car sounded awful. When I took my foot off the gas pedal, the motor just stopped, and I coasted to a stop on the side of the road.

I popped the hood, and the heat from the engine almost knocked me over. I could almost swear the whole engine was glowing red. I had driven this pristine automobile about 25 miles without any oil. All the moving parts had become so hot that it was essentially welded into one solid block of steel. I walked to the guard shack and borrowed a phone. I called home, It was answered on the first ring. When my dad knew it was me he asked where I was, I told him. He cussed under his breath and hung up.

About 25 minutes later I saw my dad driving down the ramp from the freeway in another car. I didn't know what was going to happen. By this time I realized that the car was destroyed, it was now a completely useless piece of junk, and it was all my fault.

What made it even worse is that I wasn't a kid. I fancied myself a grown man, a soldier, a defender of the nation, yet I had just done something so stupid, so...child like. I didn't know what my dad was going to do.

I didn't say anything, I just stood there. My dad walked up to the car without looking at me. His face looked like it had been chiseled out of granite, in the expression of a very angry man. He walked around the car. He looked at the engine. He started muttering to himself under his breath. I could tell he was getting angrier and angrier, and I was feeling worse and worse. It would have been better if he had screamed at me or punched me or something, I could have dealt with that better than the silence.

When he finally looked at me it was like a knife in my heart; his disappointment was obvious, it was like a smell that lingered around him and in his eyes was a look I had never seen before, and didn't like at all.

We had to leave the car there while he made arrangements to have it moved. The entire ride back home was in silence. It was one of those moments in life I remember feeling like a complete and utter failure. I later realized why he had remained so silent. It was because he was afraid that if he started talking he would not be able to control himself. He was so angry, that he felt as if he opened the bottle all the contents would come spilling out and he would not be able to control it. Even now, 36 years later when I talk about the incident he still gets a flash of anger in his eyes, and I don't blame him. I was not acting like a man that day, I was acting like a silly child, and as a result I destroyed his car.

The lesson I learned from this experience was not about me really, it was about my dad. I have always been able to reflect on this moment and remember it, and remember the way my dad handled it. He would have been completely justified to scream and yell and kick me out of the house, or start hitting me with a tire iron, but he didn't do any of those things. Instead, he controlled his anger and his actions, even though every fiber of his being was enraged. He didn't allow his anger to control him, instead—he controlled his anger. Even in this moment, he was the best example of manhood I could hope for.

For him to maintain his dignity and his manhood throughout this incident was the most impactful thing he could do for me. As I went on in life and became a man I have thought of it often, and there have been times when I had to control my anger just like he did. If it were not for his example I'm not sure that I would have been able to.

It may be that we do not have control over the things we feel, but we do have control over how we handle them. When you make the choice to handle them well, it will have a positive influence not only on you, but on everyone around you as well.

CHAPTER THIRTY-EIGHT
Race Relations

I grew up out in the country in Washington State. It was kind of a sheltered life, there were a lot of things I was never exposed to as a kid, and I'm mostly glad about that. One of the things I was not glad about is that I was never exposed to people of other races, everybody was Caucasian where I was growing up in the 70's.

I saw black people on TV though, and once when I was very small I asked my mom what the deal was with black people. I wanted to know why there weren't any around us and if there was anything else I needed to know about them. My mom told me that all people are the same and everybody is just a person, but some people look different, some people have darker skin, but it's no different from how some people are taller or shorter or fatter or skinnier than other people, and that it wasn't a big deal, they are just people, like me. When my mom told me that, I was of an age that I believed everything she said without question, and I had my answer. So that is exactly what I grew up believing.

I didn't actually meet or talk to any black people until I started boxing around the age of 14. My trainer took me up to Seattle and Tacoma to box and I met a lot of people of other races, but I never thought much about it because like my mom had told me years before, everybody is just a person, like me.

Later on when I joined the Army I went to basic training and there were lots of guys in my unit from many different races. That's where I first started to notice some racial unrest. I noticed some guys didn't like other guys just because of their race, and they would talk about them when they weren't around. Seeing this made me feel bad.

I also noticed that when we weren't training, guys of the same race used to cluster together in little groups. I thought this was strange, and being a naive country boy who was eager to learn more about the big world, I would insert myself into these groups of other races. Most of the time people were friendly to me, and I made some good friends among these other groups, but that made some of the white guys treat me different, which I thought was stupid.

I wasn't totally ignorant. I knew what racism was. I had learned about history and I was well aware of the persecution some races had gone through. I just didn't understand why it seemed to be continuing; after all my mom had told me that everybody was just people, like me, so that was my belief.

After basic training I was sent to Ft. Hood Texas. On my very first day reporting to my unit the first thing I heard was a vulgar expletive that included the phrase "another mother '*f-ing*' white-ass honky." It took me a couple minutes to realize that the guy was talking about me, because I had never been referred to that way before. Unfortunately I would soon find out, that's kind of how it was at my unit in Ft. Hood Texas.

It turned out that it was extremely racially divided between blacks and whites. For one thing, at least in my unit, the white guys were an extreme minority, there was probably 6 white guys for every 10 black guys for some reason. I was assigned to a vehicle, along with two black guys and one Italian. During the day while we were working every thing was fine. We would laugh and joke and tell stories with each other like guys will do on the job. It seemed like we were friends.

Then in the evening after work, the same guys who I had established a good relationship with during the day wouldn't even talk to me. I would say hello in passing, and be completely ignored. I would walk up to speak to them and they would walk away. I quickly noticed that just like at basic training, people only hung out with other people who looked like them. It really bothered me, I didn't want to live like this. I asked around about it, trying to understand. The white guys told me that was just how it was..."we don't bother them and they don't bother us." I asked my black coworker about it during the day when he was acting like my friend and he told me the same thing, though he was a little more apologetic about it. He advised me that I should just do like everyone else, and stay with my own kind.

I was 18 years old, far away from home, and I was miserable. I didn't understand this racial division, none of it made any sense to me. I grew up believing that every body was just a person like me, like my mom had said, and I still believed it. I kept trying to make a connection and bridge the gap between these groups of guys that I worked with during the day, and I kept talking to some of the white guys too, trying to figure out why people were acting this way.

We had a day room with a TV and a pool table. It was kind of a neutral ground it seemed. All different kinds of guys would sit in there watching TV together. That first guy, the one that called me a name on my first day had a real problem with me for some reason, his name was PFC Price. He called me names every day and made fun of me and would challenge me to fight him every chance he got. Especially when I was in the day room and other guys were there to see it. I usually just ignored him. Even though he was bigger than me, about 6'5", I wasn't afraid of him because he was obviously a bully, and all bullies were in my experience, cowards.

One day I finally got tired of it though. He was doing his usual thing, calling me names and challenging me to go outside and fight him, so I suddenly stood up, looked at him and said,"OK". Then I started walking toward the door. He said, "What?" I said, "You've been wanting to fight, so let's go…you coming?" And I walked outside and waited for him in the courtyard. A few other guys followed me outside to wait for PFC Price, but he never showed up. He completely chickened out and went to his room and never messed with me again.

This experience with PFC Price confirmed something for me. It confirmed once and for all that my mom was exactly right—people are just people. I anticipated how PFC Price would respond because he was a bully, and bullies were cowards, regardless of what color their skin was. People were just people. After that day I started hatching a plan. I won't lie and say it was a good plan, but it was a plan. I had grown so tired of all the prejudice from both sides. It hurt my feelings, it made me sad that I couldn't just talk to whoever I wanted to after work, simply because I was a white guy. I thought the whole thing was stupid, and I decided to do something about it. I kept telling myself that people were just people. And one thing I knew about people was that humor was like magic. If you could make someone laugh it created an instant connection. I also knew that it was important to be able to laugh at yourself, to not take yourself too seriously. Somehow, these two things I knew came together in my 18 year old naive country brain, in the form of a plan.

I am not recommending anyone else try it. Looking back I realize it wasn't the smartest thing I ever did, it might have been my own level of ignorance and innocence that made it work, but it did work. So here's what I did. One day after work everyone had divided up into their respective races as they always did. Out in the parking lot there was a group of about 7 black guys talking and laughing amongst themselves in a circle.

I walked right up and just stood right there in that circle with them. When I did they all stopped talking and just looked at me, as though to ask what I wanted. I began talking casually, normally, as though I belonged there. None of them responded, they just kept looking at me like I was crazy. That's when I launched plan B. I started telling jokes. Not just any jokes—I was telling black jokes that I had heard white guys telling around the barracks. These were jokes about black people, and I was telling them to a group of black guys in the parking lot.

After I told the first one, there was a cold silence. I think they may have even stopped breathing. They were not just looking at me now, they were looking at each other, and then back to me. Like they were silently asking one another what they should do. I just kept going. I told two more jokes, I laughed myself at the punch line because no one else certainly was. That's when I started to think that perhaps this was a bad idea. They all looked very angry.

I knew there was a certain amount of risk going into this, I realized I could get beat up, but I thought the possible benefits outweighed the risk. I was prepared to get beat up, but I wasn't prepared to go on living this segregated lifestyle. After the third joke I said, "C'mon guys...doesn't any body know any white jokes? Lets hear one." Again...silence. Then to my great relief one of the guys, I think his name was Harper, started telling a white joke. He got done and all the other guys laughed, and I did too. Then another guy told a joke and we all laughed again.

This is exactly what my plan was, for all of us to laugh together. Then I told another black joke and this time they laughed at it, too. Then I got off the racial jokes and just started telling regular old jokes and we went back and forth like that, laughing together, laughing at each other, and at ourselves. All of these guys became friends of mine then. Partly because they thought I was a little crazy and perhaps I was, but also because we got to know and respect each other.

After that evening I was able to walk freely between the groups of races with impunity, until I eventually left Ft. Hood and went to Germany several months later. There were some hold outs on both sides, some grumbly redneck white guys and some black guys too that didn't agree with me or my position on things but I didn't care, because they weren't the kind of guys I wanted to be friends with anyway. When I got to Germany the racial situation was much better because we were no longer identified by our race alone. Now there was another title that gave us all something in common in this foreign country; we were all Americans.

That's the end of the story; You can all draw your own conclusions about the lessons I learned, but for me, this experience was more of a validation of something I had learned when I was a tiny boy, from what my mother had told me about people. I have found it to be true my whole life. If I had to summarize the things I got from this story it would go like this: People are just people. Don't take yourself too seriously. Laughter is good for the soul, and the ability to laugh at yourself is priceless—and, all bullies are cowards.

Now head out into the world and treat every body you meet like they are another person just like you, because they are. Also, if you get a chance to have a laugh at your own expense, take it. Never take yourself too seriously.

CHAPTER THIRTY-NINE
Throw Alf Out The Window

I spent my 18th birthday traveling to the airport, to get on a plane that would take me to basic training for the US Army.

They were exciting times— war with Iran seemed imminent because they had taken 52 American hostages and tensions were becoming very heated.

My recruiter had not been totally honest with me. I scored very high on the entrance test so I could basically have any job I wanted but I had just turned 18, and I didn't really know what I wanted. I had heard the infantry wasn't a great job because you were gone for long periods of time and it didn't teach any skills you could use when you got out. On the other hand I had just finished 12 years of school, and I was not excited to sit in more classrooms. I really just wanted to have fun and adventure. I told the recruiter I for sure did NOT want to be in the infantry. Every other job he offered me required extensive schooling, extra courses like intelligence, computer technician, medic, etc., so he and I were at an impasse.

The recruiter was becoming visibly frustrated.

Then suddenly, as if he had a brilliant idea, he said, "What about heavy anti-amour weapons crewman?"

"What's that?"

He said, "It's an awesome job...you get to blow up tanks and stuff."

I thought, "Hmmm, that sounds like fun."

Then he said, "And...with this job you get a $3000 cash

enlistment bonus when you complete your training." Now I was very interested. I asked how long the training was he said, "Only three months, you'll be home in time for Christmas."

I said, "Sign me up."

So there I was, at Ft. Jackson, South Carolina getting herded around like cattle with all the other trainee's. They were separating us according to our jobs and where we would go for training. They were shouting, "All the cooks form up over here...all the mechanics... over there...all the artillerymen over here, infantry over there." And so on, until they went through all the jobs. When they were all done everyone was in a new group of men according to what their job was, except me. I was the last guy standing there all by myself.

A very angry looking drill sergeant saw me and walked, almost running toward me, until he was within two inches of my face. Then he yelled "Whats your problem, boy? Why didn't you leave when you were called?" Ignoring his spit on my face, I calmly replied, "They never called my job drill sergeant." This seemed to make him angrier, then he asked, screaming of course, asking what my job was. To which I proudly replied, "Heavy anti-armor weapons crewmen." He scoffed, and then he yelled and I quote, "Get your goat-smelling ass over there with the infantry, your nothing but a glorified grunt." I felt extremely betrayed by my recruiter. I joined the ranks of other infantrymen with a sinking feeling in my stomach. That is how my military career started.

Later that day I got on the infantry bus, headed for Ft. Benning, Georgia.

In spite of the fact that I was tricked into joining the infantry, I enjoyed basic training a great deal. I loved the physical and mental challenges of it, I enjoyed being tested to my limits, and I very much enjoyed going to the ranges and firing all manner of weapons. Upon returning from a particularly muddy weapons range one day, my rain poncho was filthy, covered with mud. The other guys started cleaning their gear as soon as we got back but I, thinking I was smarter than them, figured that could wait. I reasoned that this time would be better spent catching up on much needed sleep so I could be at my best the following day. This thinking it turned out, was a mistake.

The next morning we were at formation and my name was called with a few others, we were to get ready for something called guard mount. We were handed a diagram of exactly how our uniforms were supposed to be. Our utility belt, known as 'web gear' was to have certain things on it in certain places. Our boots needed to be highly shined, our uniforms pressed and clean, our weapons sparkling and our helmets worn correctly. We were supposed to get our uniforms together and then meet again for formation where we would be inspected, and then brought to some building to be on guard duty. This was all an integral part of our training.

I had clean uniforms, I had a pair of shined boots, and I had cleaned my weapon the night before but then I saw the diagram said my rain poncho had to be folded, and rolled into a tight bundle exactly 6 inches wide and be fixed to my web gear on the back. This was a problem, because my poncho was still filthy, covered with mud and thrown haphazardly in my wall locker. We only had 30 minutes before we had to report for inspection. I figured, aww...it can't be that big of a deal, they won't notice that one more green thing isn't where it is supposed to be on my uniform. I'll just show up without my poncho and act like everything is perfect and they won't even notice. So, that's what I did.

I showed up for inspection. We were brought to attention and the drill sergeants began at one end, inspecting every detail of each soldiers uniform. I was at the end of the line, the last to be inspected. The drill sergeant noted something undesirable on every soldier— a button undone here, a scuff on a boot there, a wrinkled shirt, a smudge of dirt. As he got closer to me I became increasingly nervous. I realized that the absence of my poncho might be noticed after all. Finally, he got to me. He started in the front, looking me up and down. Everything seemed to be in order, he didn't have any criticisms. Then he moved around to the back. I heard him grunt, then I heard him gasp, then he mumbled under his breath something I couldn't understand. Then he almost ran around the formation so he could be in front of me again. Suddenly his face was about two inches from mine—a common communication technique for drill sergeants. Then he screamed at the top of his lungs, asking me why I didn't have a poncho on my web gear?

Again, ignoring the spit I calmly apologized, and said that my poncho was in my wall locker, thinking he would make me do some pushups and that would be the end of it. Instead to my surprise, he commanded me to fall out of formation and double time, which meant to run, back to the barracks and get it. I did as he asked, but when I started running back up the hill towards my barracks I noticed he was running right behind me. He was very angry at this point, in fact I was a little concerned about his emotional stability, he was making an awfully big deal out of this missing poncho. Then, as I was running, I felt a big boot crash into my butt. He was continuing to yell and scream a tapestry of insults and threats at me and now he was also kicking me in the butt every few steps as he chased me back to my barracks. (I'm not sure how you kick someone while you are running, it must be something they teach them in drill sergeant school.)

We got to my barracks, which were totally empty; we were the only ones there. My bunk was on the second floor. We were lodged in very old, wooden WWII barracks with an open bay. It was essentially a big room lined with bunks and wall lockers down each side. He was screaming at me to open my wall locker, his chest was pushing against me and he was yelling right in my ear, which made me fumble with the combination lock, but I finally got it open. When the doors of my wall locker opened, right there— the first thing you could see was my dirty, filthy rain poncho. He started trembling with anger. I think he was holding his breath because veins were starting to bulge out on his forehead and neck. It was summertime in Georgia, and extremely hot weather so the windows were all open wide. I was standing next to one of these windows. The drill sergeant erupted in a torrent of vile insults that included members of my family, and any girl I might have had affection for. Then he proceeded to explain in a similar manner how unfit I was to be a part of **his** Army. It was during this portion that he noticed the large open window next to me.

He said he was going to throw me out of that 2nd story window. At first I thought it was just part of his rant, but then he grabbed me and together we were moving quickly toward the open window. I realized as we got to the window, judging by the enthusiasm of his grip and momentum, that he was serious. Right before I went out the window I reached out and grabbed both sides of the four foot wide opening, stopping us both. He screamed at me to let go. Then I calmly replied,

"With all due respect drill sergeant...I can't let you throw me out this window." I was larger than him thankfully, both taller and wider, younger and stronger. He renewed his efforts to throw me out the window, the whole while screaming at me and giving me orders to let go of the sides of the window. I kept repeating the same thing; "I'm sorry drill sergeant, with all due respect, I just can't let you throw me out the window."

I kept repeating that phrase over and over again. It's the only thing I could think of to do. The whole thing was very surreal and It was difficult to believe it was really happening. I was actually torn between obeying an order, and allowing myself to be seriously injured, or worse. In the end, self preservation won out. Finally, after ten minutes or so of trying to kill me, the drill sergeant was getting tired, and his anger was being replaced by disgust and intense dislike, but he knew he couldn't get me out the window. He stopped his attack. I kept hanging onto the window until he had moved far enough away from me that he couldn't surprise me with a rush.

He told me to report, in proper uniform within ten minutes and he left. As soon as he was gone I did the fastest poncho wash ever done in the showers. Then I folded and rolled it, still wet, into the prescribed shape and put it on my belt. Then I sprinted back to formation and we all went to guard duty.

I certainly did learn a lot of lessons from this event. I learned things everyday while I was in basic training about myself, other people, and the world at large. On this day however I mostly learned things about myself.

I was glad I didn't let him throw me out the window, that felt like sort of a victory that I had won. But I also realized that I wouldn't have gone through that if I wasn't busy trying to be smarter than other people by taking short cuts. The whole thing helped me realize that I was part of an organization, a team. For that team to run smoothly everyone, including myself had to do the things required of them. My actions not only affected me, but everyone else on guard duty that day. They all had to remain standing in the sun while I was being disciplined. In short, I realized I had not done my best, and I suffered the consequences of that. For the rest of my time at basic training my uniform was always perfect, and I never let my team down again.

Don't ever let anyone throw you out a window, but more importantly try to make sure no body wants to. Do the things you're supposed to do, and don't take those shortcuts.

CHAPTER FORTY
The Saga Of Dr. Pepper

When I was a kid I had the privilege of being a member of the Boy Scouts of America. I was part of troop 48, and it was a great experience that I am very grateful for. We went on awesome campouts every month and I learned so much about the flora and fauna of Washington State. I learned a lot of other great skills as well like how to tie knots, and how to start a fire. I would say that over all, being in Boy Scouts gave me some tremendous advantages that I would not have otherwise.

One of the great things about being a Boy Scout was that every year there was a week long summer camp in a beautiful area, on the shores of Summit Lake. Summer Camp was great because of the lake of course, also because there were lots of other troops of boys from different parts of the state and it was an opportunity to make new friends. We ate our food in a big military style mess hall. There was a gigantic fire place at one end, and during all of our meals we were entertained by people singing goofy songs and it was just generally a great time. So at my second year of Summer Camp I was 12 years old. It was 1974. The first year of summer camp, the year before, I had impaled my leg with a pocket knife. This year would be different because I was older now, and wiser.

At the first breakfast of summer camp I went to put salt and pepper on my eggs and someone, almost certainly one of the older boys, had unscrewed the lid on the pepper shaker. There was always mild hazing going on toward the younger boys of which, I was still one. A pile of black pepper fell out onto my plate, burying my eggs and sausage. I heard the older boys laughing, but I remained motionless for a moment. I knew what was going on. I knew they were trying to get a reaction out of me, and I wasn't about to give them that satisfaction.

I calmly retrieved the pepper lid and screwed it back on without a word. Then I proceeded to spread the pile of pepper evenly out across all the other food on my plate, even onto my pancakes. Then I just started eating it as if nothing had happened out of the ordinary. The perpetrators of this prank were obviously disappointed and confused. In my peripheral vision I could see them looking at each other and then back to me. Finally one of them asked me why I was eating so much pepper on all my food.

I stopped eating for a minute, as though he had interrupted my meal. I looked at him as if I didn't hear the question and asked him to repeat it. He asked me again why I was eating so much pepper all over my food. I answered simply, that I loved pepper and then went back to eating. The older boys kept watching me until my plate was empty.

To be honest it tasted horrible, but the victory I felt in having ruined their joke tasted very sweet. I felt I had earned some points and had climbed a rung or two higher on the pecking order with that response.

There is always a pecking order of some kind, and in a climate like Summer Camp with so many boys between the ages of 11 and 18, it was really all about the pecking order. How tough are you? How much can you take? How funny are you? How many friends did you have? How good of a swimmer are you, etc., etc.? These are all things that would increase or diminish your standing in the pecking order, which was like an invisible ranking system in which everyone by the end of the week, would know their place.

Breakfast ended and we all went to our respective activities. I was glad that meal was over. Later that day at lunch time, I was surprised to see that a good number of boys seemed to have an interest in my food. They were watching me. Apparently the news of my breakfast pepper antics had spread quickly. I ignored every one of course, pretending not to notice that they were all watching me. I overheard one or two boys mention the word "pepper" in their whispered conversations. Crap, I thought! Now they are waiting to see if I pepper my food again.

I could have just ate normally from there out and the whole pepper thing would have ended, but I felt like I was in a situation that had gotten out of control. I felt like if I didn't pepper my food then I would have a reputation of being dishonest, that I was not really the person I made myself out to be at breakfast. So, I reached for the pepper shaker, and emptied it to the ooh's and ah's of the on-lookers, and then—I ate it.

Even though my food tasted horrible, there were some positives; there were like 160 boys at camp and suddenly they all knew who I was. I had become infamous and they had started calling me 'Dr. Pepper'. Every meal was the same. Everyone would watch as I buried my delicious camp food in mounds of pepper, so much that I could no longer see my food. Then they would squeal with delight as I ate it, savoring every bite as though it was the most exquisite thing I had ever eaten. I had most of the kids fooled, but not the adults. My scout master took me aside one day and basically told me I could drop the pepper charade. He said he knew what was going on. I acted as though I didn't understand what he was talking about. I told him I loved pepper and that I enjoyed it on everything. He wasn't prepared to force me not to eat pepper, so I went about my business.

Dr. Pepper was quite famous by the 4th day of camp. I found that I had to keep increasing the amount of pepper to keep my new fans happy, and I had to put it on things that pepper was not intended to go on. That week I put pepper on strawberry shortcake, Ice cream, and I even put it on my cereal in the morning. I really hated the pepper but I did love the attention and the respect I seemed to be generating. I loved the fact that everyone knew who I was and that I was called Dr. Pepper. My celebrity status outweighed the fact that I hadn't enjoyed anything I put in my mouth since I had left home.

The rest of the week went on as usual, except for everyone in camp acting like they knew me. I had a great week. Friday was the last day at camp. We got all packed up to leave and prepared for one last big meeting at which our parents would attend, and then we would go home.

My parents could not help but notice how popular I had become.

They asked me why everyone was calling me Dr. Pepper, I just told them that was my nick name. Later I saw my parents in a deep conversation with the scout master while we were on stage, engaged in some kind of performance, I suspected the gig might be up.

My parents didn't say anything to me about it though. They drove home while I entertained them with all the stories and adventures I had gained during the week. I didn't mention pepper. The next day my mom served breakfast; First to dad, and then my brother and sister. I was so looking forward to eating something that was not covered in pepper but, when my mom brought my plate to the table lo and behold, it was covered with a mound of black pepper.

I was stunned, and shocked, and embarrassed, and disappointed all at the same time. My family was all just watching me now, seeing what I would do. Problem was, I didn't know what to do. If I eat this pepper then it will start all over. I would have to eat pepper on everything for the next 6 years until I left home, just like at camp. I couldn't do it.

I slumped in my chair, I was deflated, and defeated. Now my parents started chuckling a bit, saying things like, "What's the matter Dr. Pepper? Not enough pepper?" When I didn't see the humor in their jokes they got more serious. They told me the scout master had told them about my behavior during the week, and they invited me to tell them how it all came about.

My mom brought me a new, pepper free plate and I proceeded to tell them the whole story, the same story I'm telling you right now basically. After that I went back to a regular portion of pepper, on appropriate foods.

As you might have guessed, I learned some good things in this experience. Among those lessons I learned the importance of being honest with myself and everybody else about who I am. I learned that trying to be something you aren't is not sustainable and when it falls apart, you look like a fool.

I also learned that fame and popularity are fun, but fleeting and hollow at the same time. Now I was back home in my regular life and all those guys I was trying to impress were somewhere else. I had gained nothing from all the suffering I had gone through with the pepper. Yep, I learned it's always better to just be yourself.

Forging A Man

The only person you should really be trying to impress, is yourself. Be true to yourself, be true to who you are, be really clear about it. It's one thing no body can ever take away from you.

CHAPTER FORTY-ONE
The Flatulent Reader

7th grade was an awkward time for me. I was 12 years old, and it was 1974. I was all arms and legs, my body was growing so fast that I was always just a little out of sync with it— like I was wearing somebody else's clothes all the time. Socially, going to school every day was similar to entering a war zone. There were all the cliques, all the different groups of kids I was trying to figure out and navigate through without compromising my position on the pecking order. It was really quite exhausting.

Everyday at school I waded through a gauntlet of threats, insults, taunts and jibes, and then decided how to best respond to each. There were fights, and the rumors of fights. Alliances were formed and dissolved several times throughout each day. If you were lucky, you might have two or three friends that you could count on no matter what, but everything else was a crap shoot.

Then there were the girls. Around 7th grade was when I first started really admitting to myself that I liked girls, a lot. I couldn't really define why I liked them yet, or what I was supposed to do with them, but I seemed to fall in love several times a week, over the slightest of things. I would become smitten by the tiniest gesture, like the way a girl would smile, or laugh, the way she looked at me in passing, the way she walked, how she chewed her gum. It really didn't take much to spark my interest in those days. My problem with girls was that I didn't really know how to talk to them, or what to say. It was like they were an entirely different creature whose language I didn't yet understand.

For example, there was one girl I liked a lot, her name was Connie, and instead of talking to her I would lightly punch her in the arm every day. It wasn't a hard punch, it wasn't intended to hurt her. In my tiny cave man brain punching her in the arm accomplished many things. For one, it got her attention, it forced her to notice me. The second thing it did was allow me to touch her. For that split second when my fist was on her shoulder, we were touching, and that seemed like a good thing in my still primitive mind.

I thought we had a great arrangement, until the day she finally got fed up with it, and kicked me in the crotch so hard that my feet came off the ground. I crawled to the bathroom in unspeakable agony, and passed out for 30 minutes. The next day, as a means of getting back at her, I told her that my parents had taken me to the doctor and he had told me I would never be able to have children because of the kick I had received. She began crying hysterically from guilt, I let that go on for about five minutes before telling her that I was just kidding. Then she chased me around for the rest of the day trying to kick me again, it was great fun.

So that's what life was like when I was 12. It seemed like everything you did or said was a big deal. News traveled fast through the school and a reputation could be won or destroyed with the slightest error in judgment. One of my classes was reading class. As the title implies all we did was read in this class, and occasionally we would do a book report or something.

The teacher was Mr. Cheney. He was a tall lanky guy with an uncombed mop of coal black hair, which was contrasted by ghastly white skin, as though he had never been outside in his life. Even when he was close shaved the blackness of his beard showed under his transparent skin and turned his face sort of blue underneath. He never talked to us much. He may have actually been born without a personality. He just sat up at the front and read during the entire class. He was reading, and we were reading. Nobody talked, it was extremely quite in this class room. There were about 30 kids in the class, and my seat was right in the middle of the room. One day as I was reading, I felt like I had a bit of gas. I tried to ignore it, but the pressure was building. This bit of gas was quickly maturing into a full blown fart, and I knew I would not be able to control it forever. I had become a master of the 'silent but deadly' technique. A technique in which you manipulate your posterior anatomy in such a way, as to allow the gas to escape without making any sounds. I decided to give that a whirl. So, in the perfect silence of reading class I got into position, and let her go.

Something went horribly wrong. What should have been as silent as a gentle breeze sounded more like a chainsaw starting up. It was incredibly loud, and it seemed to be amplified by the hard plastic seat I was sitting on. The pristine silence of reading class had been violently shattered. People jumped in their seats, startled by the noise, and then every head in the room swung toward the center of class, where I was sitting. I tried to do the same thing, to look in another direction as though my gaze would shift the blame off of me —but because of my placement in the center I couldn't get away with it. Every direction I looked in, were people looking back at me. I just stared at my desk in resignation.

Then I started hearing groans and gasps from my fellow students as the methane bomb I had released began radiating outward from my location. One by one students were standing up, hands over their nose and mouth, and they were heading for the door. I have to admit, as far as bad smells go, this was in the top three of all time; it was pretty bad.

I remained motionless, staring at my desk. I didn't know what else to do. As people were filing out of the room I would catch some of the looks they shot at me. They ranged from pity, to total disgust. The last one out was Mr. Cheney. He didn't say anything, he just shook his head as he walked by. Then I heard the door close, and I was all alone, sitting in the middle of an empty room, languishing in my own filth. I turned around and looked at the door. It was a typical classroom door with one tall skinny window in it. There were three faces of kids stacked up in the window just looking at me. Occasionally one face would leave, only to be replaced by another.

It was about 20 minutes before everyone started coming back in again. No one spoke to me, it was as though I had sunk so low on the social pecking order that I wasn't even worthy of being spoken to. I had become an unclean, untouchable, unspeakable thing. At least, that's how I felt.

Somehow, I got through the rest of that day. I was certain I had caused irreparable damage to my reputation. For the rest of the week I would hear remarks and comments made about it, a few insults were shot my way, but I expected that. Then, the weekend came. Weekends were kind of magical, in that they seemed capable of purging the memories of people, wiping them clean. By Monday my life was pretty much back to normal, almost like it had never happened.

So that's the end of the story, and what it taught me was that time really does fix almost everything. Throughout the rest of my life, whenever I would commit some horrible blunder or social faux pas I knew that once I got past the initial embarrassment that everything would be OK. The passage of time would occur, and people would forget, and life would go on. It's an important lesson to remember, because sometimes people get stuck in some past action, and it affects the rest of their life. Even though time has purged it from the minds of everyone else you are still hanging onto it, letting it define you. So with this story, I encourage everyone to remember that every day is a new day. No matter how bad you might have screwed up, every new day is an opportunity to start over with a clean slate and live a life that you intend.

Now head out into the world and remember to learn from your mistakes and not to hang onto them— do not allow yourself to be defined by the things you have done wrong. Instead, be defined by the actions you take that make you a better man.

CHAPTER FORTY-TWO
Waiting For Bigfoot

I grew up on a farm, out in the country in the beautiful Pacific Northwest in the state of Washington, where I still live.

The Pacific Northwest is well known for being a sanctuary for the legendary Bigfoot, also called the Sasquatch, which was the name the American Indians gave it many, many years ago. The lore of local tribes is full of Sasquatch stories. We moved to the farm when I was seven, and by the time I was eight years old, besides becoming a super hero, all I thought about was Bigfoot. I grew up surrounded by tales of this mythical beast. I would seek out information in the school library and anywhere else I could get my hands on it. The idea that this huge, hairy, man-like creature might be lurking somewhere out in our woods was absolutely fascinating to me.

My father had a friend named Larry who was about 10 years older than him, so he seemed very old to me. One day while he was visiting he gave us a personal account. He said he was driving down a road at night. He went around a curve and his headlights illuminated something in the distance. Something huge and hairy, standing next to one of those yellow aluminum arrow signs. Larry told us that as the lights hit it, it threw up its arms as though to shield its eyes, then it angrily struck out and hit the sign with its arm before running back into the wood line. Larry said he sped straight home after that, but the next day he went to that location and he saw the sign—folded over like a taco shell. He was convinced he had seen a Bigfoot.

My imagination was already churning with thoughts of the Sasquatch. I would sit around for hours drawing pictures of it and just thinking about it, wondering how they lived and what their babies looked like, all sorts of things. Then, hearing a personal account from someone I knew and respected sent my imagination into overdrive.

Strangely, I never considered the fact that Sasquatch would be mean or ill-tempered. I had never heard stories about them hurting anyone. I wanted desperately to find one, to know it, to become its friend, so—I devised a plan. At this time in my life my favorite thing to eat was peanut butter and jelly sandwiches, stuffed with my mother's home made strawberry jam. It made sense to me that if I found them irresistible, Bigfoot would as well.

My plan was simple; I would make some sandwiches and travel deep into the forest, into the dark part where very little light sifted through the branches of the Douglass fir trees overhead. Once I found a good spot I would sit down quietly, put a sandwich out on the ground a few feet in front of me, and wait.

I wasn't foolish enough to believe that I would immediately meet a Bigfoot. From all I had read they were very shy, very mysterious creatures who didn't trust people for obvious reasons. I did believe that they would see me though, they would know I was there, they would watch me, and that through many of these waiting sessions, they would kind of get to know me, and gradually come to understand that I was a friend.

After I would sit quietly for about an hour I would take out my own sandwich and eat it very slowly, relishing every bite, making it look as tasty as I could. I would usually stay out there three or four hours, completely quiet, and perfectly still except for when I was eating my sandwich. I always went to the same spot, and sat under the same tree. When I would leave, I would leave the Bigfoot's sandwich there on the ground, and there was never any trace of it when I came back again. This went on for several months, once or twice a week depending on weather and my chores and homework. Whenever I would have the time I would make two sandwiches and head out. I didn't have any expectations of Bigfoot, I didn't want to make him a pet or anything. I just wanted to see him, to be in his presence. I felt like if I could do that, I would be better off somehow.

The weeks and months went by, perhaps more than a year

before I finally stopped. Bigfoot never did come to eat his sandwich with me, but the other things I got from the experience were amazing in their own right. Sitting quietly in the forest for an extended period of time is like traveling into another world, because after a while the forest forgets you are there, and you begin to see things you would never see otherwise. Bigfoot never came out to meet me, but all the other animals of the forest did. Squirrels and chipmunks and deer would come so close I could have touched them. I saw all manner of birds, and insects and coyotes and skunk and snakes and raccoons. It was like looking through a secret window that people didn't normally get to look through. It was like I became a part of everything.

It was from this perch waiting for Bigfoot, that I watched the seasons change. I watched new things grow, and then die and return to the soil. I watched the weather change, and saw the fur of animals get thicker with the cold. I was meditating on nature without even realizing that is what I was doing. It gave me a certain kind of peace that has never really left me. I began to look inward, I began to know myself as part of something much bigger.

In trying to meet a Bigfoot, I unwittingly gave myself a rare and special gift at the age of 8 and then 9, the gift of silence, and stillness, of quiet contemplation and observation. I learned that even though I didn't find what I was searching for I was provided with something else equally as wonderful. The key to that, was being willing and able to receive it.

I could have gotten frustrated after 2 or 3 attempts. I could have been upset that my plan did not unite me with a Sasquatch. I could have gone home and turned on the TV and forgot about the whole silly thing. Instead I waited, and kept waiting. For that I was rewarded with sights and sounds and memories and sensations that will remain with me until I die.

It's never too late. No matter how old you are or what you have been through, being alone and quiet and still in the middle of nature is something everyone can benefit from. No matter where you live, anyone can wait for Bigfoot, and in doing so begin to see all the other things you might have missed otherwise. Look, I know that everybody doesn't live on a farm in Washington State, but it doesn't matter. Maybe you are in the middle of a big city, go to the town's park, or drive a couple hours until you hit the wilderness, or find a state park. I have readers from all over the world and maybe you live in the desert, in the Middle East, in China, the Savannah, the Mongolian Steps, wherever you are, nature exists right along beside you. Some of you may have to travel to find it but it's there, and it's worth it. Go be alone in it, wait for Bigfoot, and let me know how that experience was for you.

The lesson here is that life is a lot bigger than the things right in front of you. Take the time to wait, and wonder, and see yourself as part of a bigger picture.

CHAPTER FORTY-THREE
Prey In School

The Elementary school I went to was right out of the movies; it was a wooden structure, with a bell tower, and it actually had a big bell in it with a rope hanging down.   The Principal of the school, Mr. Thompson, would pull on the rope and ring the bell to signal when school was starting, when it was lunch time, when recess was over and when school was out for the day.   There were only around 100 kids in the whole school from kindergarten up through 5th grade.   I started at this school in 1969 when my family moved to the area, I was 7 years old, in 2nd grade.   Life was pretty good for the most part.   My teacher didn't like me, but I spent recess catching frogs with a guy named Jay or playing dodge ball in the play shed, or playing war games out in the field with all the other boys, so I was having a pretty good time— until one fateful day.

Somehow, someone found out that I was ticklish. Kids would try to tickle me and I would run. I became a prey animal. The groups of people that would chase me got bigger and bigger as time went on. Of the one hundred students in my school many of them were much larger than I.   It was only a matter of time before they caught me. They would corral me in until there was no escape.

Having caught me, several of them would hold me down and the tickling would commence. Tickling doesn't make me laugh; it makes me crazy, and I HATE it. I would beg and plead for them to leave me alone.   Of course these older kids would not stop simply because I begged them.   They tickled me beyond the thresholds of my endurance. They tickled me until I wet my pants. That was the goal, getting me to pee my pants was their pay off. Before very long it had become a daily lunchtime activity.

Mr. Thompson would ring the lunch bell, and I would immediately go into "prey" mode. Emerging from the school onto the playground, I was a gazelle emerging from the safety of the forest, warily on the lookout for predators. The chase would then be on and soon I would be crying, pants wet, sitting in the middle of the field like an abandoned carcass as the predators swaggered back towards the school, their bellies full again; full on the pain and embarrassment of someone smaller than them.

I would call my mom and she would bring me dry pants. She didn't know why I had wet them because I didn't tell her. She and my father were both becoming very concerned about me, because it isn't normal for a kid to wet his pants at school every day. I have often wondered about this; why didn't I tell her? Just like many other abused children who never report the crimes against them, I think it was because I was too embarrassed. I was embarrassed and ashamed that this was happening to me, as though it was my fault somehow. So I didn't tell my parents or the teachers, I just tried to deal with it on my own the best I could. As time went on it was no longer just the older kids, or just boys who took part. It became a spectator sport for many of the girls, the younger kids, and kids my own age.

There were two evil twins at my school Lowell and Lorn. They were small built, but vicious little boys who looked for all the world like demented, freckled, leprechauns. One day there was an exceptionally large crowd in attendance of the spectacle, there were probably 30 kids involved, including around 10 girls. After I had wet my pants for the amusement of this group, the twins got the idea of taking my pants off, since I was already restrained. This had never happened before.

Then, it wasn't enough for them that I was lying there, half naked, my wet pants bunched up around my shoes. They decided to pull down my underwear too, exposing my privates to everyone who was there. Fueled by the hoots and hollers and cheers of the crowd the twins kept going. They decided to get sticks and began to poke and prod and knock my privates back and forth for a bit. They continued

216

doing this for a while, encouraged by the squeals of the spectators, many of whom were covering their eyes at this point, realizing they were watching something that wasn't good.

I had become kind of numb by this time. I couldn't cry or yell or scream any longer, and it wouldn't do any good anyway. I had two or three older kids holding down each of my limbs, there wasn't anything I could do. The bell rang, signaling the end of lunch time. All the kids just got up and ran off toward the school. They left me laying there naked in the middle of the field. Eventually I got up and went into class late with my soiled jeans and dirt and grass all over me. As usual, the teacher instructed me to go to the office and call my mother. I did, and she brought me dry clothes.

Later on that evening my mother received a phone call. Apparently, one of the kids who had a conscience told their mother what they had witnessed in the school yard that day. Their mother then called my mom. When I was asked about it, I finally erupted in a tearful confession, there wasn't any more reason to be quiet, the awful secret was out in the open now. Understandably, my parents were enraged. The following day my mother tore the school down, figuratively speaking, and an end was put to these lunch time shenanigans.

It sounds awful and indeed, it was. I didn't suffer any long-term effects however, I didn't become a victim. It's just another in the long stream of happenings that have shaped me into who I am. In later years, I became an advocate and protector of the underdog. There are few things in life that enrage me, but one of these things is the mistreatment and abuse of the small and weak. By the time I was a senior in high school I had a virtual flock of downtrodden underclassmen that looked to me for protection. No one would mess with them if they mentioned my name. Had I not endured my own personal torture, perhaps there would have been no one for them to turn to.

So it all works out, everything does. Things happen for reasons and there is some good that can come out of every bad situation. It all goes back to the formula for life; life is 10% what happens to you, and 90% what we do about it. Its up to us to squeeze every drop of good out of every situation, and then use that to make ourselves better.

Here's the deal though; it's almost impossible to make anything better or discover an advantage when you are being a victim. When you are a victim, things are happening to you, you have no control, and no hope. Even long after the situation ends, you will continue to be a victim if you focus on your victimization. Remember, the things we focus on expand so if you are focused on being a victim, that is what you will remain. It isn't until we break out of that victim mentality that we can finally move forward.

Become someone who is prepared to squeeze the good out of every situation. That's how you will be able to help yourself, and also help others who might be going through their own bit of hell. We are the sum total of all our experiences, and it's up to each of us individually to figure out how to use them, to become a better man.

CHAPTER FORTY-FOUR
The Herigstad Ostrich Ranch

T.H.O.R.

My family were always farmers, people of the land. When they immigrated to America from Norway around the turn of the century, they settled around Glendive, Montana and started a cattle ranch. It was called the Herigstad Red Angus Ranch.

Decades went by, eventually my father was born. My dad's family moved around a lot but they always had some connection with farming and agriculture.

When my dad started his own family, we eventually settled on our own little farm in 1969, for a 7 year old boy like myself, it was a paradise. We had cows, chickens, pigs and a big garden with about a quarter acre of potatoes. My mother would can vegetables that would last us through the winter and we had several fruit trees as well; apples, pears and plumbs— we even had grapes.

In keeping with my families tradition, after I got out of the Army in 1985 I had my own animals. I raised pigs and chickens, with some turkeys and rabbits.

Then one day around 1993 I got a big idea. I pitched this idea to my dad, I wanted him to be my partner because I trusted him as a man, and I trusted his knowledge and common sense. My idea was to start an ostrich farm. At the time ostrich were a pretty big deal. You could produce more meat, on less land, in less time than you could with cattle. And the meat was delicious, lean and red— kind of like deer without the gaminess. I made a persuasive argument and he agreed. The Herigstad Ostrich Ranch was born, the Acronym was 'T.H.O.R.', which I found interesting, being Norwegian and all.

It was a tough start. We started with three huge eggs that we paid a fortune for. We had to buy lots of specialized equipment as well like incubators and dehumidifiers. I had to build new barns and fences specifically designed for these prehistoric birds. Of those original three eggs, only one hatched, but it hatched with problems and ultimately didn't survive. So then we went ahead and bought some young animals; they would become our breeding stock. Time went on, and we were learning as we went. I had learned everything about these flightless giants that I could, and finally our first eggs started hatching. Everything was going pretty well and it was fun having these unusual beast on our property, and it was rewarding, working on it with my dad.

The male ostrich can weigh 400 pounds, and they are not friendly at all. During the breeding season they had one job, and that was to kill anything that entered their enclosure, including us. We had to gather the eggs daily in order to incubate them, because our climate was too humid for them to hatch properly. Being from Africa they had evolved in a much dryer climate. My dad would give them food at one end of their 125' long pen. When they were distracted, I would open the gate and dash in to get the egg at the other end, hopefully before the male spotted me and got to me first. They can see almost 360 degrees, and they can hit 35 miles per hour in three strides, topping out at 45 mph. So it was always a close call, every time. As soon as I would open the gate his head would come up. He would wheel around and start sprinting toward the egg. Meanwhile, I had to ignore the fact that he was coming and concentrate on the egg. I had to get to it, pick it up and escape back through the gate before he got to me without dropping the egg, which I might add, weighed about three pounds. Every time I closed the gate behind me he was right there, hissing and ramming the fence and kicking. He never did get me though.

As time went on we made a lot of mistakes, but we learned from them and kept improving every aspect of the operation. We became efficient at slaughtering and processing. We found a market for the hides and we sold egg shells and feathers, too. My dad had a booth at the local farmers market and we also sold meat directly to several local restaurants. Schools would take field trips, bringing kids to our farm to see the living dinosaurs.

The ostrich were unlike any animal we had ever dealt with before. You never really got to know them individually. They were still technically wild, rather than domestic. Their brains are smaller than their eyeballs, so they aren't very smart. Everything they did, they did by instinct. There was no reasoning, no thought, and no true emotion, Everything they did was a reaction to something else. They made a cow or sheep look pretty intelligent by comparison. This was illustrated to me in a dramatic way one day.

We had a young male, who weighed about 300 pounds in one pen. Apparently he saw something in the adjoining pen he wanted to peck at. There was a gate there, and where the gate was hinged it created a gap between the gate frame and the post. He put his head below the gate and raised it up so that his long neck was in the gap and he could reach whatever it was he saw. The problem came when he tried to leave. He backed up, but his head, which is larger than his neck, would not fit through the gap. All he had to do was lower his head and neck out of the gap and go on about his business but, being an ostrich, he was just stuck instead.

When I arrived it took a minute to figure out what had happened. What I saw was an ostrich head on one side of the gate. Then a very large puddle of blood. A few feet from that, lay his headless body. When he thought he was stuck, he panicked, and began pulling and pulling, until he actually pulled off his own head. It impressed me on one level, because I don't know of any other animal that would be capable of doing that. On another level it really drove home the fact that we were dealing with an animal who was very basic, intellectually. I never looked at them the same way after that.

Our ostrich farming spanned a length of around 14 years, and during that time I learned many, many lessons. So many I hardly know where to start. One lesson that always sticks with me when I think about the ostrich is that the whole thing, all the adventures we had, all of the crazy times and all the hours my dad and I spent together because of it, all started with an idea. It was just a notion in my head, an electrical impulse in my brain, it had no mass or form. From that, because of translating that idea into words and then actions, it became something solid and real in the world.

How many ideas do we have in the course of a lifetime? How many of those ideas do we never act on? We just let them float away because of fear or apprehension, or something else. I think the lesson of this story is for all of us to pay attention to our ideas. Every great thing that ever happened on earth started with someone having an idea. The lesson of this story is to *take action*. Even if your idea doesn't pan out, it could lead to other ideas and teach you things you would not have known otherwise. One idea can change a life, and provide you with memories you will treasure until you die.

Begin to regard all of your ideas as something valuable. Don't let them just float away without consideration, and don't let fear of any kind prevent you from acting on them. Taking action is an important step down the path of being a better man.

CHAPTER FORTY-FIVE
Cheating Death

Back in the early 1990's I had been a long haul truck driver for a few months. I started out as a driver for a company and was issued a brand new Peterbuilt truck with all the bells and whistles. My regular run was from Washington State down I-5 all the way to southern California, and then back again, around a 2,400 mile round trip. It was a pretty good run, I got to know all the stops and where all the best burgers were and I was feeling pretty comfortable with what I was doing.

A few months into it I got an opportunity to buy my own truck from my uncle, who was also a truck driver. I jumped at the chance because then I would essentially be my own man, running my own business, and I would be more in charge of my life. The thing was, the truck I was buying was not brand new. In fact it had several hundred thousand miles on it. It was a Freightliner cabover truck. A big blue, flat-nosed truck with zero bells and whistles. Beyond a heater and a radio that worked sometimes, it had nothing; no air conditioning, a lumpy mattress, and no Jacobs brake. The truck was basically a tool I could sleep in, nothing more but, it was mine, and I felt like it was a start.

Nowadays most all trucks come equipped with a Jacobs Brake, commonly known as a 'Jake Brake', but not back then. The Jake Brake is a pretty handy thing. Without getting too technical, it is a method of braking using only the engine itself. What it does is use the compression of one engine cylinder, against the upstroke of another, forcing the engine to run slower. It is a compression brake. You have probably heard them on the road, sometimes they are loud. They sound like, "g-g-g-g-g-g-g" like a big growl. Coming into cities you will see signs that say, "Use of compression brakes prohibited," because they can rattle widows on houses. The Jake Brake would be used mostly when you are traveling down a mountain. When a semi trucks brakes get too hot from use, they will stop working all together, and many truckers have died losing their brakes going down a mountain. Maybe you have seen a big truck coming down a mountain with smoke coming off all of their wheels? That means their brakes are too hot. The Jake Brake allows you to go down slower without relying on your foot brake, so the chance of your brakes getting hot and failing are much lower.

On the Northern border of Oregon and California there is a mountain pass you have to go over; the Siskiyou Pass. As far as mountain passes go it isn't the most treacherous, but it does present it's own challenges. In the brnd new truck I started out driving, the one with the Jake Brake, I could go over that pass headed South in 7th gear, use my Jake and coast down no problem fully loaded.

On the very first run in that old truck I bought from my uncle I had forgotten that I didn't have a Jake Brake. When I got to the top of Siskiyou I started grabbing gears and got up into 7th like I normally did, and then I started going down. Pretty quickly I realized my mistake, because my truck was picking up speed and there was no Jake Brake to slow me down. I needed to downshift, I needed to get in a lower gear and quick. The problem was, I had already built up a lot of momentum. I was able to slow down some with the foot brake, but I was afraid of trying to down shift, because once I put the transmission in neutral I would be at great risk. If I was unable to slow my road speed enough to grab a lower gear then I would be flying down the mountain in neutral without anything to slow me down, I would be free-wheeling, a runaway truck. They would have to pick me up with a stick and a spoon.

So, I decided I would have to stay in the gear I was in and hope for the best. The southbound side of Siskiyou is not as bad as the Northbound side. There is one steep stretch that goes for a couple miles at a 6% grade, and there are a few curves. I felt like I had a 50/50 chance of making it down the hill without wrecking. I was trying to only use my foot brake when the engines rpm's read critically high. I was trying to save my brakes as much as possible because I knew I would need them more a little later on. Being in 7th gear though, I was just going way too fast most of the time.

My brakes started smoking pretty quickly. I could smell that very unique smell that only burning brake pads make. I had to really stomp on them hard to make it through a couple curves and I wasn't even at the steep part yet. My heart was pounding, I was sweating bullets, I was probably holding my breath as well. With every moment that passed I became more certain that I might not make it out of this in one piece. When I hit the steep part I had no choice but to get on my brakes hard. By this time I was leaving a black contrail of brake smoke behind me as I wound down the mountain.

My brakes started to fail. I knew this because it required more and more pressure for them to work. Before long I had both feet on the brake pedal and my butt was up off the seat. I was literally standing on the brake with all 260 pounds, trying to apply as much pressure as I could. I had one more big curve to get through, and if I wasn't going slow enough, instead of the truck just leaning like it had done on the previous curves, I would plunge right over the edge into the abyss.

As I hit that last curve I really thought I was going to die. My butt was still off the seat and my heart was about to explode. I took the inside lane so that I would have some room to maneuver and it turned out I needed all of it. I felt the whole truck start to lean like it was going to tip over and then I could give it just enough road to correct it, then again, and again, until I was almost on the far shoulder, out of room.

Somehow, through some miracle, it had been just enough. If the curve had gone on much longer I would not have made it. The road straightened out. Then the grade became less steep. I was able to lower myself back onto the seat and eventually take my foot off the brake all together. Not that it mattered, they had failed completely at this point.

Now I was in gentle curves and rolling hills that didn't require any braking. There was an agricultural check point where I would have to stop up ahead a few miles. I was hoping the brakes would cool enough so I would be able to stop when I got there. Using down shifting as much as possible, I was able to come to a stop at the check point. As I stopped I looked in my mirrors and saw actual flames coming off my trailer brakes. The tires were not on fire yet thankfully, but the heat had ignited all the other grease and oil around the wheels.

I told the check point attendant I wasn't transporting any produce, then I calmly got out of the truck. Got my fire extinguisher from under the seat and walked around my truck putting out fires as though it was something I did every day. The attendant just watched me with a strange look on his face, not saying anything. Then I got back in the truck, waved goodbye to the attendant and I was on my way. The next few miles were surreal. I had come very close to having a major wreck. I thought my death was imminent and now, I was just driving along as though nothing had happened. Something seemed out of place, wrong, like I had missed something, and then it came. Back up on the mountain I didn't have time to really feel anything. I didn't have time to be afraid, I only had time to react in the moment and focus every shred of myself into the task at hand, which was staying alive. Now it was as if those feelings I hadn't had time to feel up on the mountain were catching up with me. They came up through the back of the truck and swept into the cab with a tremendous force. They would not be denied. Suddenly I was shaking involuntarily, trembling from the latent emotions of almost dying. I was shaking so bad that I had to pull the truck off the road and just sit there.

So I sat there for a while and experienced all the thoughts and feelings you might expect someone to feel and think after they had cheated death. I thought of my kids mostly, who were still small at the time. I thought about all the things I had meant to say, and never said. About all the things I had meant to do...and never did. After I finished dealing with all these things, I got back on the road.

This experience changed me. I've had several other close calls in life, many of which I will tell in other stories, and they all changed me, each in their own way. There are certain things a person can learn about themselves only when they are faced with their own mortality. I believe all these things ultimately made me a better man, but while I am thankful for the positive changes, I would not want to repeat any of them. I'm not suggesting someone should go out to tempt death in order to find enlightenment. I am however, suggesting that we make time occasionally to consider our mortality in very real, present terms. We will all die one day. My advice is to not wait until you are on the brink of death to think of all the things unsaid or undone. Make time to think of them regularly now, while they can still have an impact on the life you are living.

A lot of people manage to cheat death from time to time, but in the end, death will always win. So make the most of your time right now.

CHAPTER FORTY-SIX
The Unforgettable Beer

In the summer of my 15th year I was always on the lookout for ways to make money. Most of these methods including doing odd jobs at other people's places; mowing lawns, weeding gardens, splitting firewood and stuff like that.   Out in the rural farming community I lived in, there was also another way. Helping farmers bring in their hay. I could always count on hay season to make some extra cash.

For those unfamiliar with how it works, the farmers would cut their hay and after it was raked into big rows another machine would drive over it and it would turn the cut hay into square bales that could be easily stacked in a barn. The bales would be scattered randomly all over the fields, so it had to be gathered up, brought into the barn, and stacked.

It was hard work. It almost always happened during hot weather. The bales ranged in weight from 50 pounds to 125 pounds, depending on the farmer who made them. I had been working in the hay field since I was about 13. I was strong for my age, and I had developed the right leverage that allowed me to throw the bales up over my head, which made me valuable when we were stacking. I had worked for several different farmers in the area.   Some paid better than others, but the farmers wives would always prepare a wonderful lunch that rivaled a Thanksgiving dinner, and after all the hay was in, everyone would sit down to eat. That was the ritual.

A friend who was a bit older than me told me about a farmer I had never worked for, who needed help with his hay. I didn't drive yet, so I rode with my friend out to the farm of Ernie Morgan.

Ernie Morgan was a very unique man. He was a big man, tall and strong, his skin looked like wrinkled leather from all his years in the sun. He was friendly, but gruff and blunt, very to the point. He didn't mince words at all and I appreciated that, because you always knew exactly where you stood with Ernie. Another remarkable thing about him was that he was 70 years old. I knew this because he was proud of the fact. He liked telling people how old he was and then watch them marvel at his healthy, youthful demeanor. While we were waiting for others to arrive he showed us around his farm. It was a well kept place. He took us into a barn where he presented his pride and joy; a 1956 Thunderbird convertible in mint condition. It had less than 10,000 miles on it. It was beautiful and it looked brand new for a car that was already 21 years old. He said he only drove it to weddings and funerals.

When the other hired hands arrived we got ready to start working. That's when I discovered that Ernie had the biggest, heaviest bales in the county. We were bringing in oat hay, and the bales weighed 125 pounds, more than half of my weight at the time. We started work by 8:00 am when it was still relatively cool, but by noon it was already approaching 90 degrees, it was gonna be a hot one. I was covered in sweat, and all the blowing hay chaff was sticking to me. Grass seeds and itchy little bits of hay were clinging to every part of me, under my shirt and even under my pants, along with all the dust and dirt.

The bales became heavier and heavier as the day went on. We were stacking them on a flat bed trailer 12 feet high. After a while, instead of throwing the bales, we were rolling them because we were getting too tired to lift them any more. The entire time this 70 year old man was working right along beside us. He inspired everyone to keep working hard and doing their best, because if he could do it, certainly we could. Occasionally Ernie's wife would drive the pickup out into the field for a water break. We would find some shade and renew our strength with the water, made extra special by a slice of lemon in the glass.

On one load we had stacked the trailer very high, too high actually, and we were heading to the barn with it. It was an unstable load and we became concerned that it would fall and we would have to re-stack it. I got a bright idea and volunteered to go up on top of the stack, lay on it spread eagle while hooking my fingers into the twine of the bales and try to keep it together with my body, like a human load strap. It turned out to be a stupid idea, a wheel ran over a tree root and the whole thing started falling apart, which threatened to tear me in half. I was falling through the air with all the bales of hay but miraculously I landed in a sitting position on a bale and none of the others fell on me. So we just re-stacked the trailer and kept going.

The sun was still in the sky when we finished, but the air had taken on a pleasant coolness. We all went to the house and washed up in preparation for the grand meal. Without a doubt, it had been the hardest day of work I had ever endured up to that point. Ernie's wife had prepared several long tables outside, complete with table cloths and napkins. We all sat down to eat together. Ernie was in a very good mood, no doubt happy that all of his hay was in and the job was complete. I was the youngest person there, at 15. Most of the workers were grown men, but I had definitely earned my keep for the day. Ernie started passing out ice cold beers to all the men, and then he did something I will never forget. He came over to where I was sitting, and put one of these ice cold beers down in front of me.

I looked up at him quizzically. Being under age no adult had ever offered me a beer. The only beers I ever drank were ones that my friends and I would occasionally sneak. I thought Ernie might be testing me. I said, "Ernie, I'm only 15." Ernie looked at me for a minute, grinning. Then he laughed and waved his hand dismissively in the air and said, "You could have fooled me, on my place if you work like a man, you get treated like a man. That's my rules, and you earned every drop of that beer today, son."

It was only the one beer, but it meant so much to me. It was the first time in my life I had been regarded as a man, as an equal among other men, and I loved the way it felt. I went on to work for Ernie on several other occasions before I left home. But I'll always remember that first time, when I was 15, the day I was treated like a man.

That's the end of the story, I learned a lot of things from this experience, and from Ernie. One great thing I learned is how important it is to be an example for younger people. I have gone through my life looking for ways to pay it forward, to provide the same gift Ernie gave me to some other young boy who deserves it. I have found a few of those occasions and it always feels great.

Ernie wasn't my dad, or a relative. He was just a farmer I met and worked for, but in the brief time I spent with him he was an exemplary example for me of what manhood is. The way he worked, the way he lived, his vitality and zest for life, and the way he found joy in simple things. Ernie was an example when I was watching. And that's why I always say how important it is that we all be examples of manhood everywhere we go, because we never know who is watching us.

Now when you head out into the world, be that example of manhood for whoever happens to be watching you.

CHAPTER FORTY-SEVEN
What Matters Most

I tell this story with some reservation, because it doesn't cast me in the best light. Keep in mind as you read, that I was only 22. That is not an excuse, just a fact.

At this time I was a soldier in the Army. I was stationed in Germany and I had managed to secure passage for my wife and children to come and live with me. I had to 'live on the economy' as the Army states it, which is to say that I was not an NCO, or non-commissioned officer yet, so I was not authorized base housing. I had to find a place to rent, and I did. I had to extend my tour in Germany to three years instead of one, and I did, because I knew I would not survive without being in the proximity of my children.

The place I found to rent was on the 5th floor of an apartment type building. It wasn't too bad, until you had to haul groceries up all those flights of stairs. There was a meat shop on one corner and a bakery on another, all within walking distance, so we were doing OK. The year was 1984. At this time in life I was living with my first wife, my step daughter who was about three, and my son who was just under two years old. My youngest daughter was in the oven, almost ready to be born. The apartment we lived in probably dated back to the Second World War. Like I said, we were on the fifth floor, but they had these huge window's that opened like a giant door. The window was at least four feet tall and six feet wide. It hinged on one side and the whole thing opened up toward the street.

Germans liked this style of windows because they could hang all their bedding out on the window sill and let it get aired out. The window sill was about 12 inches wide, like a small table. I thought it was cool because it was like opening a portal up to the sky. I would often sit and feel the air, and watch the pigeons fly around. I loved these big windows.

One day, my wife and I were home with our daughter and my two year old son, Clinton. He was just a toddler, you know, little kids that can walk, but they walk like they are drunk. They stagger back and forth and fall down on their butts a lot.

I'm not sure where it went wrong, I don't remember. Bottom line is that whoever was supposed to be watching the toddler had failed. I walked into the living room and my heart almost stopped beating, because my little son had climbed up onto the sill of the huge 5th story open window. He was standing there on that 12 inch wide sill…wavering back and forth like a drunk sailor. His little toes were actually hanging over the outer edge of the sill, and there was nothing between him and the pavement below except five stories of air.

I was frozen at first. He was pointing and gesturing at the pigeons flying just out of his reach. It was a big room, maybe 20 feet across. I knew that one slight misstep by either of us, would mean his death. My instinct was to yell, but I was afraid to make any sounds. In my minds eye I imagined him wheeling around at the sound, and falling over backwards. So I started creeping towards him, as silently as I could. My eyes were riveted on him. I knew it was possible that at any minute he could launch himself off the window sill— his little body that he wasn't that used to operating yet. He was unstable, he was just a toddler. Sweat was pouring off me as I made my way toward him. In that moment I faced the most awful thing I could imagine happening. I was trying so hard not to make any sounds as I inched my way toward my son.

I decided, during that painful 20 foot trek across my living room that if he fell, I would dive out after him, knowing it would mean my own death, because I knew I would not be able to live without him, and I thought his young spirit would be comforted if I was there with him in death. So right or wrong, that's what I decided.

He was cooing, and laughing and pointing at the pigeons who fluttered just inches from his grasp. My heart was beating faster and harder than it ever had before. I was in the waking presence of my worst nightmare. Finally I arrived, I was right behind him, but he didn't know I was there. Now I was faced with a new challenge. How should I grab him? What if I miss, and accidentally push him off the ledge? Standing in my apartment next to my son, with nothing but air on the other side of him is the most afraid I have been in my whole life. I spread my arms wide, and I made a huge exaggerated grab, making certain that my arms were on the other side of him before I brought them in. I got him! I sucked him into my chest like a starving man might cling to a bit of food. He was complaining about the force of my grip but I kept holding on. Once I knew I had him and he was safe I started crying, and shaking, and I kept holding him.

I couldn't let go of him for 30 minutes or so. The whole time my mind was playing over and over again the awful possibility that had been averted. My wife eventually came in, unaware of the drama that had transpired, and wondering what my problem was. She went over and shut the window. Eventually, I was able to release him to toddle about the house as he always did.

That is the end of this story. It remains the most terrifying moment of my life. The moment when I almost watched my son plummet to his death. A death in which I would have shortly followed him. The lessons I learned from this are almost too profound to convey. It was in that moment that priorities were made real to me. It was in this experience that I gained a life long appreciation of the things that really matter. This is one reason I always say that relationships are the most valuable things we possess. My son is a man now. A good man, with children and a wife of his own. He is not just a man, but a friend and a kindred soul.

I believe this experience was integral later on when I was going through divorce and custody battles, and impoverished by child support for a time. Through it all, there was one overriding theme in my mind—it's all about them. It's not about me. Whatever is in the best interest of my children is what matters most. I believe that because of those priorities, I eventually got custody of my kids and was able to finish raising them.

So, this story is for everyone who has kids, but also for those of you who may have kids in the future, and every single one of you has a potential for that to happen. I hope this resonates with you, because it is so important. Kids are literally the future. I believe a man can be measured by the care he has for the weakest and most helpless around him. The children of today will be the men and women of tomorrow, as my son has now become. The influence we have on them in the interim is of profound significance.

Please remember the things that matter most. If there are children in your life, whether they are yours or someones else's, give them your time, your care, and your love because—it matters. It matters the most.

CHAPTER FORTY-EIGHT
The Secret Project

I was a hungry kid. Not because my parents didn't take good care of me, they did. It was just that I seemed to have been born with an unnatural appetite, and a metabolism to go along with it. So, as a result, I was always hungry. It started when I was a baby. My mother has told stories about having to feed me every 20 minutes around the clock for the first four years of my life. I don't know if she was exaggerating or not.

My unusual eating habits followed me all through childhood, through adolescence and into adulthood. Everyone in my family has a story about me eating. At a neighbors BBQ one summer I ate an estimated 22 chickens in a 5 hour period. We would go to all-you-can-eat places and I would just continue eating long after my family was done...it was a little embarrassing for them. As an adult I once ate 6 big macs on the way to work.

I simply could not get full, and luckily my body seemed efficient in making use of all these calories because I was not over weight. Fortunately for my parents we lived on a farm and raised the majority of our own food, otherwise we would have been in poverty. Our freezer was always full of meat and my mom had a big garden, and she would can produce to eat during the winter. I could often be found in the garden eating corn right off the stalk or filling my pockets with carrots I had just dug up. We also had around 15 fruit trees that kept me going.

As a small boy I often wore bib overalls. I liked them because they had a lot of pockets, and I would fill every pocket with some kind of food from the house or the garden or the fruit trees, and I would just continuously be eating. When all the pockets were empty, I would re-load. My mother had started hiding food out of necessity. I would eat all the cereal in one sitting— snacks and other goodies didn't stand a chance! If I found them I would eat them, so Mom started hiding things that she wanted to last.

I was good at finding things though, it became kind of a game for me. There were only so many places to hide stuff in the house. There was a little space between the kitchen cupboards and the ceiling. It was just big enough for my nine year old body to slip into. One day I was crawling along in this space looking for food when I came across something on a cookie sheet, wrapped in tin foil. I knew it had to be food.

Some food was strictly off limits, and I knew it. My mom made extra money baking cakes for people because she had a great imagination and was a really good cake decorator. I knew if this was one of these cakes that I would not be able to eat it, but I might be able to have a small piece.

As I was peeling up the corner of the tinfoil to see what was under it my mother walked into the kitchen. She shrieked, and then collapsed into a chair and started crying hysterically. That was not the response I had anticipated. Normally she would have snatched me down, swatted my butt and sent me outside. She was really quite upset, and I became worried. I scrambled down off the cupboard and went to her, asking what was wrong. Through her tears she was saying that I saw it, that she was a terrible mother, and other things like that, things that didn't make any sense to me.

I tried to assure her that I hadn't seen anything, and that she was a good mom, but she was inconsolable. Eventually I was able to piece together why she was so upset. She felt embarrassed about the cake, she thought I had seen it. When she realized I hadn't really seen it yet she felt a little better, but she knew that she would have to tell me about it now anyway, because she knew my curiosity would not be satisfied otherwise.

She got the cake down, but before she unwrapped it, she tried to explain. There was a young woman that was getting married, and her friends were throwing her a bachelorette party. As kind of a joke they had ordered a cake shaped like a man's 'parts'. It was a penis cake. And that is why she was so embarrassed for me to find it.

This was around 1971, and women of my mom's generation were very modest. She had never even owned a two piece bathing suit. Sex was still a taboo in many circles, and that was the case for my mother. She was relieved that I was not horrified. I actually thought it was kind of funny, and...a little bit gross. She unwrapped the cake. She had not gotten very far, it was still just cake. A long part with two round parts at the other end.

Then she confessed to me that she didn't know how to decorate it. Even though she birthed three children she acted as though she didn't know where to begin. Then her eyes lit up as she had an idea. She said since I already knew about it, that maybe I could help her. I was always eager to take on a new creative adventure. I decided that I would help my mom make the best penis cake there ever was. She very seriously instructed me that I wasn't to speak of this cake with anyone else, it was too embarrassing and she didn't think other people would understand. This was between me and her...I agreed to her request.

I went into action. I told her we needed flesh colored frosting, blue frosting, red frosting, and some purple frosting...I also said we needed some shredded coconut. She was confused by the red and blue frosting. I told her to trust me. She didn't realize that these would eventually become veins. The shredded coconut, died brown with chocolate would become hair, one guess what the purple was for.

Mom made the frostings I requested and then stood back and let me work. I transformed this delightful desert into a graphic display of epic proportions. Probably more graphic than the customer expected. The final product was— obscene, even to me, but there was a deadline and there was no time to start over. My mom delivered the cake and she said they were thrilled with it, it exceeded all their expectations.

It was fun to work on a secret project with my mom. I felt like I was of some real value to her, and it felt good. I perceived that I had been elevated in her eyes somewhat, because we had acted as colleagues— she noticed my competence. Afterward we agreed to never speak of the penis cake again, and we didn't...until after I was grown of course. She would still get embarrassed any time it was brought up. I had a lot of fun re-telling the story at family gatherings and watching my mom get all flustered, but she enjoyed the story, and the laughter, too.

The whole experience served to deepen the bond between my mom and I, but the primary lesson I came away with was about cooperation. Even though I was a kid, I got to experience cooperation for the first time. My voice was heard and acknowledged, my opinions were valued, and we worked together to create something.

The fact that what we created was a penis cake is just kind of funny. It could have been anything though, it set the stage for a lifetime of projects that I worked on with my mom; costumes, school projects, science projects, and even landscaping our yard. She was a good partner, and I miss her a lot. The things she did for me and with me continue to bless my life in many ways. One of those things was learning how to cooperate, to work together with someone else.

The other lesson here is that everything we share with other people matters. My mom probably didn't realize at the time that she was giving me the skill of cooperation, a skill I would use later in life. So it pays to remember, especially with children—that everything we do, matters.

CHAPTER FORTY-NINE
Dead Weight

It was around 1982; I was about 20 years old and I was in the Army, serving in Germany.

I was stationed in a town called Aschaffenburg, which was about 45 minutes south of Frankfurt. I had befriended a group of guys, there were 6 of us that had become friends, and we were tight. At this point I had not been able to bring my family over yet, so I was still living in the barracks. This group of friends was really important to me at the time. Whenever we were not working, we would hang out together and do things.

Having these friends made it easier to be away from home, and lighten feeling separated from our families in a foreign land. Sometimes we would just stay in our rooms and play cards. Other times we might hit a few bars together, on weekends we would often travel as a group to attend German rodeos. (Yes, they had rodeos in Germany!)

We were from all different parts of the country, but we were like minded, and that is what brought us together. The two main friends in this group were a couple guys named Robert Stiles, and Roger Cornelius. They were both from Tennessee, one of them was from a place called Copper Hill, if my memory serves me.

We had some really great times together. I remember sometimes right before payday we would all be out of money. There was this German place where you could buy a gallon of wine for a handful of change. The wine was made locally, and there weren't any words on the label, just a picture of strawberries.

So we would pool all of our change together and buy as many gallons as we could, then we would sit out in the middle of this big field and drink wine, and tell each other stories of our lives back home. We would talk about our families and the girls we knew. We would sing songs that we all knew the words to, and we would laugh and laugh. I have great memories of this youthful time.

One night we decided that we should all go to Frankfurt together, to the Topper Club, because we had never been there. The Topper Club was a military establishment in the town of Frankfurt. It was called an NCO club, but lower enlisted guys like us could go there, too.

None of us had cars, so we took a combination of trains, busses and cabs, until we finally wound up in Frankfurt. We had to walk the last few blocks, past the infamous red light district of Frankfurt, to reach the club.

At this point in my life I only listened to country music, as did my buddies. That's one of the things that brought us together; we all considered ourselves cowboys. We all had cowboy hats and cowboy boots, and we all came from rural areas and were used to working hard. We had similar values, we respected honesty and hard work. We came to the Topper Club on this night specifically because they were featuring a country music band.

The night started off great. We were having a blast listening to country music and drinking German beer. We were dancing a little, too. We were all having so much fun that it was easy to lose track of how many beers we had. We were all getting fairly lubricated, but I know that I in particular was starting to get a little sloshy.

That is when the girl in the blue dress showed up. I was married at the time and had no intention of fooling around...but that didn't stop me from admiring the absolute beauty of this woman. It was like she walked right out of a fairytale book. Her dress was sky blue, and high class, like a formal dress you would expect to see at some fancy ball. She was brunette, with flawless skin and an enchanting smile that had every guy in the place paying attention. I decided to dance with this woman, because I knew if I didn't that I would regret it. I asked her to dance, and she said, "Yes!"

Dancing to country music doesn't work out with everyone. There are different styles and ways of doing things, and sometimes dancing with strangers can be awkward because you are trying to move in different directions. For some reason this woman and I were able to dance together like we had been doing it all our lives. It was amazing. We danced several songs together, neither of us wanting to stop. We just waited on the floor for the next song so we could continue.

That, unfortunately, is one of my last memories of the night.

It was someone's birthday, and the next thing I knew I was being beckoned over to our table where three huge serving platters waited. Each platter was covered in tequila shots— it seemed like an infinite amount. So, we started toasting and making speeches. After each person said something then we would all have a shot of tequila. That is my very last memory of the evening.

The next day I woke up back in Aschaffenburg, back in the barracks, in my own bed. When my eyes opened I was very confused. I had a splitting headache, but the confusion came from the odd awareness that I didn't have any memory of traveling back home. I had no idea how I ever made it back to my bed. Then I tried to move; that's when the pain started. Every square inch of my body was screaming in pain. I realized that my headache wasn't just on the inside of my head, it was also on the outside. I was black and blue on every part of me!

I got kind of scared because I had obviously suffered some kind of severe trauma, and I had no memory of it. Along with very tender bruises there were also cuts and scraps. The back of my head felt like it had been hit with a baseball bat, several times. Had I been jumped and beat up? Was I in a car wreck or train wreck? Maybe I was hit by a car as I was walking home? I needed answers, but moving in any way was difficult so I called out into the hallway for my friend, Roger.

He was just a couple rooms away and he heard me. He came into the room grinning from ear to ear. He walked around, inspecting me, shaking his head in mock disapproval. I asked him what had happened to me. He acted like he didn't hear the question at first but he finally answered, "What happened to you is: I saved your life, that's what."

Then he went on to tell me the whole story. After the tequila, everything had gotten a little crazy. Most of the guys went off to a different place. They had met another soldier who had his own car, and not everyone would fit in it. I was completely out of it, and Roger got stuck with me. I weighed about 220 lbs at this time, and Roger was only around 150. As long as I was walking under my own power he could handle it, but if I lost the power of mobility then he would have a real challenge on his hands.

That is exactly what happened, I walked out of the Topper Club, but at the first bus stop I fell asleep and didn't wake up again. Roger told me how he had to roll my dead weight in and out of cabs. How he had to drag me by my feet into busses and off trains. That explained how the back of my head felt, from getting dragged down concrete stairways, my head bouncing off every step. He said I rolled down a hill at one point and he had to drag me back up out of the brush.

He told me I almost got cut in half by a train, because I was half on and half off when it started to move…he got me on all the way in the nick of time, before I hit something solid. As he was telling me this I started to get a little angry at the abuse I suffered at his hands, but I quickly realized that he probably had saved my life, and he had done the best he could.

I was obviously too heavy for him to carry, and there were some bad characters in the dark alleys of Frankfurt who would have enjoyed finding an unconscious young G.I. If he would have abandoned me, I may have never seen daylight again.

But, he didn't abandon me, it never crossed his mind, because we were friends. Getting me home must have been a horrible chore and he did it willingly, without being asked. It's just what you do for friends, and I'm sure I would have done the same thing for him.

Of course I thanked him at the time, but I have always wished I could see him again, after all these years, and thank him again. At the time I don't think I truly appreciated what he had done…not like I do now. Sadly, after we all left Germany I lost touch with them. I have tried many times, unsuccessfully to find them on the internet. Some people are just harder to find than others.

So Roger Cornelius, I am telling you thank you right now, in this book. Thanks for being a real friend. Maybe Roger, or someone who knows him, is reading this— and if you are, I hope you get ahold of me, I would like very much to thank you in person.

One thing this story taught me is that we should never take anyone for granted. I'm sure back in 1982 that it seemed like it would always be that way; that we would always be in touch and be a part of each others lives. We were 20 years old, living in the present, with no thought or care for the future. The next thing you know, that person is gone and you can't find them. This story also taught me to not drink tequila. I have stayed away from it all these years since.

This story serves as a reminder to all of us to not take anyone for granted. Cherish all the people and relationships in your life because they are the most valuable thing you possess.

CHAPTER FIFTY

Hard Times On The Big Road

By the time I was 30 I had done a lot of things.

I had been in the Army, I'd held a variety of other types of jobs, and I was a construction contractor with my own business for a few years. I decided one day that I should become a truck driver as well, there was a lot of money to be made in the transportation industry. So, I went to truck driving school and got my license. I got a job with a shipping company that went to California and back from Washington State three times a week. After a couple months of that I figured I had enough experience to get my own truck.

My uncle was a long time truck driver and he just happened to have an old truck he was willing to sell me. It was a Freight-liner cabover, with no AC, no power steering, and a radio that worked sometimes. Mechanically it seemed sound though.

How 'owner driver' worked: you would lease yourself and your truck to a freight company. They would find loads for you to haul and agree to pay you so much per mile, or a flat rate for the load. They would also provide insurance for the truck, but I was in charge of maintenance and I had to buy my own fuel. It wasn't a horrible deal, and it wasn't a great deal—but it was a way to get started, and you have to start somewhere.

One reason I decided to do this is because I thought it would be a great opportunity to take my kids on road trips around the country and spend a lot of time with them one on one. Had I leased myself to a reputable company it probably all would have worked out great.

Unfortunately it was back in 1991, when the transportation industry had a lot of shady characters.

When I was out on the road I depended on the leasing company to provide me access to money; this was before debit cards. There is a system called "com-checks". A company would have a com-check account with money in it for drivers. They could wire your pay to any truck stop in America, so that you could access it. They just had to give you a really long number over the phone. If it matched the number the truck stop had then they would issue you your money. Most of the time, it worked.

Summer came and school was out, so I got my nine year old son, Clinton, and told him we were going to have a big adventure. I put him in the truck and we took off, heading South.

We were having a great time! We went down into Oregon and on to California. I was dropping off loads and picking up new ones on the way and Clinton thought it was awesome.

We talked about all kinds of things from time travel to cartoons, to music. I told him stories and we sang songs together and even made up a couple new ones. Initially, the trip was going exactly how I had envisioned it. We came out of California and went into Utah. I was getting low on money, so I called the dispatch office and requested a com check. I had quite a lot of money owed to me for the runs I had just made.

My dispatchers name was Chris, kind of a smarmy young guy with a bad hairdo and a waistline of a much older man. I always thought he must have been related to the owner, and that's why he got this job. Chris told me some story about how the com-check system was temporarily down. He said to call him after I dropped my load and he would take care of it.

I said ok, because I didn't have much choice. I was delivering my load the following day. I still had a little money, it would be OK.

The next day I called Chris when I was empty again. I told him I needed money. He asked me how much fuel I had, and did I have enough to get to this other town to pick up a new load. I told him I did have enough fuel, but what did that have to do with me getting some money? He said they were still having trouble with the com-check system, and to give him a call back after I got loaded. I was starting to get irritated, but I didn't have too many other options.

Forging A Man

I went to another town and got loaded with some freight that was headed to Southern Idaho. I called Chris after I got loaded and he still couldn't get me any money. I delivered the load to Idaho. While I was there I used the last of my cash to buy Clinton and I dinner, get a shower and top off my fuel because Chris had promised me for sure that when I got back into Utah with my next load, that I would be paid.

The next day we got loaded and started out again for a town in Utah. It was hot, and since the truck didn't have air conditioning we spent a lot of time with the windows down, always talking loud above the noise of the highway. We were still having a great time together. I was trying to not let my irritation with my dispatcher affect my time with Clinton, who wasn't yet aware there was a problem.

After about 9 hours of driving I made it to the destination and got unloaded, then we went and parked at a nearby truck stop. I was eager to find a phone and get some money, ever since I had spent the last of my cash I had an uneasy feeling, because Clinton was with me, and he needed to eat. We both needed to eat. Our last meal had been dinner the day before, and we were both hungry and hot and tired.

I got Chris on the phone. I could tell by his voice that something was wrong. He told me he still could not get me any money. I told him that he had promised, and that I needed money right now, I had a nine year old boy with me and we needed to eat. I told him I have been watching other drivers get their com-checks without any problems. I demanded that he get me some money immediately. Finally, he confessed that they did't have any money in their com-check account. He said someone had made a mistake and it was just a matter of time before they got money back in the account. I said that I didn't have any time.

I told him that since he had promised me, that he should wire me some of his own money, since I was sure he had money and food to eat. He refused. Then he had the nerve to ask me to go pick up a load somewhere, I couldn't believe it. I was furious! I told him the truck wasn't moving again until I got paid, and I hung up the phone.

I am not a person that is quick to anger, unless I am extremely hot or extremely hungry, and right now, I was both. Not to mention the reality sinking in that Chris had been lying to me the whole time.

There was no problem with the com-check system, there was only a problem with the mis-management of their business.

Clinton was hungry, and he could see that I was unhappy. He asked me what was wrong. I tried to explain it to him in a way he could understand. I tried to make a game out of it, like we were adventurers who were stranded in the desert, and we had to survive on our wits for a couple days, and we had to be brave. That seemed to work, Clinton was an imaginative boy.

The next day I called the dispatch office once every hour. Every time I was told they didn't have money yet. They tried to give me this whole song about how they were waiting on another company to pay them, but I didn't believe anything they said at this point. As soon as I heard they had no money, I would hang up. We spent that day in the driver's lounge, watching TV and playing games. Whenever someone had food delivered to them, Clinton and I would just look at each other.

The following day it was pretty bad. Neither of us had eaten for over 24 hours. I wasn't so worried about myself, but I was becoming very worried for Clinton. I continued to call every hour, and I continued to hang up the phone when I was told they didn't have money. I was starting to get angry in a different, more dangerous way.

I still had $3.65. I had been saving it. I looked around on the floor of the truck and came up with 73 more cents, that made $4.38. I decided the time had come to use it, so Clinton and I went into the truck stop. I looked at the menu and determined that it was enough to get us both a large bowl of the daily soup, which was tomato. I figured if we did that, and then asked for as many crackers as they would bring us, that it would get us through the day.

When I ordered the waitress look confused. "That's it?" she asked. I confirmed that was our entire order. She looked at Clinton and then back at me. She asked where we were from, and a couple other questions. She was good at her job, apparently she had seen this situation before. Finally through clever conversation on her part, she had the whole story, she knew what we were going through.

When she came with our soup she didn't only bring lots of crackers, but two big giant sandwiches she had made herself, and a big smile. Clinton was normally kind of a picky eater, but not today.

He tore into that sandwich like his life depended on it, and it kind of did. I thanked the waitress profusely for her kindness. Clinton told her she saved our life. We were in much better spirits when we went to bed that night.

The next day I didn't start calling right away. I was kind of afraid to. Afraid of how angry I would become when I was told there still wasn't money. Finally, around noon I decided to call. I had Clinton wait at a table so he wouldn't hear my conversation. I got Chris on the phone. One more time he told me they didn't have money...and I lost it. I was screaming at him, letting him know exactly how I felt about the whole thing.

When I was done, in response he said probably the worst thing he could have said to me in that moment. He said, "Hey just go down to 'Balony Joe's' and wait in line for a sandwich." Then he laughed at his own horrible joke. Balony Joe's was another name for a homeless shelter. I didn't say anything for a few seconds. He finished laughing and was waiting for my response. In a very low, slow, quiet voice I said, "Chris, when I get back there you should know that the first thing I'm going to do is find you. Then I'm going to beat the hell out of you, and I'm going to keep going, until someone else makes me stop." Then I hung up.

The next day I found myself dealing with another dispatcher. He said Chris was at an appointment, but he would help me. Miraculously, they finally had money in their account and I got paid the money that I was due. I told this new dispatcher I wouldn't accept any load except one that took me back home. He agreed, and pretty soon we were heading north with full bellies, a pocket full of money, and a big score to settle.

I arrived at the yard in Portland, Oregon. I set my parking brake with a loud release of air and a cloud of dust that marked my arrival. I am not normally a violent man, but I was really looking forward to making Chris regret his "Balony Joe" comment. I had been fantasizing about it for a few hundred miles. Had I been alone on this trip I would not have taken it so personally, but he was messing with the welfare of my son, and making jokes about it. That crossed a line with me.

I marched into the office and went straight to Chris' desk. I was met by an empty chair. I asked loudly where Chris was, because I needed to talk with him. One of the receptionist meekly came over and informed me that Chris knew I was coming back, he had been a nervous wreck, and about 30 minutes earlier he had quit his job and walked out. Well crap, I thought, that was disappointing, but it was probably for the best, especially for Chris. I hoped he learned something from the experience. Then I went to the owners office and informed him I was tearing up my lease, I was no longer affiliated with them, and I would find other means of employ.

That is basically the end of the story. We went home, I found other outfits to work for, and to this day I have some precious memories of my son and I on our big trucking adventure. I learned a lot about myself in this story, and a lot about the world as well. I remembered how precious one on one time with a child can be, I found out what some of my boundaries were, and I also had to take responsibility for putting my son in that situation in the first place. Going without food for three days is unacceptable.

I considered that my fault. I trusted the welfare of my child to people I didn't know well enough. OK, lesson learned, that never happened again. We can't blame other people for the things that happen to our children—it's OUR job, no one else's, to make sure their safety cannot be jeopardized.

These were all tough lessons to learn, but ultimately they were the lessons I was supposed to learn, and they helped me become a better man. Wherever you are reading, and whoever you might be, I urge you to pay attention to what is happening in your life right now. Your story is currently unfolding before your eyes. We all have a choice; to learn the lessons life gives us—or to repeat them over and over until we do. When you DO learn them, you become a better man today, than you were yesterday.

CHAPTER FIFTY-ONE
The Ugly Years

This story is about one particular incident that took maybe 4 seconds to happen, but I dealt with the ramifications of it for years afterward.

I was 11 years old, in sixth grade. Before I continue I want everyone reading to think back to 6th grade. Remember your classroom, the other kids in your class, your teacher, try to remember the things that were important to you at this time in your life. Try to remember being in 6th grade.

Speaking for myself, I only had a very vague understanding of who or what I was at eleven years of age. We were still figuring out what we liked and didn't like, and trying to understand how we fit into the big picture of everything.

So anyway, there I am in my 6th grade class and I have to pee.

I get a hall pass from my teacher and I step out into the hallway. The hallway was completely empty because everyone was in class. The walls of the hallway were made completely out of metal lockers. Each kid was assigned a locker where he could keep his books and personal effects, this array of lockers on either side caused my footfalls in the empty hallway to resonate with a metallic echo.

About half way down the corridor I see another kid come out of the bathroom and start walking towards me, returning to his own classroom. I didn't know this kid, I had never seen him before. I remember he was a little smaller than me with unkempt, blond hair.

He wasn't looking at me as he walked, he was just plodding along back to his own classroom. Finally, when we were maybe 5 feet apart he glanced up at me, and stopped in his tracks— he almost seemed to recoil. Since he stopped, I stopped, and for a moment we were just standing there looking at one another. Then, he uttered the sentence that altered my life for many years to come. As he was looking at me he said; "Man...you are UGLY!"

Then, he just resumed walking past me toward his classroom as though nothing had happened. I was dumbfounded. He left me standing there by myself in the hallway and it was several moments before I moved or did anything. Prior to this moment in time I had never considered whether or not I was 'ugly'; I just figured I looked like a kid. So I stood there, processing what had happened.

It wasn't like this kid had anything to gain; there wasn't anyone around to hear him, except me. His shock and revulsion at my appearance seemed authentic. When he said that, he didn't seem to care if I heard him or not, as though he wasn't saying it to me, but rather just expressing what was on his mind in the moment. I couldn't understand what would compel someone to say something like that, if it wasn't true.

I finally made it to the bathroom, where I immediately went to the mirror hoping to relieve myself of the burden of ugliness this boy had just bestowed upon me. I looked in the mirror everyday, but this time I did so with brand new eyes. I was trying to see what this boy had seen. I studied myself, every little bit, and finally, I came to the horrifying realization that this boy had been exactly right— I was hideous. He had sold me 100% on the fact that I was perhaps the ugliest creature walking the earth. I couldn't understand why I hadn't realized it before. I could barely stand to look at myself after that.

When I went home it began a long, and I'm sure heartbreaking struggle for my parents. Not because they had an ugly son— but because they had a son who believed he was ugly. This ugliness I had acquired affected every area of my life. I could only relate freely with my closest friends, because they didn't care what I looked like. It made me painfully shy with girls and everyone else I didn't know. I felt like if I tried to interact with anyone that it wouldn't work because all they would be thinking about, was how ugly I was, and I didn't really blame them.

Just getting me to school became a chore for my mom. Imagine a child screaming and crying, begging not to go to school, because he was too ugly to go to school. That was me, almost every day. It hurt my parents on several levels, and it made them concerned for me, with just cause. It totally took them by surprise because one day I went to school a happy, healthy, well adjusted boy, and I returned home that same evening a hideous monster, with plummeting self esteem and a whole new set of neurotic behaviors.

I eventually got out of it. I emerged wiser and maybe even more emotionally stable than I would have been otherwise, but it took three years. I spent three years being the ugliest boy in my school, my town, the whole world.

Three years crying myself to sleep and wondering why I had been made this way, and avoiding situations where my ugliness would become a spectacle; which happened to be everywhere.

I didn't go to any therapy or counseling for my ugliness, but I still overcame it, and I did it on my own. I believe I got out of it through a combination of pure reason and logic. I'm not going into that right now, that may be fodder for another story. The important thing for this story is that I overcame it.

Sometimes I wonder what would have become of me, if I did not overcome it? How different would my life have been? Would I even still be alive today? All good questions that I'll never know the answer to, and it doesn't matter anyway, because I did recover from it.

What made me think about writing this story is seeing a friend's Facebook posting one day. He was talking about body image. He is currently in the act of losing weight, and he has lost a ton now, I'm happy to say. Even though he is doing awesome and has lost all this weight, he was feeling bad about himself, because he was comparing himself to other men who are on the heavy side. Pictures of other men really, in magazines and stuff— they are paid models, for crying out loud.

The only true, accurate, worthwhile comparison, is to compare one's self, to one's self. It doesn't make sense to compare ourselves to other people, because we aren't them. We are ourselves though, and that's why I started my podcast back in January 2016, and telling men to go look in the mirror and make an honest assessment of themselves.

If we compare ourselves to the men we were yesterday—**that** is an accurate, meaningful, worthwhile measurement. If you can accurately measure something, then it is easier to find a way to improve it.

Unfortunately for me when I was eleven…there wasn't any way to improve my ugly face, I was stuck with it. I ultimately realized by the time I was 14 that the only opinion that really mattered was my own, and I happened to like the person I was. My father's council was also instrumental in shaking off that ugliness.

So the lesson for today is to be careful about caring too much about what other people think. The only opinion about you that really matters is your own. Other people don't know what struggles you face, they don't know how your brain works, they can't appreciate how far you have come; and if they are superficial enough to make a character judgment based on something external, you probably don't want these people in your life anyway.

I'll tell you, when I stopped caring what other people thought and started caring more about what I thought of myself, it was so liberating! It was true freedom— the freedom to be exactly who I am. I've said it hundreds of times by now; 'being a better man' is about being committed to improvement in every area of your life. I believe in that, I advocate it. You cannot measure your improvement against anyone but you— the guy you were yesterday.

One way to shed all of this socially induced unhealthy anxiety, is to be content in the knowledge that you are always improving, always becoming a better man.

CHAPTER FIFTY-TWO
The Unwelcome Passenger

I was still pretty young, in my early 30's, and I was long haul trucking around the country. I had not gotten custody of my kids yet, and I was paying so much child support I couldn't afford rent anywhere, so, I was living in my truck as I worked, while I tried to figure everything out. It wasn't too bad, I had a comfortable bed in the truck, and all my other personal hygiene and nutritional needs were met at the many truck stops that dot the countries roadsides.

It was early in December, I had just made it back to the Western side of the country after spending a few grueling weeks hauling freight back East. I had been gone for over a month and I was on my way home, to spend Christmas with the family in Washington State.

As a rule, I never picked up hitch hikers. For one it was illegal because the truck's insurance didn't cover it, but also…it just wasn't too smart. You run into a lot of strange people out on the road and you never know who you might be picking up.

I was on the last leg of my journey and I was really looking forward to getting home when I pulled into a truck stop in Boise, Idaho. Now only about 535 miles separated me from my kids. I went in to get something to eat and I noticed an older woman standing by the front door talking with people who came and went. She looked like somebody's grandma — white curly hair, kind of a plump body, and she was wearing modest clothes that added to the 'Grannie' appearance. I thought it was kind of strange, she didn't look like a typical homeless person or 'lot lizard'. Maybe she was a stranded

257

motorist, looking for help?

I ate my dinner, and made a phone call home. I watched a little TV in the drivers lounge and then I got up to head out to my truck to continue my journey. As I left the truck stop, the old woman was still there. She asked me if I could help her, so I stopped and asked her what kind of problem she was having.

For the next five minutes she told me a horrible story of how she had been evicted from her home, and she was trying to get out West, where her family was going to care for her. She said she had not seen her kids in over five years, she had already come a long way, and she was almost there and she was shooting for Seattle. With tears in her eyes she asked me again if I could help her. She just needed a ride.

I could feel my rule about hitch hikers becoming weaker. Her story really plucked at my heart strings, she kind of reminded me of my own grandma. The sun had gone down and it was getting very cold outside, dipping down into the 20's. I explained to her that it was against the rules, that the company I drove for did not allow passengers. She nodded as if she had heard that before from someone else, and shivered a bit in the cold, as her eye's fell down to her feet.

I went back to my truck and started it up— but I just didn't feel right. I kept wondering what was going to happen to this old woman after I drove away. She was trying to get home to her family, just like I was. What kind of man was I, that I could leave this poor woman to the fates?

I got out of my truck and went back to her. I asked her if she had any luggage, but all she had was a very large purse. I told her I could take her to the outskirts of Seattle, then I had to turn south but she would be close enough for her family to come and get her.

She was gushing with thanks and gratitude as we walked back to my truck together. She climbed up in the passenger seat and got settled in, and we took off. I was feeling pretty good about myself, I was happy I had made the decision to help her out. As it turned out, that was a decision I was going to start regretting very quickly.

We weren't even 10 miles down the road when she lit up a cigarette. I don't smoke, and I didn't allow smoking in my truck — it's where I lived. I explained this to her and asked her to put it out.

She grumbled a bit, but did as I asked.

The conversation in the truck started to take on a whole different vibe. She started talking about crazy things, things that didn't make any sense at all...like a story a little kid will tell when they make it up on the spot, and none of the parts fit together.

Some of her stories were just outlandish and obviously, untrue. I started wondering how much of her original story was true. After a bit she said she was tired and asked if she could lay on my bed. I didn't like the idea of a stranger getting on my sheets...especially a stranger as strange as this. So I told her she could lay down, but she would have to stay on top of the blankets, not under them. She climbed back into the sleeper and I was grateful I wouldn't have to listen to her incoherent babbling anymore for a while.

It was fully dark now, both outside and inside the cab. I started smelling something funny. It almost smelled like something was burning. Wait, something **was** burning. I turned on the dome light and looked back into the sleeper to find my guest smoking under a blanket, as if that would conceal it! I don't raise my voice often, but I did then. I told her to put it out and let her know exactly how I felt about the whole thing. About her disrespecting my wishes when I was just trying to do her a favor.

I told her she would have to sit in the seat for the rest of the ride. She was very unhappy after that, and was even yelling back at me. She even called me a few names. I was very upset, and angry with myself for getting in this situation. Now I was driving around with a crazy old lady that thought she could do whatever she wanted.

She had become a liability. I realized also that being a woman, an unbalanced one, that she could easily take revenge on me by making false allegations at the next stop. I decided I would put her out at the next safe place to do so.

She tried smoking two more times. She tried to start a few wacky conversations, but I had stopped replying to her. We drove the next two or three hours in silence. The whole time I was trying to figure out the best place to unload her. We had traveled about 397 miles together when I pulled into a truck stop in Ellensburg, Washington. I parked and explained to her that this was the end of the line. Trying not to be a total jerk, after all— she was still an old lady (or so I thought), I told her I would buy her a meal and pay for a shower. She agreed.

We went in, she ordered her food and while she was eating I went and took a shower of my own. Somehow being in her proximity had made me feel less clean. When I got out of the shower I found her and told her goodbye, and left her in the lobby. When I got to my truck, something told me I should inspect the passenger side where she had been sitting. If she forgot something I didn't want any remnants of her left in the cab.

I opened up the passenger door, and then I screamed. Yes, I screamed. Not a high pitch girl scream, it was a man scream, but a scream nonetheless. On the floorboard in front of the seat were two, bloody, feminine napkins. No effort had been made to conceal them, they were just sitting there starring at me. Apparently they had been removed and replaced in the darkness of the cab as we rolled down the highway, unbeknownst to me.

I found a stick in the parking lot and immediately scraped them out of my truck. Now I was really angry. I ran back into the truck stop to find this woman and give her another large piece of my mind but, she had vanished. She wasn't anywhere to be found.

I was angry with myself for the rest of the way home. I felt like such an idiot to be taken in by her sob story. I thought about all the other things that could have gone wrong, but fortunately didn't. I was also angry with her, for taking advantage of my kindness.

I learned a few things from this. In trying to be a good guy, I put everything in jeopardy; my truck, my job, and even my own life. She could have easily had a gun in that big purse. I was also reminded that my gut instinct should never be ignored. Before she even got in the truck something felt off about the situation, my gut was trying to tell me something— and I simply didn't listen because I had been so taken in by her sad story.

It might seem like the lesson would be to not trust strangers, or that no good deed goes unpunished, but I don't think so. I've helped out other strangers since then. I have tried to do good when the situation calls for it, and I have not had any other problems because I follow my gut instinct first and foremost. If a situation seems dicey, then it probably is. And following my gut has kept me out of a lot a bad situations.

Now when you are out into the world, don't be afraid of helping people out. There are people who need help sometimes and if we can, I think we should. However, do be afraid of what can happen when you don't follow your gut. One of the greatest kindnesses you can do for yourself, is to pay attention to that little voice inside your head.

CHAPTER FIFTY-THREE
It Looked Good On Paper

Kids are very impressionable.

In 1969 I was 7 years old, and I pretty much believed everything I saw, or was told. I didn't have a dubious bone in my body, and I trusted everyone.

One day I saw the movie "Mary Poppins" for the first time. I enjoyed the movie very much, but I was particularly fascinated with the way Mary Poppins could fly around effortlessly, just hanging onto her umbrella. I thought how cool it would be to be able to do that.

It was fall, and the leaves were turning color. We have an enormous maple tree on our property and it was starting to drop its seeds. If you don't know what maple seeds look like, I'll tell you. They have a fin, about an inch and a half long. It grows out of the seed itself and looks a lot like an insect wing.

At the right time, the seed breaks from the limb and the seed falls, but the fin doesn't let it fall, instead it rotates in the air like a tiny helicopter, and falls very slowly. Sometimes these seeds could travel quite a distance from the tree they fell from. We called them 'whirligigs'.

On this particular day I was looking up at all the whirligigs spinning through the air, they were kind of mesmerizing to watch. Then, out of the blue I was struck with a brilliant idea.

I went and got my little brother who was about 4 years old, and enlisted his help. Together we started gathering up whirligigs from the ground. We filled an entire shopping bag with them, we probably had four or five hundred altogether.

Then I stole some thread from my mom's sewing stuff, and we went to work. I had my brother cut of the thread in four foot lengths. Then I would tie that thread to a whirligig, and set it aside nice and straight so they wouldn't be all tangled.

My plan was fairly simple. When I got string tied to all of the seeds, I would tie the other end, all the loose ends, together. Then I would climb up on top of the barn and holding the tied end in one hand — I'd jump off. Then I would proceed to float around like Mary Poppins to the amazement of anyone in attendance, with 500 spinning maple seeds keeping me afloat!

As we spent a few hours tying string to maple seeds, I really felt like I was some kind of genius. I was so proud of myself for coming up with this idea, and I couldn't believe no one else had ever thought of it. In my mind it made absolute, 100% perfect sense.

My brother got bored and tried to quit a couple times, but I kept talking him into staying with some brotherly force. Eventually, we got them all tied. It looked like a big, unidentifiable brown mass tied to a bunch of string—but I knew what it was. Holding my arm out I spun around to observe the action of the seeds in the air. I saw several of them spinning in the air I created…this was going to work.

The barn wasn't too hard to climb. It had a lean-to on the West side that was fairly low. A barrel, a pallet, and a bucket were all we needed to get up there. Then we could shimmy onto the pitched roof of the barn. It would have been a lot easier if I didn't have to help my brother, but he had come with me this far and it wouldn't be right if he couldn't share the glory and see the fruits of his labor.

When we got up to the peak of the roof things started to look a little different. It's amazing how much difference elevation can make in ones perspective. The wind was blowing, and I was hanging onto my brother to make sure he didn't fall. We finally got to the barn gable on the East end of the barn. As I looked down over the edge something seemed to change inside me. I didn't understand what my problem was…I had thought this whole thing out, I was certain it would work. I suddenly felt, well—kind of afraid.

I spent a few minutes, trying to talk myself into stepping off the barn. I was telling myself to do it, to just jump, but something inside was holding me back. Eventually my brother started asking me what

I was doing. Wasn't I going to jump? That's when I had my second brilliant idea of the day.

I looked at my brother and said; "You know, I've been thinking. You have been such a good brother today, and such a big help, that I decided to let you go first!" Then I handed my brother the bundle of string. At first he looked happy and proud that I was giving him this honor. Then he crept to the edge and looked over. He stuck his little fist with the strings out towards me and said; " No Alf, I don't want to."

Then I had a third brilliant idea. I told my brother to sit down and wait for me, with the seed bundle. Then I climbed back off the roof onto the ground. I got a metal bucket and filled it with rocks. Then, lugging the bucket along with me, I climbed back up on the roof where my brother waited.

I told him we would do an experiment first. I tied the string bundle to the bucket handle. I told my brother that we would try it with the bucket first, and then I would do it. He agreed. After a ceremonial pause, I swung the bucket out into space, and let go. To my horror...it did not go as planned.

The bucket filled with rocks, and all the whirligigs plummeted through the air and crashed into the earth below as if nothing was even slowing it down.

We both stood there in silence for a moment. The realization washed over me that I had almost killed myself. Then a second wave of realization...that I had almost killed my brother. It was not a good feeling. All the pride and elation I had felt earlier gave way to a sick feeling in my stomach. I didn't understand how I could have been so wrong. It looked so good on paper!

I nodded toward the other end of the roof and we both made our way back down to the ground. I put my arm around his shoulders, and we both went into the house to eat some sandwiches.

This story taught me something in a very visceral way. In my mind I can still see that bucket hitting the ground, and imagine the sound of all my bones breaking. It stuck with me, that image, and probably saved my life many times over the years because I learned to always test things that are untried...no matter how sure I am it will work. This experience caused me to understand exactly how much I didn't understand, about how things work. It gave me a new way of discovering things — instead of just jumping.

When you are out into the big world test things that are untried, be smart, and listen to the little voice inside your head when it tells you to go get a bucket, even if the plan looks good on paper.

CHAPTER FIFTY-FOUR
Dreams Ignite Ambition

When I was 12 years old I started to develop a dream, an ambition. Like most ambitions mine didn't show up out of the clear blue sky, rather it was promoted by something very specific. What prompted my dream was a book.

In 7th grade I had found a book in my school library. It was about the life of a famous boxer named Rocky Marciano from the 1950's. He wasn't just a famous boxer, he was the heavy weight champion of the world. Not only that, but he was the only heavy weight champ to ever retire undefeated. I didn't realize when I checked out that book, how it would change my life.

Rocky Marciano became a hero to me as I read the story of his life from his humble beginnings in Brockton Massachusetts to his winning the most coveted title of the day, heavyweight champion. Along the way I developed a sense of the man, his character. He was small for his weight class, with short arms but he had a head made of granite. Ultimately it was his heart that I respected most, his courage and fortitude. He overcame his physical adversities with sheer determination and grit. He trained longer and worked harder than all of his competition, and that's why he won. I was also impressed by the influence he had over kids and fans in general. The public loved him, and he was an excellent role model for thousands.

I read the book through, then I read it again. I read it several more times until I could recite the action of his most famous fights punch by punch— something I would do without too much provocation. One day I made a decision that I was going to follow in Rocky's footsteps and also become the heavyweight champion of the world. If I couldn't be a super hero, I could be a boxer. I told my parents and anyone else who would listen of my decision. Most people thought I was going through a phase, but I was deadly serious.

The problem was that living way out in the country as we did, there were no boxing facilities. There were no trainers, there weren't even any stores that sold boxing gloves. I didn't let any of that dampen my spirits though. I got an empty feed bag, it was large and made of burlap. I filled it with other feed bags, some clothes, a little hay and even some dirt until it was the weight and consistency I thought I needed. I hung that bag from the apple tree in our yard. I checked out some more books about boxing technique and read them all, then I started punching on that bag.

Very quickly all my knuckles were bloody from the rough burlap. My mom had a whole box of gloves that she used for gardening, so I started wearing them. I would wear the gloves out pretty quickly, and then I would just grab another pair and keep going. I would be out in the yard for hours just punching away on that home made bag. I would go until I was exhausted or something else made me stop, then the next day I would be back at it. The entire time I didn't have any idea if I was doing anything right, but I figured doing something was better than doing nothing.

This went on like this for a couple years. During that time I had to replace the bag several times.

I took $45 I earned from my first job picking strawberries to get my very first pair of boxing gloves, via mail order. I'll never forget the feeling I had when I put them on for the first time. After two years my parents started to realize that it wasn't just a phase, I was actually serious. Unbeknownst to me they started searching for someone locally that could teach me how to box. Who they found was a guy named Al Vitolo. He was a cantankerous little Italian guy who was tough as nails— and a former New York City featherweight champion. He was looking for guys to train. When they told me about him I thought I was dreaming, this seemed too good to be true!

When I met Al for the first few times we didn't do much. He had me jump rope and shuffle around a little. I thought it was kind of lame. What I didn't know was that Al was spending that time just sizing me up. He didn't ask for any money. He was looking for guys who might one day turn pro, his investment of time was focused on that future, so he was very careful about who he agreed to work with. One day Al took me to the boxing gym at Ft. Lewis Army base. It was like walking into a boxing movie. Guys were shadow boxing in mirrors and jumping rope. They had an actual boxing ring, and you could smell the sweat and the blood. He had me get warmed up a little bit jumping some rope and I got to punch a real live punching bag for the first time in my life. It was made of leather and every thing!

Then all of a sudden he told me to get in the ring. Once in, he started fitting me with a cup and headgear. He wrapped my hands and put big 16 oz gloves on me. I asked him what we were doing and he said I was going to spar someone. I hadn't seen this coming, I didn't know anything yet. He saw my concerned look and just said, "You want to be a fighter right? Well, then you have to fight." The next thing I knew this beast of a man walked out and got into the ring. I weighed around 160 when I was 14. This guy weighed at least 250, he was covered with hair and muscle and he was a grown man in the Army.

We sparred three, three minute rounds. I can say without reservation that they were probably the most physically uncomfortable 9 minutes of my life. At the end of it I was covered in blood, mostly from my nose. It turned out the blood was a good thing because it covered up my tears. The guy was hitting me at will, dancing around and popping me from every angle. I couldn't see anything coming, because my eyes were so full of blood and tears. During the entire time I didn't hit him one time…not once. I had been completely out of wind after the first 30 seconds. Between rounds I couldn't hear anything Al was saying because I was too busy breathing. I had wanted to quit on several occasions but for some reason, I didn't. I had thought about this too long and too hard to just walk out of the ring on my first outing. I knew it had to end eventually, and it did after the third round.

Of course I thought I had failed miserably, but Al was full of praise and seemed genuinely impressed, which confused me. After we got the bleeding under control and I was changing clothes Al explained to me that the entire purpose of this exercise was to see if I had any heart, to see if I would quit. Also, to let me experience what it was like to be out of gas and defenseless in the ring so that I would never let it happen again. He told me, "Now that I know you won't quit, I can teach you how to box. We won't spar again until you are ready." That was actually a big relief.

True to his word, I didn't get back in the ring to spar for about six months. During that time I learned technique and gained skills and flexibility and toughness. He was very 'old school' in his methods. Once he told me to lay down on my back and close my eyes. He went to a balcony above me and dropped a medicine ball on my stomach, unsuspectedly. It was a few minutes before I could breath again, then he told me I should never relax my stomach muscles, even when I'm sleeping. For several years after that, I didn't.

The next time I got into the ring, I held my own. I was always sparring grown men though, guys much older and heavier than me so I continued to get beat up on a regular basis—but I kept getting better. I got better much faster than I would have if he had taken it easy on me. Little by little, day by day, punch by punch, I became a good boxer.

I never did turn pro, after four years of training I joined the Army instead for reasons that would be another story. Then I had kids and started businesses and just got busy with living. The original dream that was fueled by that book in 7th grade didn't fit as well with the man I eventually became. Though later I did start my own boxing gym in the town where I grew up, and I had a great time training kids and adults in the sweet science of pugilism.

I cannot over state the lessons that boxing taught me about myself, and about life in general. Much of who I am today was forged inside the ropes of a boxing ring. It's a place where excuses die a painful death and where you get to know yourself better every time you enter.

The lesson I would like people to take away from this story is not so much about boxing, that's just my personal example. The real lesson is about the power of dreams, the force of ambition. My life was permanently altered because I picked up a book when I was 12. Many other people probably read that book and had an entirely different experience. So I don't think the book gave me my dream, but I do believe it ignited or awakened the power of dreams inside me. That in turn, altered my life. In my case, that dream did not come to fruition, but it created a fabric, a foundation upon which I could accomplish so many other things. It gave me momentum, and inertia. If a human being can develop momentum and inertia in a forward direction...there is no telling what he can accomplish.

I believe everyone has within them this great potential for ambition. The ways we discover to express that ambition become the dreams that we pursue. I personally think every man, at any given moment of his life should be in pursuit of a dream. Even if you fall short of that dream, if you miss that objective, in the process you have created forward momentum and it's much easier to attach that to a new dream, and keep moving forward.

If you currently do not have a dream you are in pursuit of, I strongly suggest you find one— make one, invent one. The possibility of failure holds many people back from doing this, which doesn't make sense because failure is a requirement of success. Every man who has ever dreamed up great things has also failed on multiple occasions, then he learned from those mistakes and kept on pursuing his dream.

If you don't start thinking about your dream right now, your ambition may never find an outlet. Start thinking about it now, focus on it because the things we focus on expand. Do not let fear rob you of this, to dream is your birthright as a human. You just have to claim it.

CHAPTER FIFTY-FIVE
There Was A Man

One upon a time, there was a man. This man lived in Montana, the son of Norwegian immigrants. When this man was a boy he didn't learn how to speak English until he was 6 years old and started school. He wasn't an especially big man, but he was smart and tough. He was the eldest child with three younger brothers and two younger sisters.

When he was a young man he left home to find his own adventure. He lived with a guy who was a boxer and as a result of that, he also learned how to box. He was a natural fighter in the first place. He didn't fight out of malice or aggression, but as a means of sport...for fun.

When he came back home he put this new boxing skill to the test. He loved to fight, it was fun for him and he would fight at the drop of a hat. He also arm-wrestled and was known for beating guys much larger than himself. There is one account of him arm-wresting a man who outweighed him by 70 pounds. They were betting chickens. He brought home all of that man's chickens on that occasion.

This man we are speaking of had mechanical aptitude and was also good at running machinery. He started working for road crews, building the highways that crisscross America today.

He didn't limit his activities to road construction though, wherever he was he had animals; sheep, cows, chickens and goats. He was always wheeling and dealing, buying things and selling them for a profit. He would buy lambs in the Spring and sell them in the Fall. For a time his life was nomadic. He had a single-wide trailer he lived in with his family and it would be towed across America from North to South as he drove combines, harvesting the wheat that fed the country.

He liked to drink, and smoke, and laugh...and he was a story teller and quite a joker as well. He had a wife whom he loved, and two sons. He raised those two sons to be as smart and self sufficient and tough as he was but more importantly, he passed along to them humor, and common sense, a love of life and a sense of right and wrong.

When this man was only 55 years old there was a tragic accident. He was operating a large tracked vehicle, working on a road crew. (Here in America they are called CATS / Caterpillars or Bull Dozers.) Somehow, he fell off of the tractor and wound up getting crushed beneath it; he was killed. Nobody knows for sure how it happened, there were no witnesses.

This man's name was Alf Herigstad. He was my grandfather. He was the man I am named after, and the man responsible for creating the best man I have ever known— my father. I was only a year and a half old at the time, so even though I had met him when I was a baby, I have no memory of it.

The reason I'm telling you this story is because of the profound effect it had on me. I believe there are some lessons here for all of us. First, to have been named after someone is significant. Regardless of how different your personalities may or may not be, you are bound forever by that common name. On the cork board in front of my desk is the newspaper clipping that reports my grandfathers death; the death of Alf Herigstad. It is sobering to read your name in that context.

The main lesson though, the one I really want to impart to you, is this: My grandfather lived a certain way. He approached life with aggression and determination, while at the same time having a care and love for those around him.

This resulted in many, many stories that were told and re-told at family gatherings. I paid extra close attention because they were talking about someone with the same name as me. Through these stories I gained a sense of the man. There were countless stories,

274

some of them funny, some unbelievable, but all of them helped to fashion in my mind, the essence of this man.

Whenever my dad would speak of his father I would study his face as he spoke, and I could see the respect and love he still had for him. My mother had a great fondness for him, and she had her own stories from a different perspective, that added to my sense of who this man was that I shared a name with.

By the time I grew up I felt like I had known my grandfather. I felt like I knew the kind of man he was. I had developed a genuine affinity and love for this man, even though I had no actual memory of him. That my friends, is the power of this story.

That is the definition of legacy. It has made me very aware that everything I do in my life matters. It makes me ask the question that, if I were to die today, this minute...would there be enough stories? Not only would there be enough stories, but would they be the kind of stories that could help shape another young man's sense of his own self? Would these stories add something good to the world?

I have many different ages of listeners on my podcast, from teenagers to people older than me. I suspect that people reading this book are from many different ages, countries, religions and genders as well. The lesson of this story is that it doesn't matter how old you are, or where you are from or what gender you are. As long as you are living you have an opportunity, through your own life and how you are living it, to affect someone in the future by the stories you leave behind. That will be your true legacy—not the money and the possessions you leave behind, but the stories.

Tomorrow is not promised to any of us. All we have, the only chance we have to leave an imprint on the world, is today.

I shared this story about my grandfather because I wanted to illustrate the kind of impact a man can have. I doubt if he was even aware of it—he was just living the best he could and doing the things he thought were right. But he had a profound impact on my father, who in turn had a profound impact on me. He left stories behind, from everyone that ever knew him, rich stories of a man who met life head-on, without fear.

So as you head out into the world, regardless of who you are or where you are from, I charge you with the task of being aware every day of the stories you are leaving behind. Think about how your life will be told, think about the affect it will have on the young ears that hear your stories. Consider your legacy.

If you do this, it won't only affect future generations, but it will help you be a better man (person) every day than you were the day before. It will actually make your own life better while you are still living it.

Thanks for reading this book. Thanks for allowing me to tell my stories. Now, go be the author of your own stories, and while you're doing that, be a better man today, than you were yesterday...and then keep doing that every day.

THE END
ALF HERIGSTAD

ACKNOWLEDGMENTS

My Ancestors ~ Thanks for my Mom and Dad

Mom and Dad ~ Thank you for my existence

Lulie, my wife ~ Thank you my love, for being a true partner in love and life

Ladonna and Bart, my siblings ~ Thanks for loving me in spite of myself

Christine, Clinton, and Gurine…my children ~ For the privilege of being your dad, thank you

The people of Hawk's Hearth ~ Thank you for trusting me, and being my friend

The listeners of Being A Better Man ~ Thank you all, for listening

Special thanks to the members of the Launch Team:
Lulie Herigstad
Mitch Evancho
Clinton Herigstad
David Baldwin
Teri Roe
Steven Tessler
Continued: >>>

Alf Herigstad
Landon Brown
Tom Potter
Marilyn Murch
Eric Guillory
Adam Normandin
Anita Rasmussen
Ingebjørg Uro
Christine Riley
Johan Øberg
Laura Jimenez
Ole Jørgen Rodar
Donald Schuettke

Your efforts and support were invaluable in helping me
create this book, thank you.

I named this work "FORGING A MAN" because life is like a forge; from the moment we are born, we are but a piece of molten steel on an anvil, about to be pounded. You put the steel in the fire until it is red hot, then you beat it into the shape and form you desire.

We are shaped in the same way by the experiences of our lives. The hardships, pains, joys and victories—all of it shapes us into the individuals we become. These stories are what helped to forge me; My parents, where I lived, the friends I had, all of these things were precise hammer blows that helped shape me into who I am.

The same is true for you holding this book right now. Your experiences may have been different from mine, but forces have shaped you in the same manner. Now, this book will become another hammer in your life. As you read the stories, and reflect on your own life lessons, they will contribute to your shape as a man...as every experience we have will.

About The Author
~ Alf Herigstad ~

Alf Herigstad has loved writing since he was a child. Since then he has authored hundreds of poems and stories, just for fun. He had a love for the written word and enjoyed being able to invoke emotion and inspire thought in others. Later, he wrote professionally for a time in the Army and used his passion for writing in many of his entrepreneurial ventures.

In 2012, Alf became a contestant on a popular Norwegian Reality show called 'Alt For Norge,' it was a life-changing experience in many ways. Upon returning to America he wrote his first book, an account of his adventures based on the journal he kept in Norway. A revision of that book will be available soon in paperback and digitally. Its a behind the scenes look at being on a reality show in a different country, what its like to be embraced by a nation, and the experience of being 're-booted' to your factory settings.

Alf has done a lot of things in the past five decades; He isn't just a minor celebrity in Norway, he has been a boxer, a boxing gym owner / trainer, a construction contractor, an Ostrich farmer, a long-haul truck driver and worked in several other industries such as real estate and fitness.

Alf is currently the creator and host of the popular podcast, 'Being A Better Man.' A program that is focused exclusively on the character of men of all ages. You can listen at his website: www.beingabettermanpodcast.com, or on iTunes or Stitcher. He also enjoys contributing to his local community by volunteering time to projects, hosting gatherings, and also being a substitute school bus driver with a portion of his time.

Alf resides on a small family farm in Washington State with his lovely wife Lulie, and their dog, Wunjo. He has three grown children, and nine grand children.

Alf welcomes contact from readers and listeners, you can email him at: alf@beingbetter.men

To order copies of this book:

Individually: This book is available for order directly from the **Createspace eStore**, from **Amazon.com** all over the world, and wherever fine books are sold. In fact I encourage you to go to your local bookstore and ask them to order some copies. Bulk sales: If you are affiliated with an organization filled with people who may benefit from the content of this book, you can inquire at **Createspace** about the bulk sales option, and receive a wholesale rate.

To connect with the author:

As the author of this book I am eager to connect with those of you that have taken the time to read it.   You can find me on Twitter at: **@Alfbeingbetter** or **@AlfHerigstad**. You can join me on Facebook in my **Being A Better Man group**. I'm on Instagram at: **Being A Better Man**.   My website is **www.beingabettermanpodcast.com**.   I also love receiving emails, and you are welcome to email me directly at: **alf@beingbetter.men**. I am available for personal appearances, interviews, and speaking engagements, just inquire via email or my website.

Pay it forward:

This book was written with the intent that it would be shared.   We all know someone that would benefit from the stories and lessons found in Forging A Man. It is for this reason that it is an ideal gift.   You can probably think of at least three people right now who would be ideal recipients...I'm suggesting that you send them a copy of their own and make their day. Or, perhaps you have received this book as a gift, if so do not forget to thank the person who gave it to you. Now you have a chance to pay that kindness forward by giving a copy to someone else.

My Goal:

My goal, is that as a result of reading this book and listening to my podcast, that men will start looking closely at their reflections in the mirror every day, and make a promise to themselves The promise is; "I will be a better man today, than I was yesterday." Then, they will go out into the world and do it. I believe if this goal is reached, the world will become a slightly better place.

<<<◇>>>

www.ingramcontent.com/pod-product-compliance
Lightning Source LLC
LaVergne TN
LVHW011321080426
835513LV00006B/149